Andrea Coppola

CERTIFIED TRAINER

BLENDER
The Ultimate Guide

VOLUME 1

Blender
High School

Summary

VOLUME 1

1
BEFORE YOU START

1.1. Preface

A few years ago, when I first looked at the wonderful world of 3D modeling, I started my long search for the right tool.

It was a really exhausting research: no software really suited to my needs because of either the unfriendly interface or the extreme complexity, or the bad guides or the poor results.

I was about to give up. Maybe I'll never find the right software that would allow me to go on by myself and create the 3D models of my own projects without asking for other professionals' help (costing a lot of money, often out of budget).

However, someone showed me Blender as the solution to my problems. At the beginning I was skeptical, due to the bad experiences mainly caused by the (sometimes partial) study of other open source or free software.

It is a common opinion that "free" is synonymous with poor, incomplete, unprofessional.

Blender immediately turned out something wonderful, extremely complete and professional.

Its graphic interface seamed to me linear and well organized, perfectly clear and understandable, contrary to what is said by some users.

Specially since newer versions kept on improving over and over.

Its completeness and potential encouraged me so much that I purchased all English and Italian educational materials around and, not happy, I took private lessons.

I almost immediately felt my hardware had to be upgraded and then I bought all latest gen components that allow me to push the software towards higher performances.

Meeting my friend and colleague Francesco Andresciani, which inspired me this extensive work, showed me a new direction: a series of successful publications that make me proud even today. Then I had the idea and the desire to write the guide I always wanted to read.

The complete and full of practical examples handbook I wanted to have on my bookshelf and on which I wanted to learn Blender.

A different guide from the others, far from the index-topic scheme, a path whose secrets will grow with me.

Blender is an ever growing software, something open you can test and study on, reaching new goals every time.

My research goes on, but in the same software environment now. Daily study, exercises and the discovering of new features, plugins and techniques encourage me to continuous improvement.

I hope that the following pages could be for you what I unsuccessfully looked for and what could have doubled the knowledge in half the time.

All my best wishes for your work!

Andrea Coppola

1.2. Introduction

This guide is obviously divided in 5 main volumes and annual updates, depending on the new Blender releases.

This guide can be considered valid for all the versions of Blender 2.6x, 2.7x, and next 2.8x and 2.9x.

In the first volume we will discuss basic topics from general information to system configuration, to the customization of work environment, to the structure and the functionality of the user interface (UI), to basic and advanced modeling tools (modes, transform tools, modifiers).

In the second volume we will explore in depth the two main render engines (*Blender Render* e *Cycles Render*), the lighting, the materials in both the engines, the manifold nodes techniques and the camera framing.

The third volume will focus on the physic simulations (fluids, smoke and flames, volumetric effects, rigid and soft bodies dynamic, cloche and force fields), on the particles systems and on the *Compositing* of final images.

The fourth volume will be entirely dedicated to animations, *rigging* and armature's inverse kinematic, *Motion Tracking, Sculpting* and audio-video editing.

Finally, the fifth volume is dedicated to advanced Grease Pencil, advanced Compositing and Game Engine.

Please refer to future publications for other volumes on further topics and new features.

Blender is a really sophisticated and detailed suite, it is almost impossible to deeply know and describe all features and techniques, specially the most advanced ones.

I wish this huge effort could became a Landmark but also a starting point for all Blender users, professionals, CG fans and, why not, amateurs and beginners.

1.3. Blender history

At the end of 90's Blender started to be distributed for free and it gathered a tremendous amount of interest from 3D graphic fans.

Blender was first created in 1995 as an in-house 3D toolset of the Dutch animation studio NeoGeo, replacing the too old previous one, under the artistic direction and internal software development of Ton Roosendal.

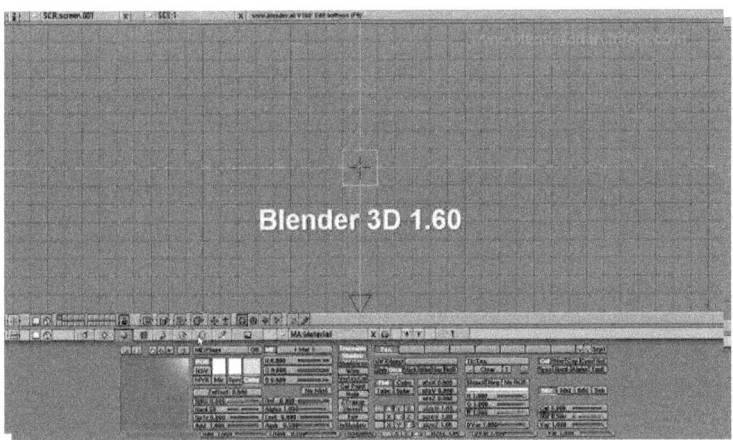

fig. 1 One of the first Blender release, the 1.60

In 1998 Ton himself decided to found a new company called Not a Number (NaN) to further develop Blender as the first great open source 3D modeling software.

In 2000 NaN secured financing of € 4.5M which enabled NaN to rapidly boost Blender development, reaching soon 250.000 registered users.
However in the following years, on the edge of bankrupt with NaN, Ton Roosendal founded the non-profit organization

BlenderFoundation; since then it continues developing and promotingBlender as the greatest community-based open source project ever.

Year after year the *Blender Foundation* developed and released for free several animation movies like *Sintel* and *Caminandes.*

fig. 2 Durian Project: Sintel

The new experimental feature film "Gooseberry Project - Cosmos Laundromat" is now being developed.

You can watch them on YouTube or download from www.blender.org.

Blender features are many: from 3D modeling to sculpting, from compositing to photo-realistic or cartoonish rendering, from animation to visual effects, from game development to programming.

From the quality point of view Blender has absolutely nothing to envy to other most known commercial software.
Its versatility, easy to use and high quality performances make of Blender an effective competitor, *open source* besides.

The non-stop development and the opening to external programmers allow Blender to be constantly improved, updated and corrected.

The new render engine *Cycles*, considered the basic render engine of this wonderful suite, is unquestionably one of the best *unbiased render engines*, that type of engines which use, at the cost of render times, an algorithm that simulate the real lighting behavior, creating extreme photo-realistic renders.

But what does *open source* mean?

This term refers to any software whose programming code is open to any programmers who want to contribute to its development.

This means Blender has a free license, is cross-platform and runs equally well on Linux, Windows and Macintosh computers.

Blender is the future of the 3D Artist job.

1.4. About Free Software and GPL[1]

When one hears about "free software", the first thing that comes to mind might be "no cost". While this is typically true, the term "free software" as used by the Free Software Foundation (originators of the GNU Project and creators of the GNU General Public License) is intended to mean "free as in freedom" rather than the "no cost" sense (which is usually referred to as "free as in free beer" or gratis). Free software in this sense is software which you are free to use, copy, modify, redistribute, with no limit. Contrast this with the licensing of most commercial software packages, where you are allowed to load the software on a single computer, are allowed to make no copies, and never see the source code. Free software allows incredible freedom to the end user. Since the source code is universally available, there are also many more chances for bugs to be caught and fixed.

When a program is licensed under the GNU General Public License (the GPL):

- You have the right to use the program for any purpose.
- You have the right to modify the program and have access to the source codes.
- You have the right to copy and distribute the program.
- You have the right to improve the program, and release your own versions.

In return for these rights, you have some responsibilities if you distribute a GPL program, responsibilities that are designed to protect your freedoms and the freedoms of others:

- You must provide a copy of the GPL with the program, so that recipients are aware of their rights under the license.

---

[1]From www.blender.org

- You must include the source code or make the source code freely available.
- If you modify the code and distribute the modified version, you must license your modifications available under the GPL (or a compatible license).
- You may not restrict the licensing of the program beyond the terms of the GPL. (you may not turn a GPL program into a proprietary product.)

The GPL only applies to the Blender application and not the artwork you create with it; for more info see the Blender License policy on www.blender.org.

1.5. The Method

Discuss all the topics of the Blender suite is a cyclopean venture, probably also because of its constant and continuous updating and new feature releases.

However, in this volumes, I tried to sum up all Blender features and explain them as easily and fluently as possible, covering (almost) every setting and tool, but also showing practical examples that allow you to start working right away.

Users are highly recommended to pay attention to the exercises starting from the beginning of the chapters regarding the basic knowledge, which often refer to practical aspects.

We will always repeat the command shortcuts, the working modes, windows and panels from which start a command, in order to let the visual memory gradually help you to learn the main software features.

You will also find some symbols at the beginning of certain paragraphs which means:

 Exercise symbol (inserted in a grey box);

 Definition or tip;

 Note icon (**bold** typed in a grey framed box);

As we love to repeat, Blender is a complex but not difficult suite, therefore you will need constant practice.

Knowing how it has been programmed and how it is meant to work is the key for the optimal understanding and use.

Keep this little advices in mind before you start this long and winding journey.

We truly believe (and we wish) that 3D graphic and the power of Blender will become a growing passion for you.

1.6. Convention used in this volumes

In this volumes, we'll use the following conventions:

LMB	Left Mouse Button
RMB	Right Mouse Button
MMB	Middle Mouse Button
MW	Mouse Wheel
SHIFT	SHIFT key on the keyboard
ALT	ALT key on the keyboard
CTRL	Control key on the keyboard
TAB	TAB key on the keyboard
SHIFT+C	Key combination (ex. Shift and C)
ENTER	ENTER key on the keyboard
7 NUM	7 key on the numpad
F1 - F12	Function key from F1 to F12
SPACEBAR	SPACEBAR key on the keyboard
BACKSPACE	BACKSPACE key on the keyboard

1.7. How to install Blender

You can download Blender for free from www.blender.org where you can choose the Windows, Mac OSX or Linux version.

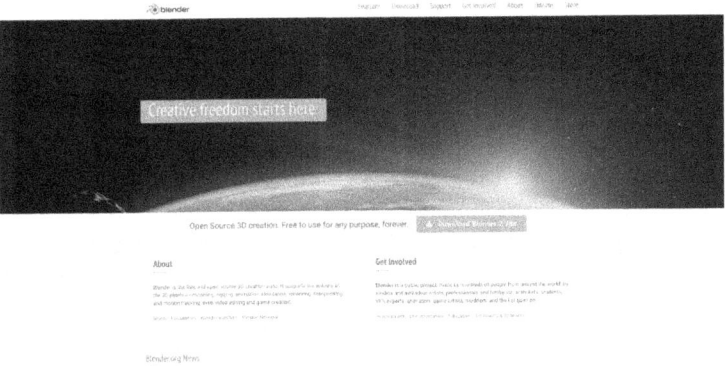

fig 3 www.blender.org homepage

From the *Download* section all you have to do is to choose your platform and download the installation file. This volume refers to version 2.7x, and the new features will be analyzed on the upgrade volumes.

Windows installation

On Windows systems you can download either the *Installer* file or the **.zip* folder (64bit is preferred if supported).

When you run the Installer (**.msi*) you'll be asked to set the destination folder and the **.blend* files relation. You must have administrator privileges to install Blender on your system.

With the *.zip* option Blender should run out of the box, without installation procedure. To use Blender, just unpack the archive you downloaded and start Blender.

Mac OSX Installation

On Mac systems just unpack the *blender.app* folder into the archive you downloaded and drag it into the Application folder. Otherwise you can run Blender directly from the packed folder.

GNU/Linux installation

On Linux systems you can download the *.bz2* archive to be unpacked.

The installation file suits most recent GNU/Linux distributions and you can directly run Blender from the unpacked folder.

1.8. Settings and customization

One of the main feature of Blender is its flexibility and fully customizability to suit all your needs, you system hardware performances and you personal habits without any specific patch.

Besides the UI customization (we'll discuss it later), from the System Preferences window (*File – User Preferences* or CRTL+ALT+U) you can adjust many settings according to your system, your aesthetic taste, the mouse use, the controls, the visualization, the shortcuts and the
Add-ons. Let's open the *User Preferences* window.

It appears as a stand-alone window and it is the only case in Blender because it is designed to allow you to view all relevant options and tools at a glance without pushing or dragging pop-up boxes around.

1.8.1. *User Preferences*

In the *User Preferences* windows the available options are grouped into seven tabs, as shown below:

Interface (where you define some settings on the interface);

- *Interface* (change how UI elements are displayed and how they react);
- *Editing* (control how several tools will interact with your input);
- *Input* (customize how Blender reacts to the mouse and keyboard as well as define your own keymap);
- *Add-ons* (manage Blender's Add-ons and plugins);
- *Themes* (customize interface appearance and colors);

- *File* (configure auto-save preferences and set default file paths for blend-files and more);
- *System* (set resolution, scripting console preferences, sound, graphics cards, and internationalization).

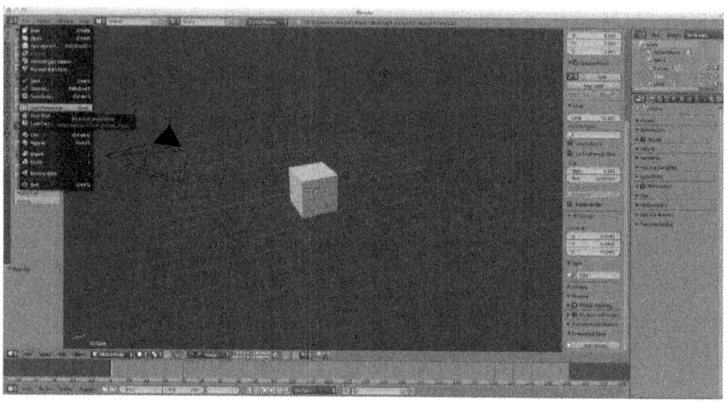

fig. 4 How to open the *User Preferences* editor

A)   Tab Interface

In this section you can manage the UI elements.

Under *Display* you can check/uncheck this options:

- *Tooltips* when enabled, a tooltip will appear when your mouse pointer is over a control;
- *Python Tooltips* displays a property's python information below the tooltip;
- *Object info* display the active Object name and frame number at the bottom left of the 3D View;
- *Large Cursors* use large mouse cursors when available;
- *View Name* displays the name and type of the current view in the top left corner of the 3D View;

- *Playback FPS* shows the frames per second screen refresh rate while an animation is played back;
- *Global Scene* forces the current scene to be displayed in all screens;
- *Object Origin Size* sets the diameter of selected 3D Object centers in the view port;
- *Display Mini Axis* shows the mini axis at the bottom left of the viewport, while the two settings below define their dimension and brightness when enabled.

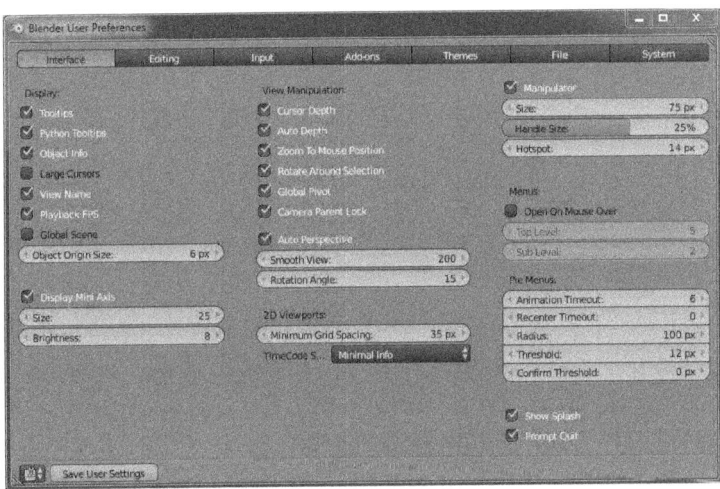

fig. 5 *Interface* tab in the *User Preferences* editor

Under *View Manipulation* you can check/uncheck this options:

- *Cursor Depth* use the depth under the mouse when placing the cursor;
- *Auto Depth* improve view pan, rotate, zoom functionality;
- *Zoom to Mouse Position* when enabled, the mouse pointe rposition becomes the focus point of zooming instead of the 2D window center. Helpful to avoid panning if you are frequently zooming in and out;

- *Rotate Around Selection the* selected object becomes the rotation center of the viewport;
- *Global Pivot* lock the same rotation/scaling pivot in all 3DViews;
- *Auto Perspective* automatically switch to perspective projection when moving from Orthographic Top/Side/Front view to User view;
- *Smooth View* length of time the animation takes when changing the view with the numpad;
- *Rotation Angle* rotation step size in degrees, when 4NUM,6NUM, 8NUM, or 2NUM are used to rotate the 3D View.

Under *2D Viewport* you can set this options:

- *Minimum Grid Spacing* the minimum number of pixels between grid lines in a 2D viewport;
- *TimeCode Style* format of Time Codes displayed when not displaying timing in terms of frames.

In the top right corner you can enable/disable the *Manipulator* (edit tool to translate, scale and rotate objects in the 3D viewport) and set its visual parameters.

The *Menus* options allow you to have the menu open by placing the mouse pointer over the entry instead of clicking on it.

Pie Menu options control the settings of this selection tool (must been abled from the *Add-ons* tab).

Show Splash simply enable/disable the splash screen on Blender startup.

B)   Tab Editing

These preferences control how several tools will interact with your input.

- *Link Material To* define the way materials are applied to objects;
- *New Object* set the insert rules of a new object into the scene. You can align it to World or View coordinates and set/unset *Edit Mode* as the default mode for new objects;
- *Undo* allows you to manage the number of undo steps available;
- *Grease Pencil* controls the starting parameters of the pen tool(radius, smoothness, default color...) you can use to draw directly in the 3D viewport;
- *Allow Negative Frames* under *Playback* enable/disable the possibility to set negative frames on the timeline.

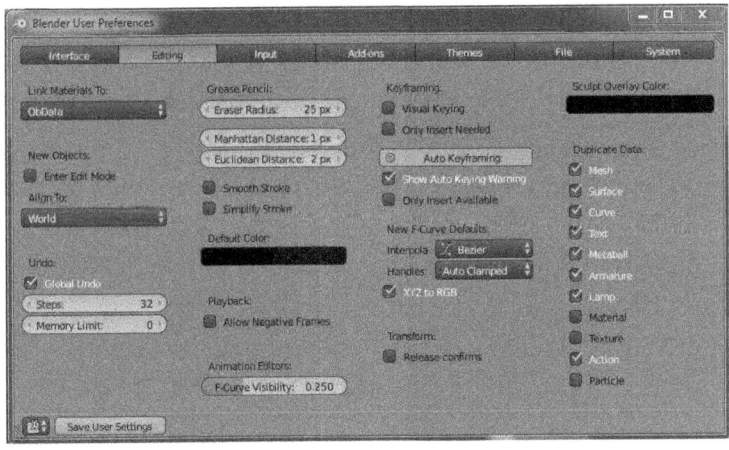

fig. 6 *Editing* tab in the *User Preferences* editor

Under *Keyframing* you find the following check boxes and controls:

- *Visual Keying* enable/disable the keyframes visibility;
- *Only Insert Needed* will only insert keyframes if the value of the property is different;
- *Auto Keyframing* enables Auto Keyframe by default for new scenes;

- *Only Insert Available* will only add keyframes to channel F-Curves that already exist;
- *New F-Curve Defaults* controls the mathematical behavior of the new F-Curves;
- *XYZ to RGB* set the same color for X, Y or Z animation curves(location, scale or rotation) as the color for the X, Y and Z axis;

When enabled, *Release Confirms* check box under *Transform* allow you to confirm a transformation (started with a drag-and-drop LMB action) just by releasing the LMB.

Sculpt Overlay Color allows the user to define a color to be used in the inner part of the brushes circle when in *Sculpt Mode*.

The last section *Duplication Data* allows the user to decide which data of the original object will be transferred to the copied ones.

C)   Tab Input

In the Input preferences, you can customize your keymap.

From the *Preset* drop-down menu you can assign to Blender the same keymapping from other 3D software like 3DStudio Max or Maya. Clicking on + or – buttons you can add a custom preset or delete an existing one.

Checking the *Emulate 3 Button Mouse* options Blender will emulate the functionality of a 3 button mouse even on an Apple mouse or a 2 button laptop touchpad, according to the following key combinations:

3 buttons mouse	2 buttons mouse	Apple mouse
LMB	LMB	LMB
MMB	ALT + LMB	CMD + LMB
RMB	RMB	CMD + LMB

Continuous Grab allows the drag-and-drop transformations (such as grabbing or panning a view) to continue over the viewport limits by warping the mouse within the view.
Drag/Tweek Threshold defines number of pixels that a User Interface element has to be moved before it is recognized by Blender as a movement.
As you may have noticed, the mouse buttons input settings are set by default as the opposite of the most common commercial software. First of all, the selection with the RMB instead of the left one.
It is a personal choice, but I recommend to switch to left button selection as the *User Preferences* window allows us to do that. So in the *Input* tab go to the *Select With* section and select *Left* (colored in blue when selected) to enable left mouse button (LMB) selection.

Double Click set the speed of double clicking (in ms).

Emulate NUM tells Blender to treat the standard number keys as Numpad keys if you have a keyboard without a Numpad (e.g. on a laptop).

Orbit Style sets how Blender works when you rotate the 3D View by default when holding MMB. If you are familiar with Maya or Cinema 4D you may want to set *Turntable*.

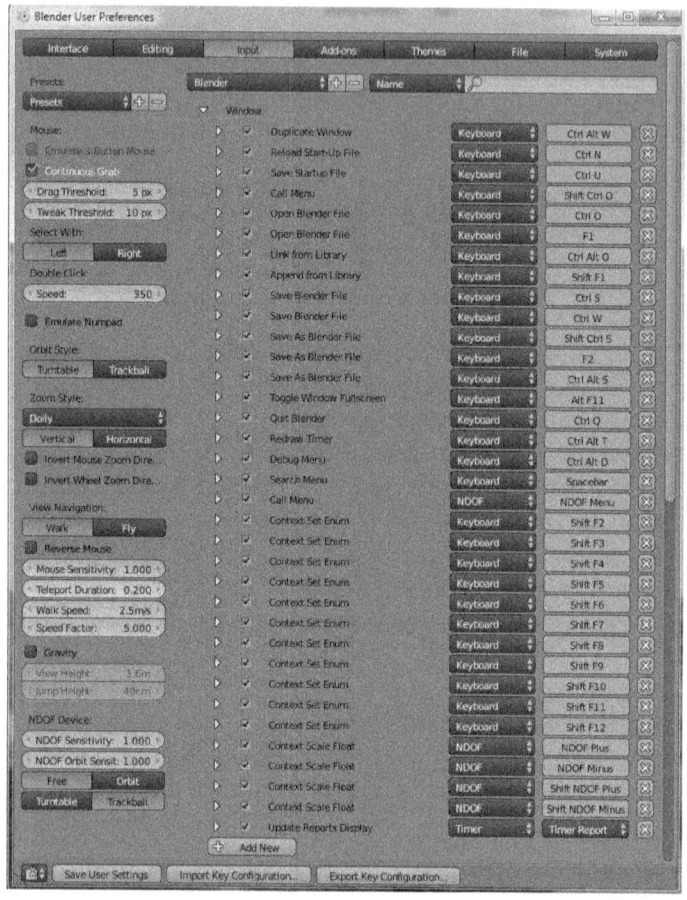

fig. 7 *Input* tab in the *User Preferences* editor

Zoom Style controls how Blender performs zoom in and zoom out actions when the CTRL+MMB combination is used, choosing among
Dolly, Continue and *Scale*.

Invert Zoom Direction inverts the Zoom direction for *Dolly* and *Continue* zooming.

24

Invert Wheel Zoom Direction inverts the direction of the mouse wheel zoom.

NDOF Device sets the sensibility of a 3D mouse.

With the *Keymap Editor* you can edit each keymap for every single windows in Blender.

On the right side of the *Input* tab you can reset or edit all the shortcuts used in Blender.

D)   Tab Addons

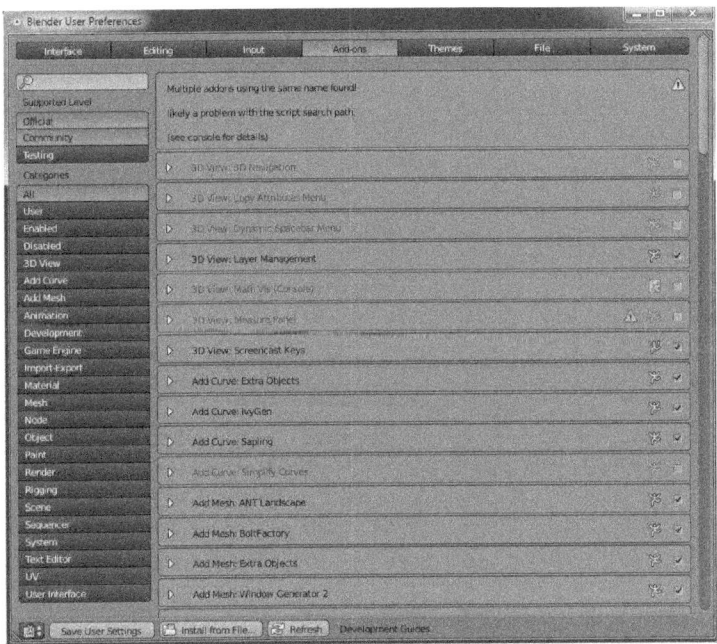

fig. 8 *Add-ons* tab in the *User Preferences* window

In the *Add-ons* tab you can easily manage secondary options, which are not enabled in Blender by default, using the searching filter or the categories list. New features may be added as well with *Install From File...* button.

E) Tab Themes

The *Themes* tab allows you to customize interface appearance and colors, windows, border colors, backgrounds, cells... Elements are grouped by categories in the list on the left. You can also click on *Reset to Default Theme*.

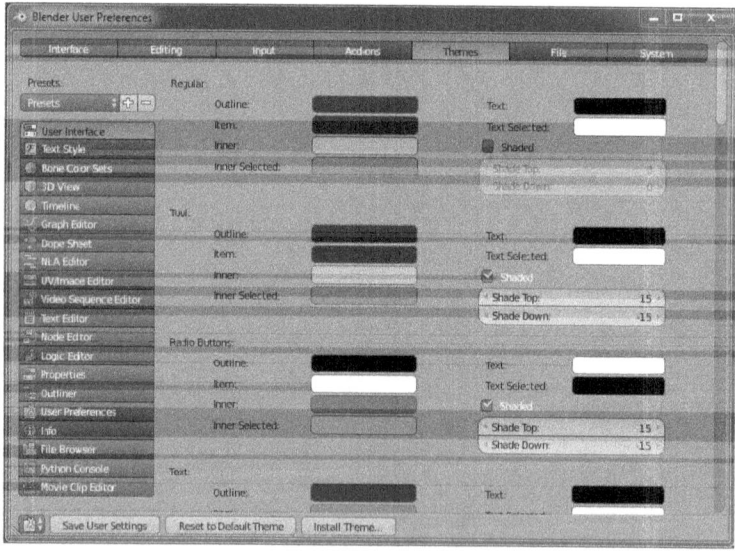

fig. 9 *Themes* tab in the *User Preferences* editor

26

F)   Tab Files

The *File* tab allows you to configure auto-save preferences and set default file paths for blend-files, rendered images, and more.

In the File Paths section you can specify the locations for various external files such as fonts, textures, render output, sounds, scripts, temporary and cache files and more.

On the right you can find the *Save & Load* section where to set the rules of loading and saving files (relative paths, *.blend* file compression, load external UI, filter file extensions and show thumbnails in the internal browser).

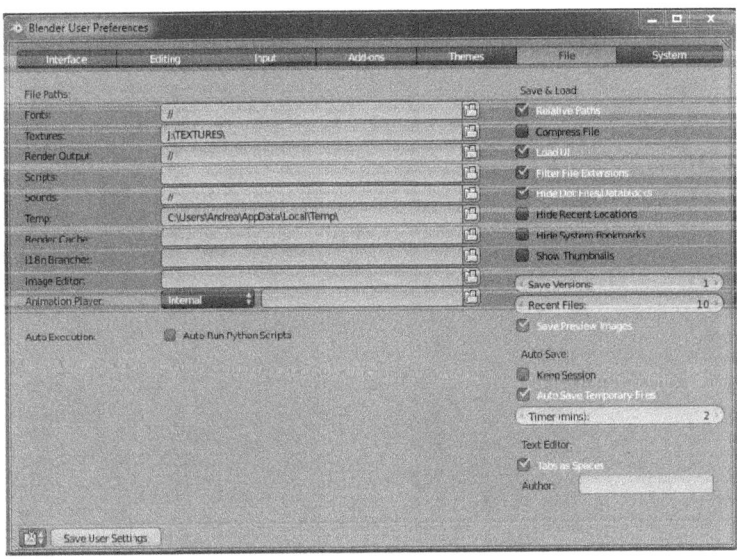

fig. 10 *File* tab in the *User Preferences* editor

You can also control:

Save Version number of versions created for the same file (forbackup);

27

Recent Files number of files displayed in *File - Open Recent;*

Save Preview Images enable the previews of images and materials in the *File Browser.*

In the *Auto Save* section:

Auto Save Temporary File enable *Auto Save* (create a temporary file);

Timer is the time to wait between automatic saves.

G)   Tab System

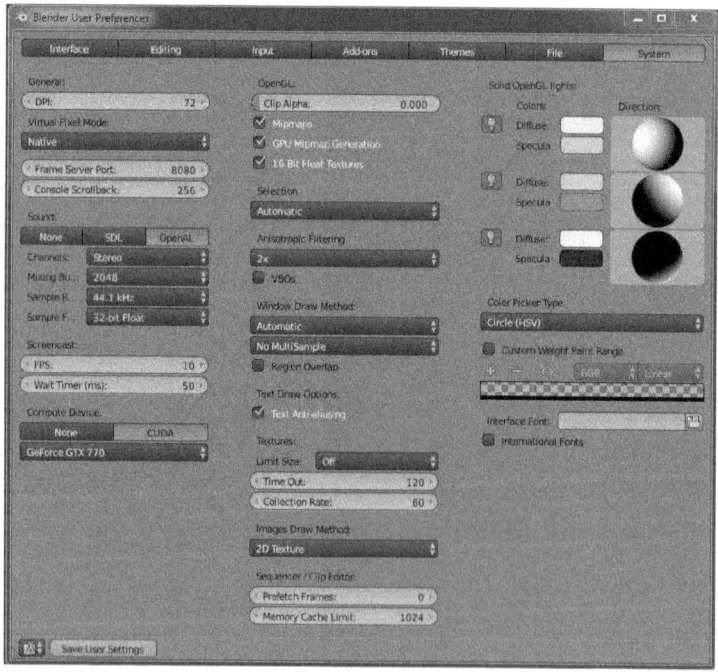

fig. 11 *System* tab in the *User Preferences* window

The *System* tab allows you to set resolution, scripting console preferences, sound, graphics cards, and internationalization (languages).

Under *General*:

- *DPI* sets the value of the screen resolution which controls the size of Blender's interface fonts and internal icons shown;
- *Virtual Pixel Mode* allows you to select global scaling. While the DPI only scales the interface, this will scale line width, vertex-size. This is intended for hi-dpi monitors;
- *Frame Server Port* TCP/IP port used in conjunction with the IP Address of the machine for frame server rendering;
- *Console Scroll back*sets the number of lines, buffered in memory of the console window.

In the *Sound* section you can set the audio output device (*OpenAL, SDL* or *None*), the audio channel count (*Mono, Stereo, 4 Channels, 5.1 Surround, 7.1 Surround*), the number of samples used by the audio mixing buffer (*512 , 1024 , 2048, 4096 , 8192, 16384, and 32768*), the audio sample rate, which is the audio sampling frequency (*44.1 Khz,48 Khs, 96 Khz and 192Khz*) and the audio sample format in bits (*32 float, 8 Unsigned, 16 Signed, 24 Signed, 32 Signed, 32 Float, and 64 Float*).

Compute Device will set the compute device used by the *Cycles Render* engine. When set to *None*your CPU will be used as a omputing device for *Cycles Render Engine*. When set to *CUDA* you will be able to use your compatible Nvidia CUDA enabled graphics card it to render with the *Cycles Render Engine*. It is highly recommended to use graphics cards when possible.

In the *OpenGL* section you'll be able to set options like *Clip Alpha* (from 0 to 1) or *Mipmap* (scale textures for 3D View using Mipmap filtering).

Other options are *Anisotropic Filtering* and *VBOs* (which speeds up the viewport rendering acting on the vertex arrays), and the *Window Draw Method* which fit the graphics card driver settings (*Automatic*)or allows to choose other methods.

Text Draw Options enable interface text anti-aliasing.

In the *Textures* sections, the *Limit Size* control limits the maximum resolution for pictures used in textured display to save memory, while the *Time Out* value indicates the time since last access of a GL texture in seconds, after which it is freed.

In the *Sequencer/Clip Editor* the *Prefetch Frame* value sets the number of extra-frames over the video playback. The *Memory Cache Limit* is the upper limit of the sequencer's memory cache(megabytes).

Solid OpenGL Lights are used to light the *3D View*, mostly during *Solid view.*

Custom Weight Paint Range allows the user to customize the default color ramp (red-yellow, blue-green) Blender use to visualize how much a bone deforms the mesh of a character.

International Fonts allows the user to use a different font set in order to translate either the UI or the tooltips into any other supported language (we strongly discourage to use a language other than English).

 Once you finished customizing user preferences, you can save your settings by clicking on the *Save User Settings* button.

1.8.2. System requirements

Blender is a very light software, but it has to be supported by a powerful hardware to ensure high performance, specially with complex calculations and heavy scenes. We show below a basic and a recommended configuration regardless the used platform.

Configurations are update to 2015.

Basic configuration:

- *CPU Intel i5*
- *RAM 4GB*
- *HD 500GB*
- *Graphic card with 2GB RAM and 512 Cuda Core*

Recommended configuration:

- *CPU Intel i7 or above*
- *RAM 16GB*
- *HD SSD 512 GB*
- *Graphic card with 4GB RAM and 1500 Cuda Core*

But what is *Cuda Core*?

Modern graphic cards, specially the professional ones, are real computers, which replace CPU in the graphic calculations.

Graphic card processor is called GPU (*Graphic Processor Unit*) and is equipped, as well as the CPU, with logic units.

Core refers to these units, real processors inside the hardware component, which manage the calculations individually, increasing their rate and speed.

GPUs work exactly like CPUs but, even if each single GPU Core is slower compared to CPU's, GPU can manage a higher number of logic units.

As an example, *Quad Core* means a CPU with 4 logic units (Cores). The latest graphic cards, like *Quadro* series, has up to 4000 Cores!

However not all the graphic cards are suitable for use in Blender.

Before you purchase a graphic card, make sure the GPU is compatible with *CUDA Core.*

We can suggest *Nvidia GTX 700, 800* and *900 series* or the advanced
Titan and *Quadro* series.

fig. 12 the new graphic board *Nvidia GTX 1080*

If your system is equipped with such a card, you better choose it as
Compute Device by selecting *CUDA* in the *System* tab of the *User Preferences* window (lower right corner) and saving you settings by clicking on the *Save User Settings* button.

Blender also supports multi-cards settings directly managing them from the *Compute Device* section of the *User Preferences* window. If more than one cards is installed, you can choose the right combination (e.g. *Device 1 + Device 2*).

IMPORTANT TIP: best performances are granted with identical graphic cards, same model, same chipset and access speed, same CUDA Cores and same RAM. Any difference, especially if significant, may cause worse performance than one card.

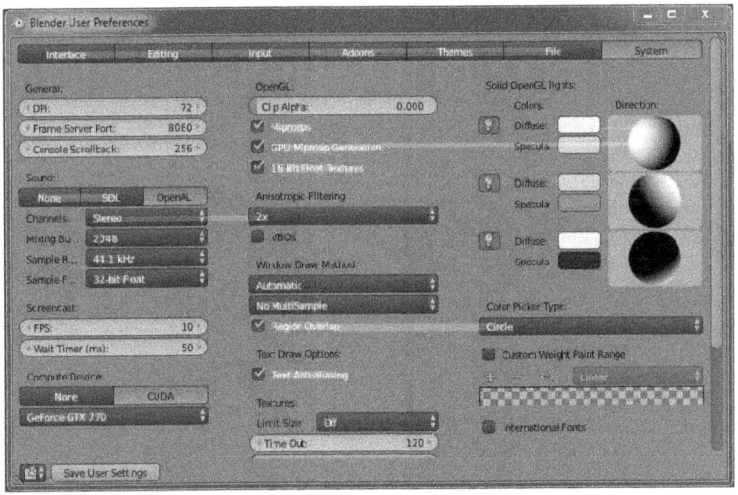

fig. 13 *CUDA* enabling in the *System User Preferences*

33

Saved settings will maintain every time Blender is started.

If you changed the main windows layout, you can also save your UI customizations as default start-up file.

Go to *File – Save Startup File* (or CTRL+U) and confirm your choice. From now on Blender will start with your own settings.

1.9. Online Resources

You can find tons of information and tutorials about Blender all over the web. Sometimes it is good quality stuff, sometimes not.

As it is open source, everyone can contribute to its development, however users must be able to get the best from online materials.

Internet is full of dedicated sites and tutorials, some of them very useful and well done.

Here is a short list of some Blender-related websites from which extract some more info, complementary to this Guide:

- **www.blender.org**(official Blender website)

- **www.blenderfoundation.com**(official Blender Foundation website)

- **www.blenderhighschool.net**(educational website from this guide's author)

- **www.blenderartists.org**(the biggest Blender forum)

- **www.blenderguru.com**(Andrew Price's website where you can find a lot of precious tips and high quality tutorials)

- **www.bledtuts.com**(high quality tutorials)

- **https://cgcookie.com/learn-blender/** (educational and content website)

- **www.blendswap.com**(Blender website from which you can download a lot of models and assets for Blender)

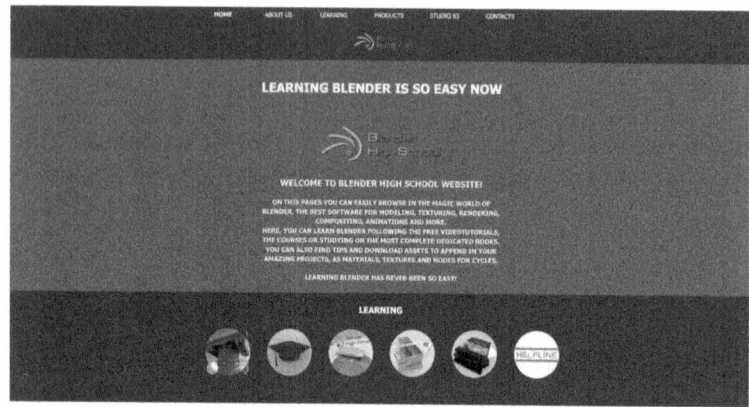

fig. 14 website *www.blenderhighschool.it*

2

BASIC OPERATIONS

2.1. Editors and Interface structure

Before starting to jump through the Blender windows, it is useful to clearly understand how they work, which elements, buttons, areas, panels and input data areas they are made of.

We must gain the full control of these windows, also named *Editor*, and understand how they can be placed, erased, splitted and resized. In one word: customized.

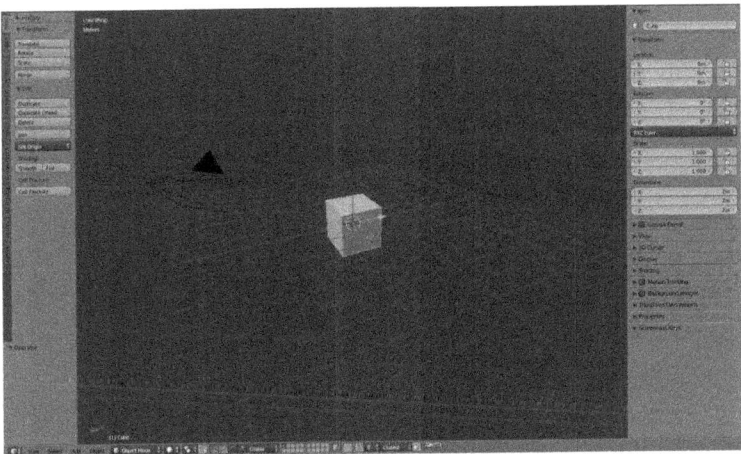

fig. 15 *3D* view Editor

Blender has several *Editors* with common features each.

We will describe them one by one.

2.1.1. *Header*

All editors have a *Header*, a strip with a lighter gray background containing icon buttons.

Each *Header* has an icon drop down menu on the left corner which allows to choose the window (or *Editor*) type. To change the features of the current window simply choose an icon on the drop down menu.

fig. 16 *Header*

All editors have a *Header*, a strip with a lighter gray background containing icon buttons.

Each *Header* has an icon drop down menu on the left corner which allows to choose the window (or *Editor*) type. To change the features of the current window simply choose an icon on the drop down menu.

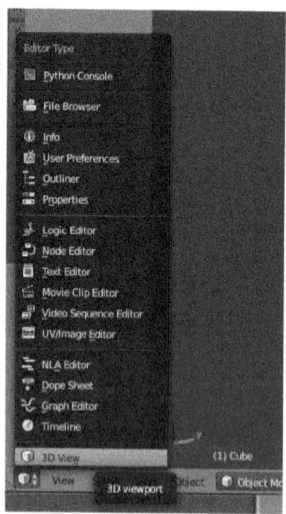

fig. 17 drop down menu

To move a header from top to bottom or the other way round, simply click on RMB on it and select the appropriate item from the pop-up menu (*Flip to Bottom* or *Flip to Top*). To gain some extra horizontal space in the header you can choose *Collapse menus.*

You can also set the active window to full screen (or the way back) by choosing *Maximize Area* or *Tile Area* (CTRL+UP-Arrow).

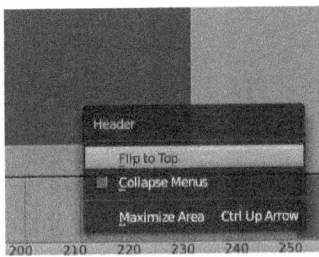

fig. 18 Header's visualization options

2.1.2. Work Space

fig. 19 work space

The work space is the main area of a window, the place where the magic happens.

41

Not every window has a work space (such as the *Properties* window).

Sometimes, such as in the *3D Viewport*, the work space can be further divided and show other related sidebars.

2.1.3. Sidebars

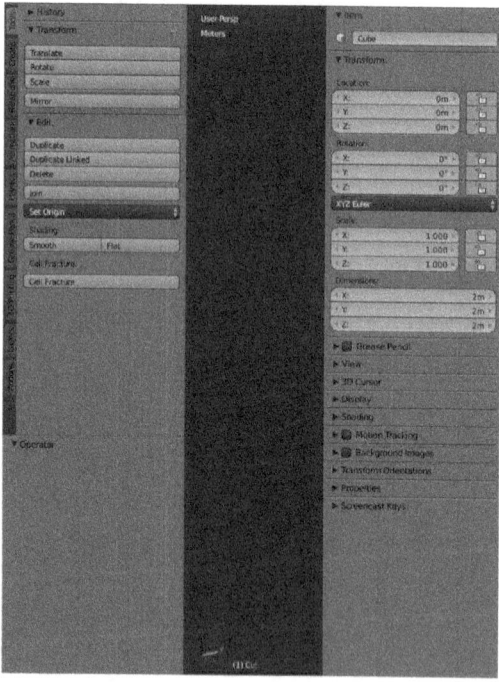

fig. 20 the two sidebars of the *3D Viewport (Tools and Properties Bar)*

Sidebars are special vertical areas at the right and/or left corner of specific windows (some window could have one, some other two, some other none), which contains additional tools and information and can be easily visualized/hidden with the same shortcuts (T for the left bars, N for the right ones).

2.1.4. Regions

Regions further subdivide a bar.

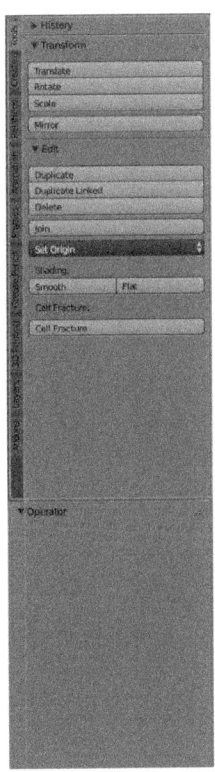

fig. 21 upper region in the *Tools Shelf*

2.1.5. Tabs

Tabs are side "flaps" used to group specific tools and features of one or more regions based on a common topic.

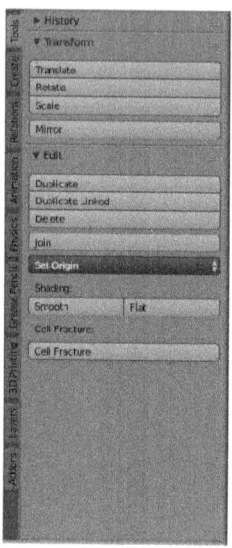

fig. 22 *Tools* tab in the *Tools Shelf*

2.1.6. Panels

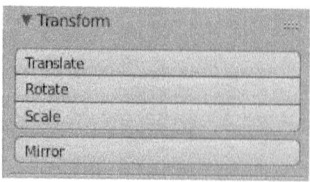

fig. 23 *Transform* panel in the *Tools Shelf*

The smallest organizational unit in the user interface is a panel, which can be collapsed to hide its contents by clicking on its upper left black arrow (or its header), or you can change the order of panels by clicking and dragging on the handle in the upper right corner of a panel's title.

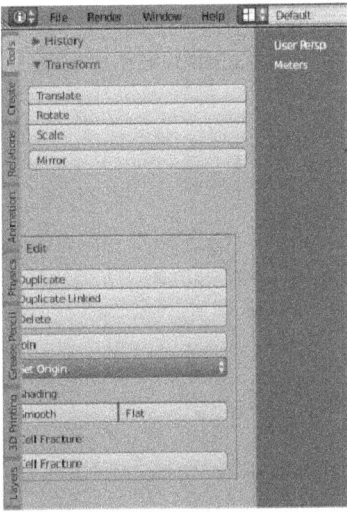

fig. 24 dragging of the *Edit* panel in the *Tools Shelf*

fig. 25 p*inning* a panel

Often it is desirable to view panels from different tabs at the same time. This has been solved by making panels with *Pin* option. A pinned panel remains visible regardless of which tab has been selected. You can pin a panel by clicking SHIFT+LMB on its header, or by clicking RMB on the header and choosing *Pin*.

2.1.7. Resize windows

You can resize areas by dragging their borders with LMB. Simply move your mouse cursor over the border between two areas until it changes to a double-headed arrow, and then click and drag.

You can maximize an area to fill the whole application window with CTRL+UP-Arrow (or CTRL+DOWN-Arrow).

2.1.8. Split or Join windows

You can manage the windows layout by splitting existing windows and then adjust its dimensions and type according to your needs.

In the upper right and lower left corners of a window are the window splitter widgets, and they look like a little ridged thumb grip. It both splits and combines window panels. When you hover over it, your cursor will change to a cross. LMB and drag it *inward* to split the window vertically (moving right/left) or horizontally (moving up/down).
To join the current window with the one above it, hover the mouse pointer over the window splitter. When the pointer changes to a cross, LMB click and drag up to begin the process of combining.

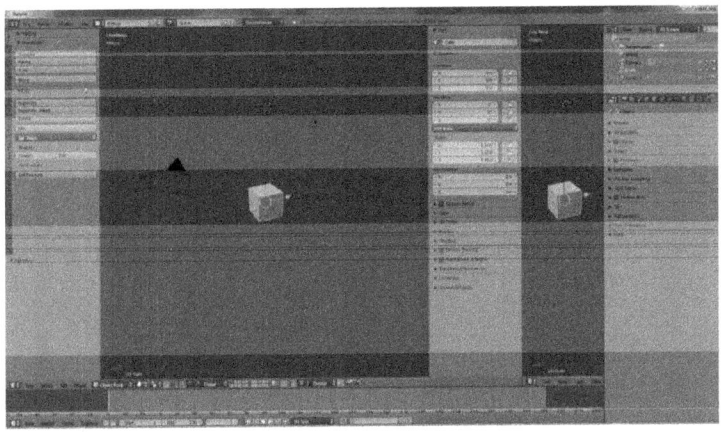

fig. 26 *splitting* a window

To join the current window with the one above it, hover the mouse pointer over the window splitter. When the pointer changes to a cross, LMB click and drag up to begin the process of combining.

The upper window will get a little darker, overlaid with an arrow pointing up. This indicates that the lower (current) area will "take over" that darkened area space. Release the LMB to join.

If you want the reverse to occur, move your mouse cursor back into the original (lower) area, and it will instead get the arrow overlay.

In the same way, windows may be merged left to right or vice versa.

In order to merge two areas, they must be the same dimension in the direction you wish to merge. For example, if you want to combine two areas that are side-by-side, they must be the same height. If the one on the left is not the same as the one on the right, you will not be able to combine them horizontally.

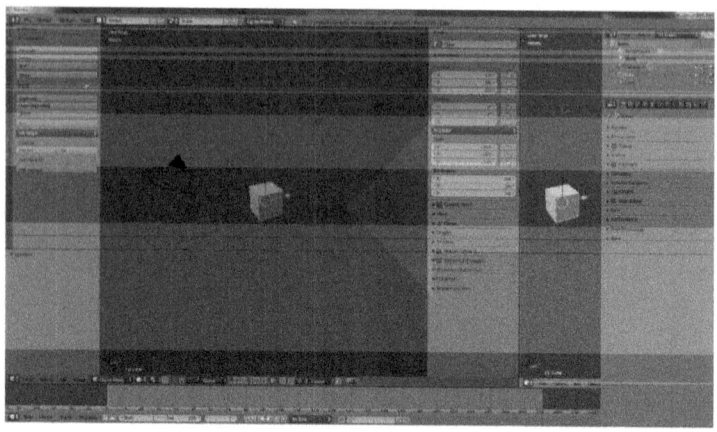

fig. 27 *Joining* two windows

2.1.9. Buttons and controls

Inside the windows you can find several buttons, icons, boxes and other controls used to assign numeric values to specific actions, to apply tools or simply to make choices. Let's check them in depth.

a) Operation Buttons
Operation Buttons are simple active boxes, which start a command on a mouse click.

Mirror

fig. 28 operation buttons

Operation Buttons are simple active boxes, which start a command on a mouse click.

48

b) Switches

Switches are similar to buttons but are grouped in two or more elements. When one is clicked the others are automatically disabled.

fig. 29 switches

c) Drop down menus

fig. 30 drop down menu

Clicking on a drop down menu (marked with two little bright arrows) will show a list of options to choose from.

d) Check boxes

fig. 31 check box

Check boxes simply enable/disable a specific option.

49

e) Counters

fig. 32 counter

With counters you can specify a value clicking on its center or increase/decrease the current value by using the side arrows.

f) Sliders

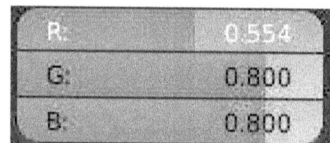

fig. 33 sliders

With sliders you can specify a value clicking on its center or increase/decrease the current value by sliding the bar to right/left. The main difference between Sliders and Counters is that sliders can only operate into a range between a min and max value.

g) Text fields

fig. 34 text field

Text fields allow you to insert alphanumeric strings fro example to name objects.

h) Color Picker (palette)

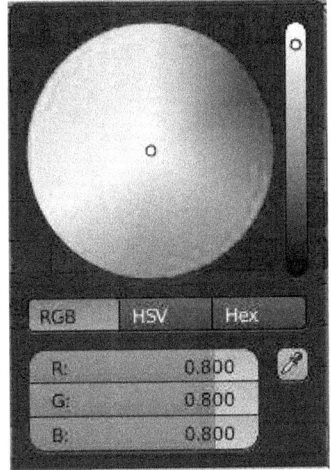

fig. 35 color picker (palette)

Color Picker (or palette) is a tool witch allows you to insert numeric values to define a specific color.

A typical example is when you has to define the color of a material.

i) Icons

fig. 36 icon

Icons, as seen previously, usually activate a drop-down menu, rather than text fields or other buttons. One example is the icon of the header that determines the window type.

2.1.10. Mathematical functions in Counters and Sliders

In the field dedicated to the numerical values entries of the Counters and Cursors you can also enter mathematical functions. The Blender calculation engine is able to calculate the inserted formulas.

For example by entering the value 0:20 + 1.30 will be automatically calculated and displayed the value 1.50m (in meters if it is set, as we shall see later).

Similarly you can use the symbols – (*minus*), / (*divided*), * (*times*), ^ (*raised*), *log* (*x*) (logarithm), *sin, cos, tan* (*sine, cosine* and *tangent*), *abs* (*x*) (*absolute value*) and other mathematical functions.

2.1.11. The – (*minus*) symbol

During transform operations that we will see below (move, rotate and scale), minus is used in case of negative transformation, which means opposite to the positive direction of the axis and the absolute counter-clockwise rotation. The symbol – (minus) can also be inserted below the absolute value, so you do not re-run the operation again in case of error or omission.

For example, to translate along the *x*-axis of 2 meters in the negative direction (according to conventional orientation) you can type "– 2" as well as "2 –".

2.1.12. Decimals

The decimal values are separated by default by the period (.), for example 12.3.

The zero at the end is not necessary (12.3 = 12.30).

Also the zero at the beginning can be suppressed for non-integer values smaller than 1. For example "0.4" can simply be typed ".4".

2.1.13. Units

It will be shown later how to set the units in Blender.

Anyway decimals numerical values will be automatically converted to the corresponding value according to the set scale.

For example, if the scale is set in meters, the value .1 will be automatically converted in "10cm".

Or you can operate in the opposite way. Blender recognizes the values "m" (meters), "cm" (centimeters), "km" (kilometers), "mm" (millimeters), etc.; it is therefore possible, without making a conversion calculation in mind, type directly "10cm" or "10 cm".

2.2. Start Blender

At startup, Blender comes (if enabled the option of preference) with a *splash screen* with a default configuration of the windows.

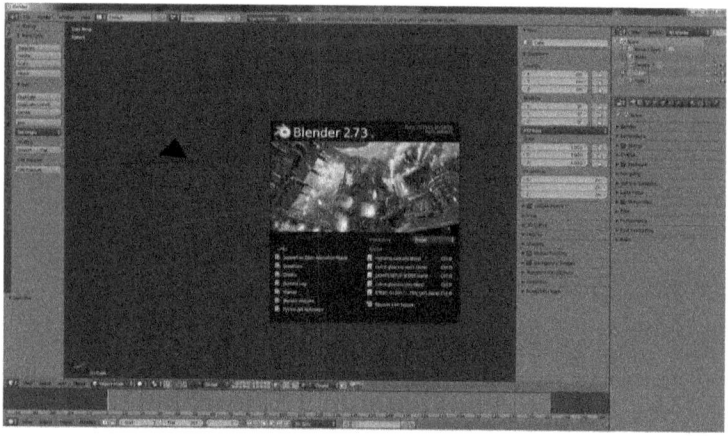

fig. 37 *splash screen*

In the *splash screen*, you can choose the interaction configuration from the drop-down menu, call up recent files, retrieve the last open session (Recover Last Session) or visit some *online link*.

In the upper side the version with the date of release is shown.

Clicking outside of this window, the window closes and Blender will present itself in its default configuration.

2.2.1. Blender interface and basic settings

Blender has been known for a good but difficult software for years because of its indecipherable GUI.

The interface was still almost the same of the initial versions up to version 2.49 indeed, that is designed primarily for developers and not for users.

With version 2.5, Blender got a revolutionary restyling, which made its user interface something very clear, understandable and user friendly.

The latest 2.7x version (which this volume refers to), the interface has been further improved with the introduction of several tabs on the Tools Shelf bar, as we shall see later.

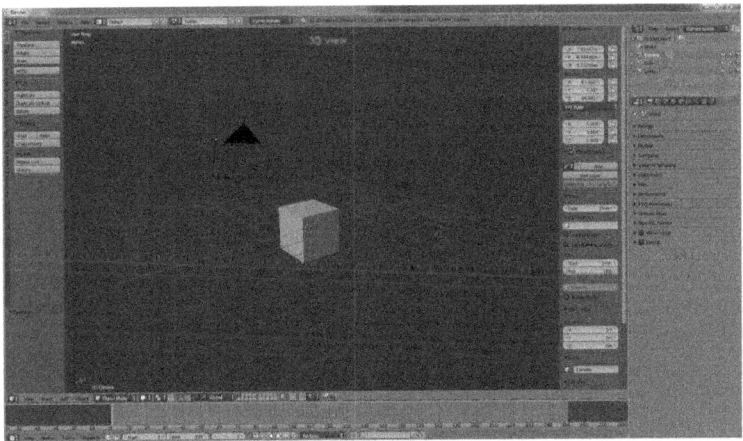

fig 38 default GUI

As seen, the Blender interface can be customized, as in many commercial programs, to suit your needs and according to the working areas.

For this reason Blender already provides some layout presets that allow you to use the interface for modeling, animation, compositing, game engine, etc.

Let's see in detail how the default interface is structured.

The default layout is divided into five fully customizable windows.

2.2.2. The *Info* header

fig 39 Info header

The horizontal upper window is called **Info**, **Info editor** or **Info Header**. It is composed of a header and a gray area, generally minimized.

The header shows some drop-down menus: *File, Render, Window, Help, Screen Layout, Scene* and *Render Engine*; and an information line.

a) File

The *File* drop down menu contains all operations relating to the imported file, or to import.

In particular:

- *New* (CTRL + N) creates a new default blank project;
- *Open* (Ctrl + O) opens the existing file;
- *Open Recent* (SHIFT + CTRL + O) allows you to open a file from the recent file list;
- *Revert* reloads the current file;
- *Recover Last Session* allows the recovery of the last unexpectedly closed session;

- *Recover Auto Save* restores the last saved version of a file;
- *Save* (Ctrl + S) saves the project with a *.blend extension;
- *Save As ...* (Shift + Ctrl + S) saves the project with a name;
- *User Preferences...* (CTRL + ALT + U) retrieves the window of preference previously analyzed;

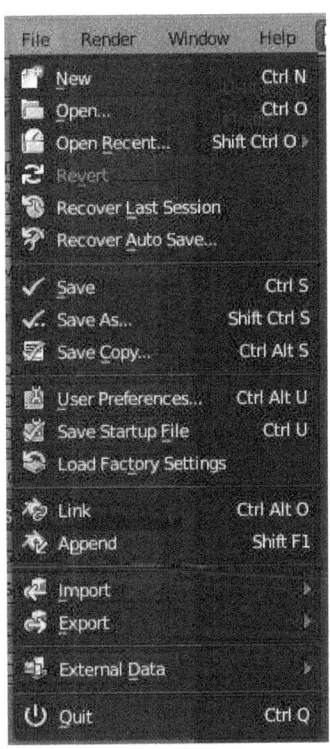

fig 40 il menu a tendina *File*

- *Save Startup file* (CTRL + U) saves all current settings: installed or open Addons, positions and size of windows, the objects in the scene, the entered numerical values, preferences, and changes made in a template file will become the default file opening program. Caution is recommended in the use of this very useful and important function;

- *Load Factory Settings* restore the default values with the default factory settings;
- *Append* and *Link* allow you to import or connect to an open file the contents of another file. The shortcut of the two functions are CTRL+ALT+O and SHIFT+F1 respectively;
- *Import* allows you to load models from other compatible formats created with other modeling software;
- *Export* saves the project in a compatible format with other software;
- *External Data* retrieves and manages the files directly related to the running files (for example, textures and videos). Simply insert in the opened browser the path of dissociated files;
- *Quit* (Ctrl + Q) closes Blender.

b) *Render*

The *Render* menu manages the tools for the rendering engine. In particular:

- *Render Image* starts the rendering process of a static image (also with the shortcut F12);
- *Render Animation* starts the rendering process of an animation (also with CTRL + F12);
- *OpenGL Render Image* and *OpenGL Render Animation* start rendering in OpenGL mode, if supported;
- *OpenGL Render Option* opens a submenu by managing OpenGL's Preferences on Antialiasing and Transparency (Alpha);
- *Show / Hide Render View* shows or hides the rendering window during the process (ALT + F11);
- *Play Rendered Animation* launches the animation after the rendering process (also with CTRL + F11).

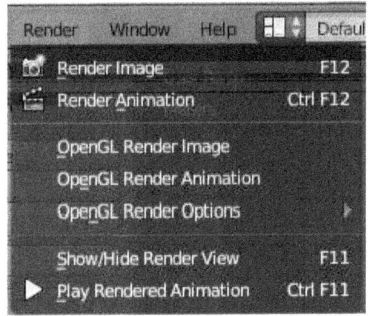

fig 41 the *Render* drop-down menu

c) *Window*

This menu manages the current interface windows.

- *Duplicate Windows* duplicates the entire opened project into a new Blender window (CTRL + ALT + W);
- *Toggle Window Full screen* maximizes Blender hiding the top bar of the operating system (ALT + F11);
- *Save Screenshot* is a shot of the entire workspace and save the files in a specified folder in the browser (Ctrl + F3);
- *Make Screen cast* start a video capture clip of the work area and saves it at the end in a /tmp folder. To start the operation you can also type ALT + F3, while click on the CAPTURE button that appears in the header of the Info window is necessary to stop it. When you start this useful operation a semi-transparent circle will appear around the cursor that will show the mouse position during playback video;
- *Toggle System Console* shows the Blender starting command lines into a Shell window.

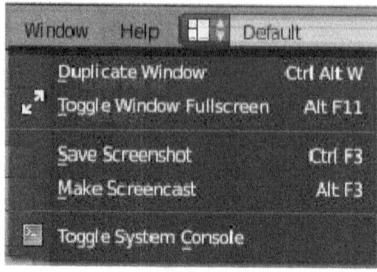

fig 42 the *Window* drop-down menu

d) *Help*

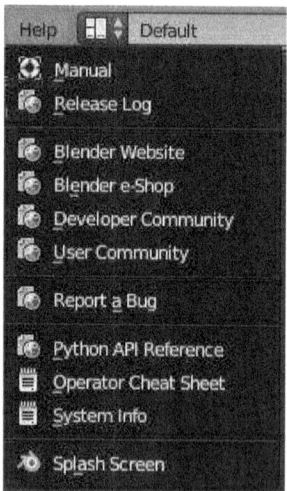

fig 43 the *Help* drop-down menu

The *Help* window contains the links to all Blender Foundation sites for manuals, commands, and other dedicated functions.

The *Splash Screen* launches and redisplays the splash window.

e) Screen Layout

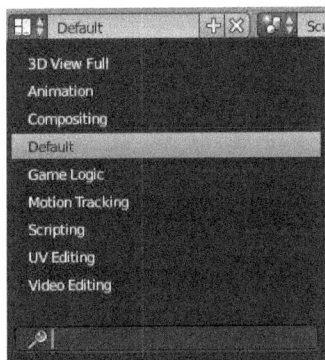

fig 44 the *Screen Layout menu*

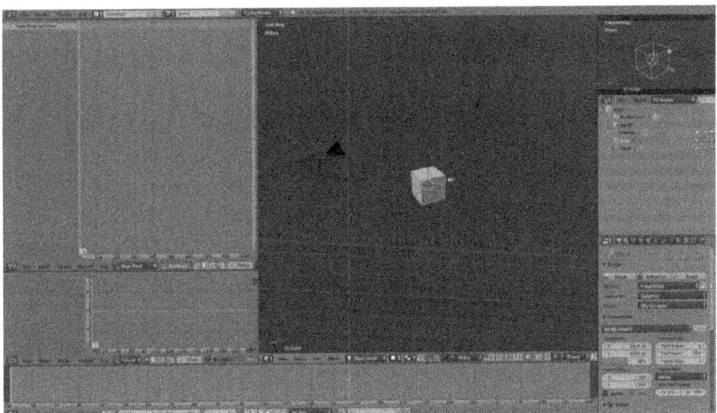

fig 45 the *Screen Layout* set to *Animation*

This window contains some common configurations (or Layout) of the work areas in Blender. *Default* is the starting configuration.

Of course, setting a different configuration and then saving in *Save Startup File* will open Blender in the new configuration until the next modification.

You can add new windows and panels configurations by clicking on the "+" button and typing the desired name, or delete a configuration by clicking the "X" button, both placed on the right of the drop down menu.

Once a configuration is cancelled, it will be impossible to recover it.

   a) Scene

The *Scene* menu lets you create different scenes inside the same *.blend work files, starting from the main one. By clicking on the "+" button, you will see a drop down menu where you can specify which elements are to be duplicated in the new scene, for example, only the settings, rather than the entire scene (*Full Copy*). The scenes in this last case will be completely independent.

This workflow is fundamental in Blender because it will be easier to manage in the same project, for example, views and different illuminations, rather than modified versions with colors and materials, or the presence or absence of objects.

To delete a scene, just click on the button "X" (on selected scene).

fig 46 the *Scene* drop-down menu

b) Render Engine

This menu is used to select the rendering engine to be used in the current project.

Blender Render is the default render engine.

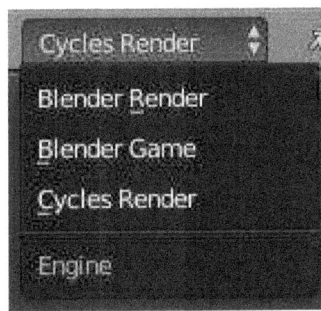

fig 47 the *Render* drop-down menu

c) The *info/statistic* line

This line provides all the statistics and information such as objects and elements in the scene. 1From left to right: the Blender used version, the number of vertices and faces of the selected object, the number of triangulated surfaces, the number of objects in the scene in relation to the selected objects, the number of selected depending on the total lamps, the memory occupied by the file, the name of the active object.

While in *Edit Mode* (as discussed below) specific statistics will be activated: the number of vertices, edges, faces and object name.

v2.73 | Verts:8 | Faces:6 | Tris:12 | Objects:1/3 | Lamps:0/1 | Mem:10.03M | Cube

fig 48 the *info/statistic* line

2.2.3. The *3D View* editor

The wide central window is called *3D View*, where the actual 3D solids construction and modeling take place.

On opening, by default, it displays a cube, a light and a camera arranged on a grid which is parallel to the Cartesian axes x (in red) and y (in green).

Below, on the left side, the set of three axes x, y, z, respectively, in the colors red, green and blue is represented and oriented according to the current view.

At the top, on the left side as well, a string in white informs you about the type of display (perspective or isometric) and the current units.

Two vertical bars (one right and one left), called **Sidebars**, contain information and tools on the project and on selected objects.

In particular, the left sidebar is called the *Tools Shelf* and includes all the necessary tools for creating and basic modeling.

The right sidebar, called *Properties* bar, provides the information and properties of the objects in the scene and the 3D view itself.

Since we have not yet discussed the specifics of the object types and methods, describing in detail all of the Sidebar feature may be difficult and not in line with the method used in this book.

We prefer therefore briefly describe the two sidebars and deeply discuss on the details of their features with clarifying examples in a second time.

By default, the *Header* of the 3D view is placed horizontally at the bottom of the window.

fig 49 the 3D View *Header*

From left to right, just after the 3D View icon, the **View** menu shows all the functions related to the current view.

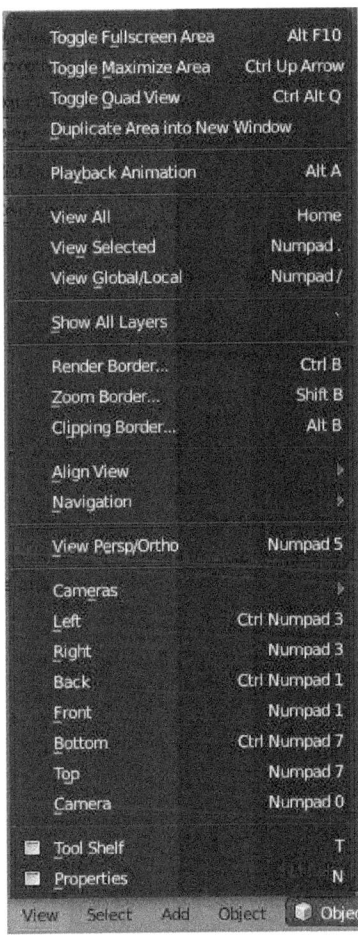

fig 50 the *View* menu

- *Toggle Fullscreen Area* (ALT + F10) maximizes the size of the 3D view in full-screen;
- *Toggle Maximize Area* (CTRL + UP ARROW) maximizes the 3D view in Blender window (CTRL + DOWN ARROW to restore);
- *Toggle Quad View* (CTRL + ALT + C) divides the work area into 4 equal parts and shows the current scene from the 4 main views (*TOP, FRONT, RIGHT* and *PERSPECTIVE*). This option is useful when you need to control the modeling process both in the orthogonal views and three-dimensional view;

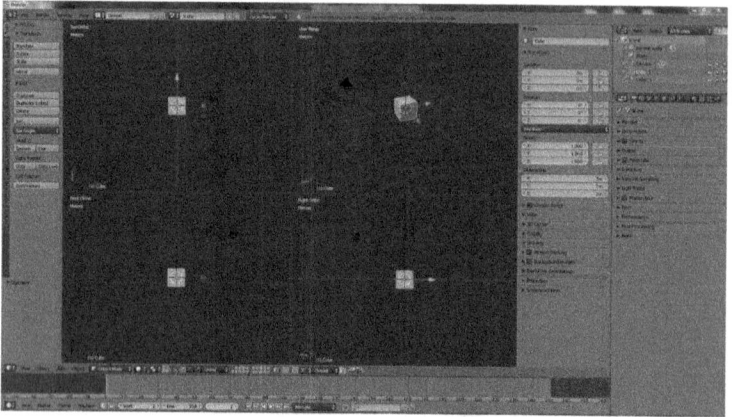

fig 51 *Quad View*

- *Duplicate Area into New Window* duplicates the 3D view with an exact clone;
- *Animation playback* (ALT + A) runs the animation;
- *View All* (Home key) makes all the objects in the scene visible;
- *View Selected* (. NUM) maximizes and focuses the view on the selected object;
- *View Global / Local* (/ NUM) maximizes and focuses on the selected object, hiding all the others. Repeating the operation returns to the original view;
- *Show All Layers* turn on all layers;

66

- *Render Border* (CTRL + B key with the mouse drag) creates a box selection that will define the area of pre rendering of the scene or the current view;
- *Zoom Border* (SHIFT + B and dragging) performs an automatic zoom to the defined area;
- *Clipping Border* (ALT + B, and dragging) automatically shows only the selected area. Pressing ALT + B again will restore the previous conditions;
- *Allign View* opens a drop-down submenus, from which you can chose some other options:
    - *Align View to Active* shows another submenu from which you can enable the default views, even with some of the NUM keys:

7 NUM	Top view
CTRL + 7 NUM	Bottom view
1 NUM	Front view
CTRL + 1 NUM	Rear view
3 NUM	Right view
CTRL + 3 NUM	Left view
5 NUM	Split from orthographic to perspective and vice versa
4, 6 NUM	horizontal rotations of 5 ° of the view
2, 8 NUM	vertical rotations of 5 ° of the view
0 NUM	Active Camera view
CTRL + 0	Set object as Active Camera

    - *Center Cursor and View All* centers the view to the3D cursor and displays all objects;

    - *Allign Active Camera to View* sets the current view as the camera view, or in other words applies the orientation and location of the current view to the active camera (ALT + CTRL + NUM 0);

    - *Allign Active Camera to Selected* automatically frames the selected object with the active camera;

- *View Selected* (. NUM) maximizes and focuses the view on the selected object;
- *Center View to Cursor* centers the view in the 3D view so that the cursor is at the center of the viewport;

- *View Lock to Active* (SHIFT + . NUM) centers the view on the selected or active object;
- *View Lock Clear* (ALT +. NUM) restores the view from the previous step.

- *Navigation* shows the main navigation methods (orbit, pan and zoom);
- *View Persp / Ortho* (5 NUM) automatically switches from perspective view to the isometric one;
- *Cameras* opens a submenu with two entries that manage camera view:

  - *Set Active Object as Camera* (CTRL + NUM 0) means that the selected camera becomes the active one, whose view can be displayed with 0 NUM key;

  - *Active Camera* displays the view of the active camera (0 NUM).
- The next 7 voices select the default views with the combination of the NUM keys (the same as *Allign Active View* but without SHIFT key);
- *Tools Shelf* opens and closes the Tools Shelf Bar on the left (T);
- *Properties* opens and closes the Properties Bar on the right (N).

Below, in the **Select** menu shows all the commands related to the selection of the objects and the geometric elements that compose them.

The items in this menu change depending on the current *mode* (*Object Mode* and *Edit Mode*). The entries concerning the *Edit Mode* will be analyzed in detail below, in the "Mode" chapter and in particular in the *Edit Mode* section.

NOTE: All of Blender menu items generally change depending on the current mode. E.g. in Sculpt Mode, the header of the 3D view menu completely changes into other dedicated items.

Let's see in detail the entries for *Object Mode*:

- *Select Pattern ...* allows you to enter a string for the selection of objects in the scene. For example * selects all objects;
- *Linked* (SHIFT + L) selects objects by grouping type criteria(object data, material, texture, particle system, libraries, etc.). it is a useful feature if you need to select objects of a specific type;
- *Grouped* (SHIFT + G) selects the objects in the scene according to a predefined grouping pattern;
- *Select Camera* select the active camera;

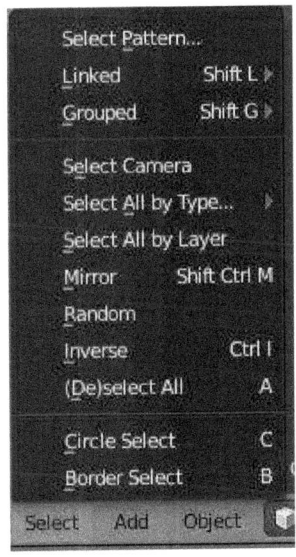

fig 52 *Select* menu in *Object Mode*

- *Select All by Type* opens a drop-down menu that allows you to select all objects which belongs to a specific category (mesh, curves ...);
- *Select All by Layer* select all objects placed onto one or more specific layers;
- *Mirror* (SHIF + CTRL + M) selects any objects mirrored by the selected ones;
- *Random* make a random selection between a group of objects in the view. You must specify in the bottom region of the Tools Shelf the percentage of selection using the slider;
- *Invert* (Ctrl + I) reverses the current selection;
- *Select / Deselect All* (A) select or deselect all objects in the scene;
- *Circle Select* is a useful tool to select objects using a circular brush, resizable with WM. By typing C and then adjusting the size of the circular brush you can select objects by clicking with LMB (MMB to deselect). To end the selection, type ESC (or RMB);
- *Border Select* (B) is the most common method of selection, using the rectangular selection by dragging LMB. This will create an area within which all objects will be selected.

> **NOTE: Selection and active objects. When you select an object, its outline is colored with light orange by default, indicating that it is the ACTIVE object, on which to perform basic editing actions. In a multiple selection (multiple objects), only the active one will have the edge in light orange, while other selected objects will have the edges colored in dark orange. In a multiple selection JUST ONE OBJECT could be active.**

Other selection and de-selection methods

You can select or deselect multiple objects by SHIFT + LMB on them, one by one.

In a multiple selection, the last object selected will be the ACTIVE one. On that list, you can simply change active object by clicking the object again while holding SHIFT.

In the **Add** menu (SHIFT + A), you can enter all the major objects in the scene.

fig 53 *Add* menu

SHIFT + A within the work area will open a drop down menu with the same options.

In the **Object** menu (while in *Object Mode*) you'll find all the controls that manage the operations on selected objects in the scene.

The menus shown while in *Edit Mode* will be analyzed in detail in the related chapter; let's now analyze the controls in *Object Mode*.

- *Convert to* (ALT + C) allows you to convert a mesh to curve and vice versa;
- *Hide* (H) shows or hides the selected object or objects;
- *Hide Unselected* (SHIFT + H) allows the inverse function, namely to hide what is not selected; while *Show Hidden* (ALT + H) shows previously hidden objects;
- *Move to Layer* (M) moves the selected object or objects on another layer. Simply select the desired Layer once activated the command;
- *Transfer Mesh Data Layout* opens a window, once selected two or more objects (one active), where you can specify which data to transfer from the active to those selected;
- *Transfer Mesh Data* (SHIFT + CTRL + T) transfer the vertex or bevel data from the active object to the other selected ones;
- *Join* (CTRL + J) combines two or more object in a single mesh;
- *Game* opens a submenu in which you define to copy, add or delete the active object properties and data in the game environment;
- *Quick Effects* quickly assigns to the active object a volumetric effects or physical behavior, such as: fur, explosion, smoke, fluid;
- *Constraints* manages chains, groups or parent relations of the active object, and in particular:
  - *Add Constraint (with Target)* (SHIFT + CTRL + C) opens a window in which to assign to the active object a relations with other objects or simulations;
  - *Copy Constraints to Selected Object*, in a selection, copy the relations of all selected objects from the active one;
  - *Clear Object Constraints* (CTRL + ALT + C) deletes all relations assigned to the active object.

- *Group* manages objects grouping, not to be confused with *Join* as each object will remain the owner of its geometry, internal relations and properties, but it will be linked to others. *Group* opens a submenu:

- *Create a new Group (CTRL + G) groups the selected objects;*
- *Remove from Group (CTRL + ALT + G) removes the selected object from one specific group;*
- *Remove from All Groups (SHIFT + CTRL + ALT + G)removes the selected object from all groups which it is linked to;*
- *Add Selected to Active Group (SHIFT + CTRL + G) add the selected object to the group that contains the active object in the scene;*
- *Remove Selected to Active Group (SHIFT + ALT + G)removes the selected object from the group, which the active object is in.*

- *Track* launches Tracking-related commands (we will discuss them later);
- *Parent* manages the functions of parent/children relations between objects (we will discuss them later);
- *Make Single User* makes the selected objects data unique and connected to itself only;
- *Make Local* (L) creates a data library related to the selected object in the current file;
- *Make Dupli Face* converts the selected object in a two-side distance;
- *Make Links* (CTRL + L) opens a submenu where you can choose what to link or copy (materials, data, modifiers, animations, groups) from the active object on the other selected objects. To do this you must select the objects on which you have to copy the data, then (while holding SHIFT) select the one to copy these data from, type Ctrl + L and then choose the type of information to be copied (or connect);
- *Make Proxy* (CTRL + ALT + P) adds an *Empty* object which locally assign the object data on;

73

- *Delete* removes the selected object or objects. You need to confirm;
- *Duplicate Linked* (ALT + D) creates an instance of the original. It is a useful function in the case of identical objects still subject to change in *Object Mode*. The changes made in the original geometry (in *Edit Mode*) will be automatically applied to all instances;
- *Duplicate Object* (SHIFT + D) creates an exact copy, completely independent from the original;
- *Animation* opens a submenu which allows you to control the main animation functions also from the 3D view:
  - *Add Keyframe* (I) adds a keyframe to a specific parameter in a given frame; *Delete Keyframe* (ALT + I) eliminates an existing keyframe on the selected parameter;
  - *Clear Keyframes* removes all keyframes on the selected object;
  - *Change Keying Set* (SHIF + CTRL + ALT + I) changesthe settings of the active keyframe;
  - *Bake Action* definitely applies the keyframed transformations assigned to the selected object;

- *Snap* (SHIFT + S) opens a submenu in which you can find summarizes the snap functions (better explained in the following chapters);
- *Apply*(CTRL + A) definitely assigns to the selected object the transformation made in *Object Mode*. This opens a dropdown menu from where you can choose whether to apply location, rotation, scale, rotation & scale;
- *Clear* restores the original *Location*(ALT + G),*Rotation*(ALT +R),*Scale* (ALT + S), *Origin* (ALT + O) settings of the selected object;
- *Mirror* lets you to mirror an object according to the mouse position (CTRL + M), or according to x, y or z axes;

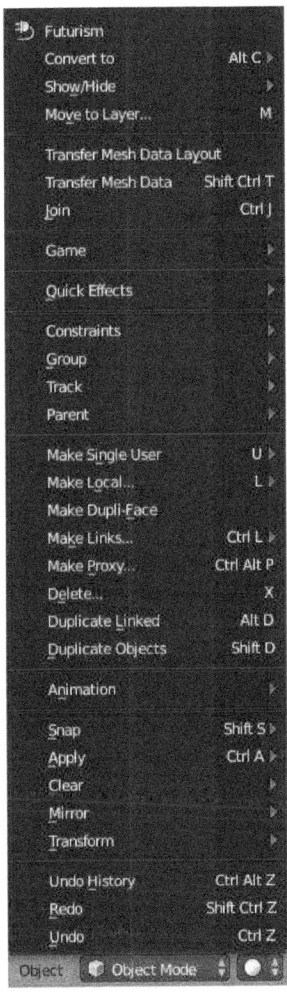

Futurism
Convert to   Alt C ▶
Show/Hide   ▶
Move to Layer...   M

Transfer Mesh Data Layout
Transfer Mesh Data   Shift Ctrl T
Join   Ctrl J

Game   ▶

Quick Effects   ▶

Constraints   ▶
Group   ▶
Track   ▶
Parent   ▶

Make Single User   U ▶
Make Local...   L ▶
Make Dupli-Face
Make Links...   Ctrl L ▶
Make Proxy...   Ctrl Alt P
Delete...   X
Duplicate Linked   Alt D
Duplicate Objects   Shift D

Animation   ▶

Snap   Shift S ▶
Apply   Ctrl A ▶
Clear   ▶
Mirror   ▶
Transform   ▶

Undo History   Ctrl Alt Z
Redo   Shift Ctrl Z
Undo   Ctrl Z

Object   Object Mode

fig 54 *Object* menu in *Object Mode*

- *Transform* allows you to perform the three main transformations: *Grab* (G), *Rotation* (R), *Scale* (S). The command may be followed by keyboard entries such as the x, y or z direction and the numerical value. For example, to

move the object by 2 meters in the negative X direction simply type "G X 2 -" (or "- 2");
- *Undo History*(CTRL + ALT + Z) shows a dropdown menu which lists the last used commands;
- *Redo* (SHIFT + CTRL + Z) restores the last cancelled operation;
- *Undo* (Ctrl + Z) cancels the last operation.

The next drop-down menu, called **Mode Menu** (*Object Mode* is displayed by default), allows you to access the various working modes, which are:

fig 55 Mode menu

- *Object Mode*, which allows you to modify the whole selected object, without editing its "internal" geometry;
- *Edit Mode*, in which you can modify the single geometry elements of the object (vertex, edges and faces), using specific geometry tools;
- *Sculpt Mode*, which allows you to literally sculpt the shape of the object with customizable brushes which make the workflow similar to a real clay sculpting method;
- *Vertex Paint,* which allows you to paint some vertices, in order to assign them specific operations;
- *Weight Paint*, which assigns a weight to each painted vertex;

- *Texture Paint*, which allows you to paint textures applied on the selected object directly in the 3D Viewport.

With the TAB key you can quickly switch between *Object Mode* and *Edit Mode* and vice versa; CTRL + TAB to switch between *Object Mode* and *Weight Paint Mode*.

There are two other modes that are available only with specific objects:

- *Particle Mode*, which contains tools to manage the particle systems;
- *Pose Mode*, dedicated to the armor posing mode. You can toggle this mode with the *Weight Paint* mode clicking CTRL + TAB.

We will go into detail later, after learning introductory concepts.

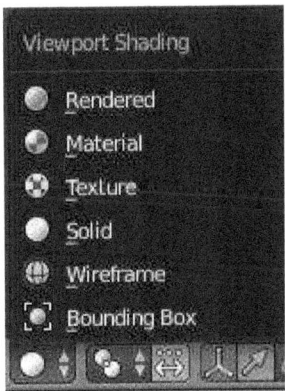

fig 56 visualization styles

The next menu is the **Viewport Shading Menu** and displays all the objects in the 3D view in six different ways.

- *Bounding Box* displays a box corresponding to the maximum object size. This method is useful in case of very dense geometries and "heavy" scenes;
- *Wireframe* displays transparent wireframe object with only edges visible. This display style is very useful to understand the totality of the objects geometry and to select parts which could be hidden by foreground objects;
- *Solid* displays the object as a solid (not transparent). In this case you can only select visible objects (or its components);
- *Texture* makes applied textures visible in the 3D view. Useful to check if UV mapping was properly assigned or not;
- *Material* provides more complete information on the material assigned to the objects, such as reflections and transparencies;

fig 57 visualization styles: 1: *Bounding Box*; 2: *Wireframe*; 3: *Solid*; 4: *Texture*; 5:*Material*; 6:*Rendered*

- *Rendered* allows you to see a preview of the rendered scene, according to the *Preview Sampling* resolution set in the *Render* panel of the *Properties* window. Useful to preview the final result without the need to launch long rendering processes. SHIFT + Z to toggle between *Solid* and *Rendered* view.

Z key allows you to quickly toggle between the two most used visualization styles, *Solid* and *Wireframe*; ALT + Z to toggle between
Solid and *Texture* view.

The next button **Pivot Center for Rotating / Scaling** will be analyzed later through practical examples.

It is used to define the center (*Pivot*) point for a transformation.

fig 58 *Pivot Center for Rotating / Scaling* button

You can set as *Pivot point* the active element of a selection (center of gravity); the middle point of an object, of a selection of objects or elements; individual center of gravity of all the selected objects or items; the center of gravity between several objects; the 3D cursor; the center of gravity of the Bounding Box, if enabled.

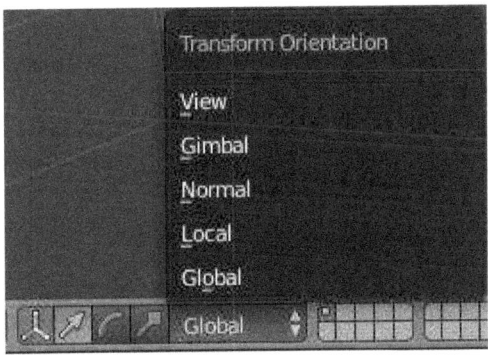

fig 59 *Transform Orientation* menu

The following buttons are used to select the object manipulators, used to manually operate on the selected object or its geometry

79

performing the three main transformations: **move, rotate** and **scale**.

The first of the five buttons enables/disables the manipulators.

The second one (a small arrow) adds the translation manipulator to the selected object (displayed as three colored arrows) centered on the pivot point and aligned along the three reference axes x , y and z. To move the object along an axis just click on the corresponding arrow and drag it forward or backward. To freely move the object, simply click and drag the white center circle.

The third button (a little arc) adds the rotation manipulator to the selected object (displayed as a set of three colored rings) centered on the pivot point around the three reference axes x , y and z. To rotate the object around an axis just click on the corresponding ring and drag it clockward or counter-clockward. To operate free rotation, simply click and drag on the white central circle.

The fourth one (a line with a square at the end) adds the scaling manipulator to the selected object (displayed as a set of three axes with handles at the top) centered on the pivot point and aligned along the three reference axes x , y and z. To scale the object along a axis, just click and drag on the corresponding square. To make a global scale, simply click and drag the white center circle.

In all the three cases, the manipulators use the conventional axes color (red = x , green = y , blue = z).

You can enable all three buttons simultaneously with SHIFT + LMB on the specific icons; it will display all of the three manipulators on the selected object.

The fifth button (with the text *Global* by default), named **Transform Orientation**, opens a drop down menu that allows to choose the reference axis system: *Global* (referred to the whole scene), *Local* (referred to the selected object), *Gimbal* (i.e. according to the active *Rotation Mode*, with Z axis fixed on Global z-axis while X and Y pointing object x and y local axis), *Normal* (perpendicular to the selected face/edge) and *View* (referred to the current view).

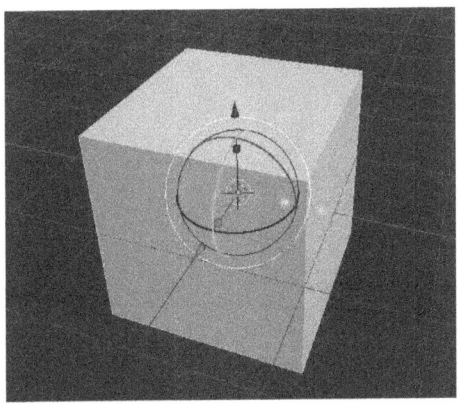

fig 60 the three *Manipulator* handles centered on the *Pivot* point of the *Cube*

Like other image editing software or CAD drawing, Blender also allows to group objects in Layers.

fig 61 *Layer Selector*

The layer system helps you to properly manage and design your object distribution on the scene.

Grouping objects by type, material, color or function can solve a lot of problems and, if necessary, to lighten up the scene from unnecessary objects at some stage simply by turning off a specific layer.

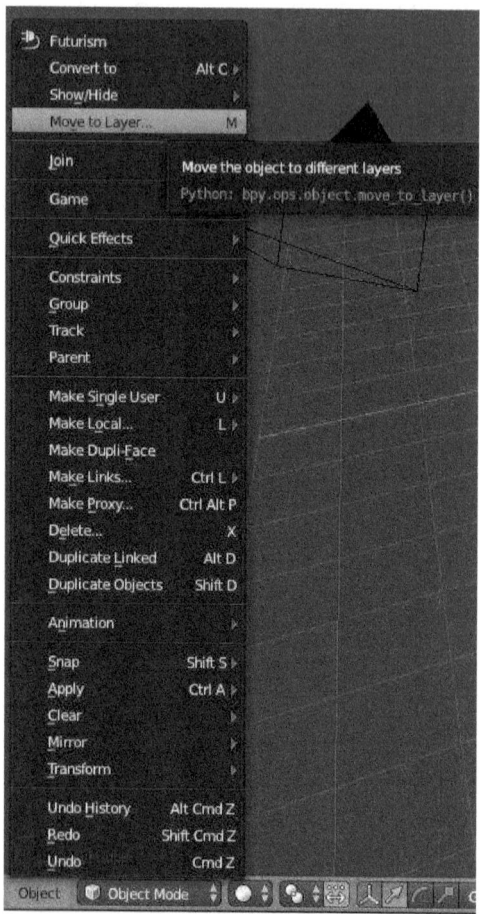

fig 62 *Move to Layer* option

Blender has 20 layers each represented by a box. In the next version 2.8 the layers will be removed and replaced with the *Collections* into the *Outliner*. Follow next *Upgrades*.

Layers which contain at least one object are displayed as a box with a grey circle (in the *Layer* selector), while boxes with the darker gray background represent active layers, meaning that the objects grouped in them are displayed in the scene and eventually rendered.

The box with the yellow circle represents the layers which contains the active object.

To move an object or objects in a specific layer simply select them from the *Object* menu and choose the option *Move To Layer* (M), then select the box representing the layer target. Alternatively you can type M and the number from 1 to 0 to move the selected object directly to any layer within the first 10.

If the *Layer Management* addon is enabled, layers can be managed from the *Tools Shelf*, where you can name layers, turn them off/on in the 3D view or in the render, and many other options.

 If the button **layers lock** is enabled (as it is by default), any changes to the layer visibility of the current view also take place in all the 3D views with *layers lock* enabled.

fig 63 *Layers lock* button

On the right of the layers icons you can find the **Proportional Editing** options, displayed as a button with a gray ball inside (meaning it is disabled – by default). LMB on this icon (or press O key) to enable it (the grey ball turn to blue): a drop-down menu named **Proportional Editing Falloff** appears on his right.

This menu is used to control the proportional influence of the transformation operations (move, rotate and scale) on the nearby objects (or elements if you are in *Edit* Mode) according to the selected distribution method.

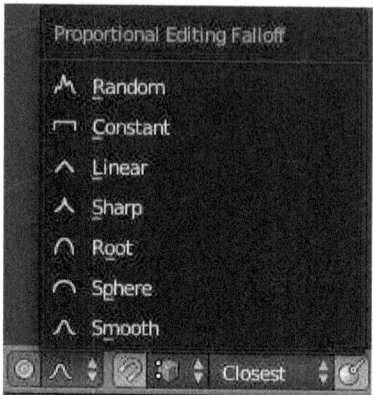

fig 64 *Proportional Editing falloff*

While in *Proportional Editing* mode, once a transformation command is activated a white circle appears on the *Pivot* point, representing the width of the influence area; scrolling the mouse wheel (WM) the white circle will scale and the transformation will be applied to all the elements within it, according to the selected *Proportional Editing falloff.*

You can choose among *Smooth, Sphere, Root, Sharp, Linear, Constant* and *Random* distribution.

The icons to the left to the individual menu items explain the effect applied.

The **Snap** icon (displayed as a magnet) is a powerful tool used to control the transformation operations, snapping object or mesh elements to various types of scene elements during the transformation itself, according to a predetermined logic.

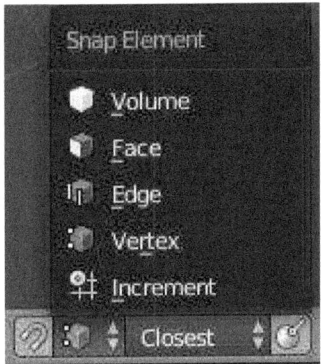

fig 65 *Snap* menu

The last two buttons launch the rendering or animation in OpenGL mode (*Open Graphics Library*), a widely used platform for video games and especially in the Unix environment.

fig 66 *OpenGL Render and Animation* buttons

2.2.4. The *3D View Sidebars* – basic knowledge

The *Sidebars* tools, features and controls may change according to the selected object, the current Mode type and the enabled Addons.

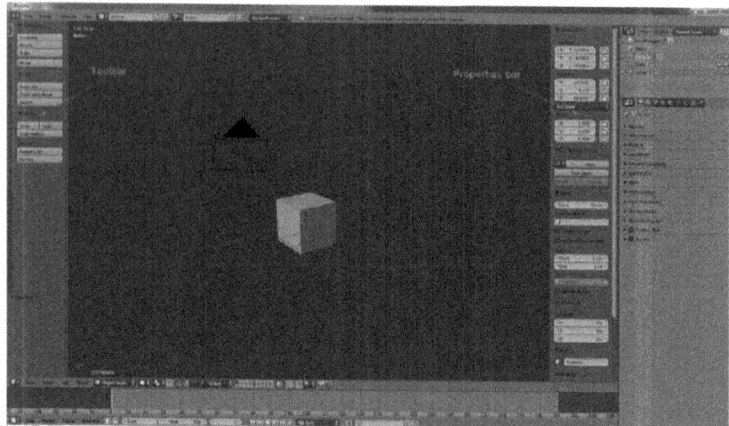

fig 67 *Tool* and *Properties Bar*

A) *Tools Shelf*

In the *Tools Shelf* you can find all the transformation and creation tools, relations management tools, physic and other tools. These may change depending on the current mode of the selected object, enabling different options.

It is divided into two main regions: the upper one contains several tabs, while the lower one is active during specific commands.

Let's briefly describe the default tabs in the upper region:

- *Tools* contains all the transformation controls for objects geometries. The parameters and panels may change depending on the mode and type of objects;
- *Create*(SHIFT + A) allows you to insert new objects in the scene;
- *Relations* manages the parent/child relationships between objects in the scene;

- *Physics* contains the main controls for the physic simulation;
- *Grease Pencil* contains the basic tools to draw freehand in the 3D view.

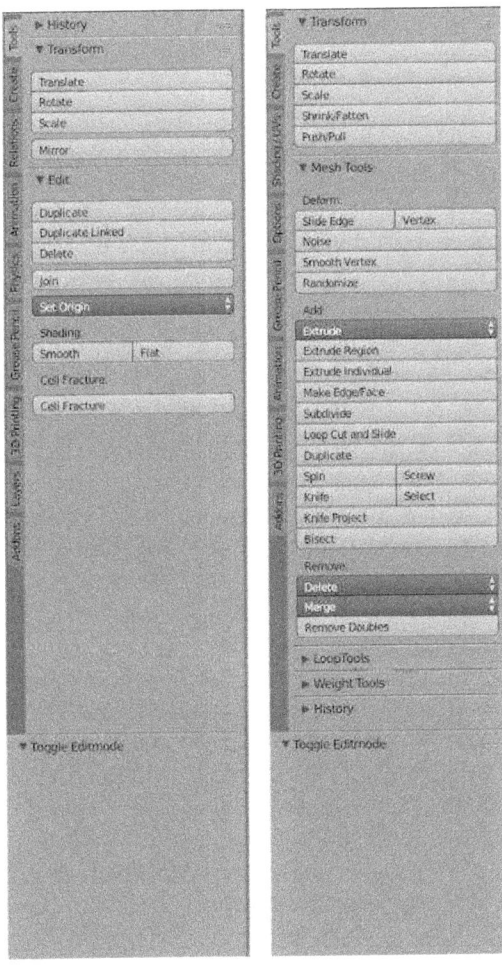

fig 68 the *Tools Shelf* in *Object Mode* (left) and *Edit Mode* (right)

More panels and tabs can be added by enabling specific Addons, such as the 3D printing tools or the *Layer Management*, previously described.

B) *Properties Bar*

The *Properties Bar*, not to be confused with the *Properties Window* (or *Properties Editor*), displays all the properties of the selected (or active)object, View options, Shading options, 3D Cursor location and other functions which will be briefly shown below, aiming to be detailed in the following chapters.

All properties are divided into specific panels (not necessarily in the order described below):

- *Item* is a text box that provides information on the name of the selected object. This can be changed by clicking within the text field. Automatically the name will be updated in the objects list of the *Outliner* and in the *Object* panel of the *Properties window*.
- *Transform* groups the location, rotation, scale and size properties to the selected (or active) object. While in *Edit Mode*, the panel can also show the chamfering information of the selected *Vertex* or *Edge* (*Mean Bevel Weight*, *Bevel Weight* and *Mean Crease*) if a geometry modifier is applied (such as *Bevel* or *Subdivision Surface* modifier). These parameters can be directly edited into the specific counters, or using shortcuts (as discussed below) or manipulators;
- *Grease Pencil*, which contains information about the brush and pencil sets, is used to draw directly in the 3D view or on a mesh object;

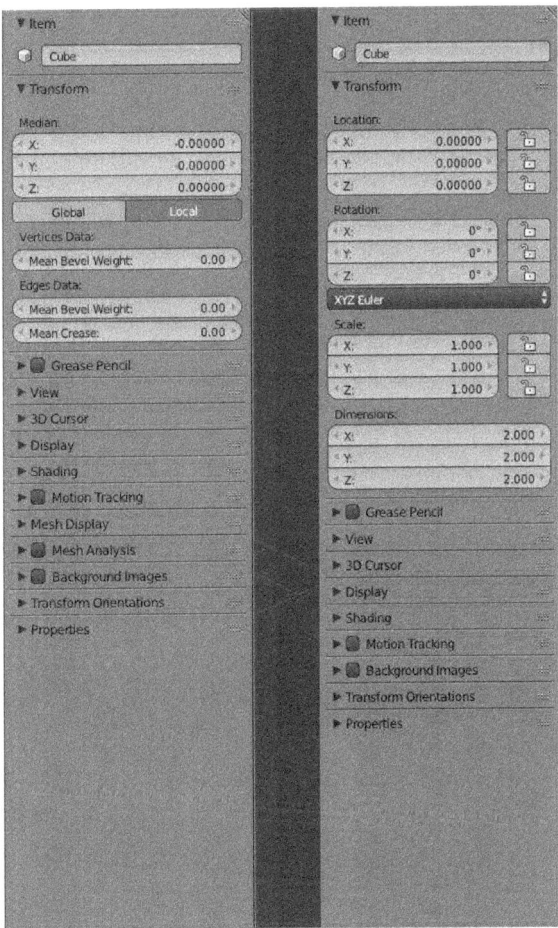

fig 69 the *Properties Bar* in *Object Mode* (left) and *Edit Mode* (right)

- *View* provides information on the current view such as the virtual camera lens angle and the clipping starting and ending distance; you can lock all navigation operations within the 3D view on a specific object (*Lock To Object*) to be selected from the pull down menu list, or on the 3D cursor (*Lock to Cursor*); with a *Camera* view active, you can lock the navigation operations in order to be applied to the

89

Camera view (*Lock Camera to View*); you can select the active camera (*Local Camera*) and render the limits of a selection in the 3D view (*Render Border*);

- *3D Cursor* provides the 3D Cursor *Location*, referred to the origin of the Global Axes;

- *Display*, where you can check/uncheck what to visualize in the 3D view and in particular:

  - *Only Render,* if enabled displays in the 3D view only what will be actually rendered;

  - *World Background,* in enabled shows the color of the background set for the current scene;

  - *Outline Selected* displays a colored outline of the selected object(s). The default colors are light orange for the active object and dark orange for the other selected objects;

  - *All Object Origins* if check, displays the origin of all objects in the scene instead of the active object only;

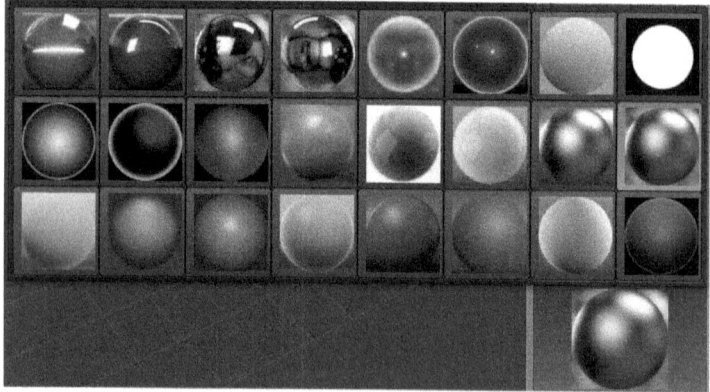

fig 70 predefined *Matcap* virtual shaders

  - *Grid Floor* enable/disable the visibility of x, y and z axes and of the grid on the XY plane in the 3D view; you can also manage the lines number, the size and the subdivisions of the grid. *Toggle Quad View* automatically split the 3D View in 4 regions representing the *User Perspective* view, a *Top Ortho* view, the *Front Ortho* view and the *Right Ortho* view.

- *Shading* is a panel that manages the shading of 3D objects in the scene. There are three options to check:
  - *Textured Solid* which forces the display of a texture, if assigned, even in *Solid shading* mode;
  - *Matcap* assigns a predefined shader to all the objects in the scene, it is very useful to better understand the geometry of the meshes, especially while sculpting. These shaders are only virtual and do not effect the actual object material;
  - *Backface Culling*, in non-solid surfaces, makes the back faces (according to the face normal orientation) transparent (not in *Rendered* shading view);
- *Motion Tracking* contains some helpful parameters for the motion tracking system used for animations;
- *Background Image* will be widely analyzed later with practical examples. Essentially it allows you to load one or more images (also called *blueprints*) as background of a specific view (or all of them) replacing, scaling and rotating them to fit your need in order to use them as references for your model;
- *Transform Orientation* is the same option previously described in the *Manipulator* icon set of the 3D view header.

2.2.4. The *Timeline* editor

fig 71 the *Timeline* window

The use of the *Timeline* is manifold. It is used to reproduce the simulation of physical effects applying transformations in a specific span of time; it is used for animations, video editing and post production.

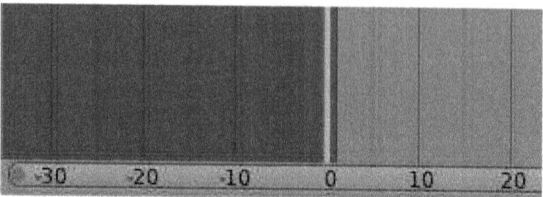

fig 72 the frames string and zoom button

The *Timeline* looks like a very simple window: a main area with vertical black and grey thin lines representing the frames and a green vertical cursor (representing the current frame), which proceeds frame by frame, second by second as the animation goes by.

Below the main area you can find a horizontal bar where the frames' numbers are indicated and two small dark grey circles are placed (one on the right and the other on the left of the frames bar), which are used to zoom in or out the displayed range of frames, simply by LMB dragging to the right/left the circles.

fig 73 *Timeline header*

Below the frames bar, the *Timeline header* is located, in which, from left to right the following buttons and menus are placed:

- The *Timeline* editor icon (a clock icon);
- *View* menu, where you can find the following options:
  • *Toggle Fullscreen Area* (ALT + F10) that sets the Timeline window to full screen;
  • *Toggle Maximize Area* (CTRL + UP ARROW) that maximizes the Timeline area into the Blender window (CTRL + DOWN ARROW to restore);

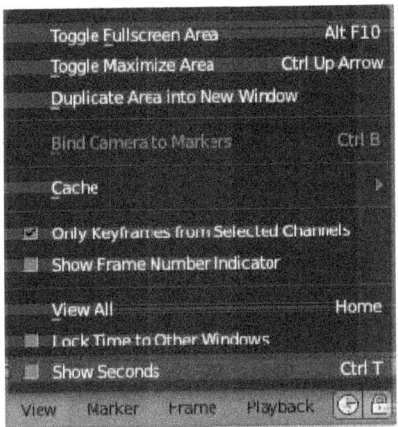

fig 74 the *View* menu of the *Timeline*

- Duplicate Area into New Window that duplicates the Timeline window in a new Blender window;
- Bind Camera to Markers (CTRL + B) will link the selected camera on the active markers;
- Cache that displays the cache of the different physic simulations applied to an object;

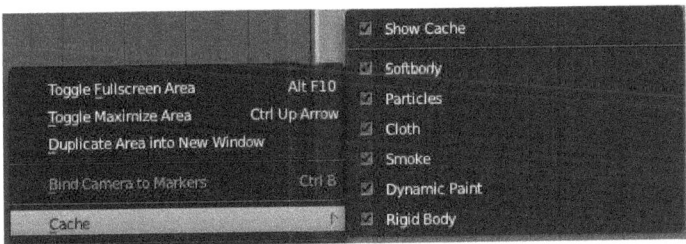

fig 75 the *Cache* menu

- *Only* Keyframes to Selected Channels if checked only considers keyframes for the selected object;
- Show Frame Number Indicator displays the current frame number in a green box on the bottom right of the green slider (vertical line) in the Timeline main area;

- View All adjusts the zoom rate in order to show the full active frame range in the Timeline window;

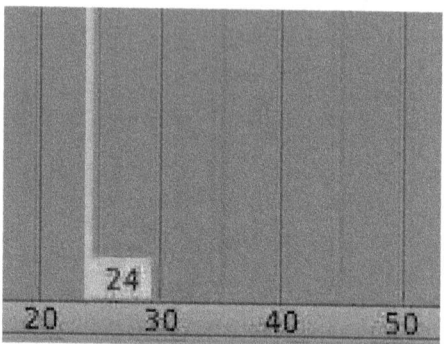

fig 76 frame number on the *Timeline* slider

fig 77 the *Marker* menu of the *Timeline*

- *Lock Time* to Other Windows allows you to synchronize the time of all the windows on the selected frame in the *Timeline*;
- Show Seconds displays the seconds together with the relative frame number ("3+12" means that the current frame is the 12th after the second number 3 of the

animation) in the green box placed on the bottom right of the green slider (vertical line) in the *Timeline* main area;

- the *Marker* menu allows you to manage markers in the *Timeline*. The markers must not be confused with the keyframes, which will be analyzed later. They are used to insert a visual mark in order to point out any useful information or note about animation sections or specific events; they can be shown on the windows that manage "time events" (*Timeline* but also *Graph Editor, Video Sequencer* and *Dope Sheet*). To insert a marker in the current frame just type M or choose *Add Marker* from the *Marker* menu. Let's see other options:
  - *Jump to* Previous Marker immediately jumps to the location (frame) of the previous marker (according to the selected one);
  - Jump to Next Marker jumps to the location (frame) of the next marker (according to the selected one);
  - Grab / Move Marker allows you to translate or move the selected marker. It is the same to dragging with the mouse;
  - Rename Marker (CTRL + M) allows you to name (or rename) a marker;
  - Delete Marker (X) doletes the selected marker;
  - Duplicate Marker To Scene... allows you to copy the selected marker into another scene;
  - Duplicate Marker duplicates the selected marker into the current scene;
  - Add Marker (M) adds a new marker to the current frame.

- The *Frame* menu contains all the information and tools to manage the frames:
  - *Auto-Keyframing Mode* allows you to choose between the types of automatic keyframes insertion, *Add &Replace or Replace;*
  - *Set Start Frame* (S) sets the current frame as the first frame of the animation preview;

- *Set End Frame* (E) sets the current frame as the last frame of the animation preview;
- *Set Preview Range* (P) allows you to graphically select few frames (with a box selection method) to play as an animation preview;
- *Clear Preview Range* (ALT + P) reset the animation preview to the full animation range.

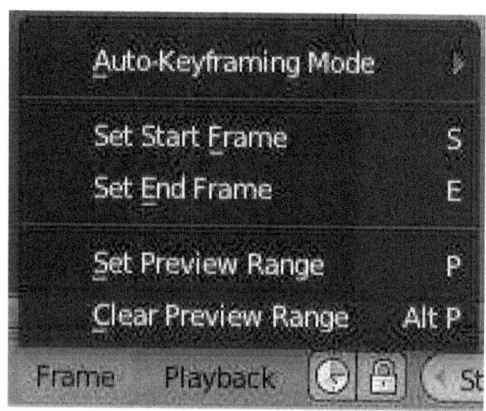

fig 78 the *Frame* menu

- The *Playback* menu shows a check list of the elements to be played during dragging operations in the *Timeline*.
  - *Audio Scrubbing allows audio channels to be listened during manual drag in the Timeline;*
  - *Audio Muted turns off audio playback;*
  - *AV-Sync plays back and sync with audio clock;*
  - *Frame Dopping causes the frames to be dropped if the frame display is too slow;*
  - *Clip Editor updates* the *Movie Clip* Editor during playback;

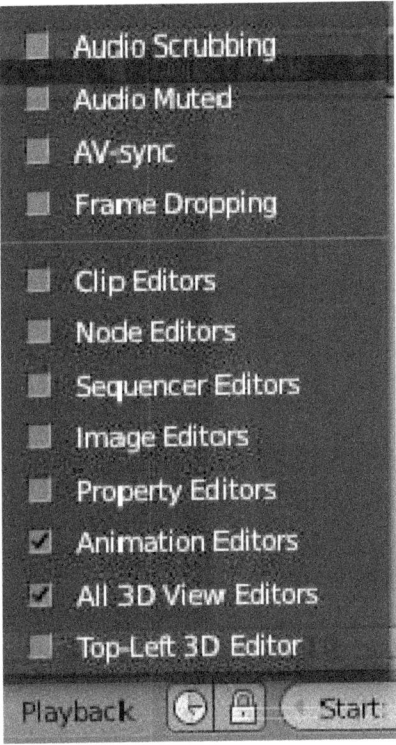

fig 79 the *Playback* menu

- *Node Editor* updates the nodes in the Node Editor during playback;
- Sequencer Editor updates the Sequencer during playback;
- Image Editors updates the Image Editor during playback;
- Property Editors updates in real time the values in the Preferences editors during playback;
- Animation Editors updates Timeline, Graph Editor and Video Sequencer Editor during playback;
- All 3D View Editors updates Timeline and 3D View during playback;

- Top-Left 3D Editors updates the Timeline during playback if Animation *Editors* and *All 3D View Editors* are enabled.

The next menus and controls on the *Timeline* header are:

- *Range Control buttons:*
  - Use Preview Range if enabled uses an alternative start/end frame range for animation playback and OpenGL renders instead of the Render Properties star/end frame range;
  - Lock Time Cursor to Playback Range if enabled doesn't allow frame to be selected with mouse outside of the frame range in the Timeline main area.

fig 80 *Range Control* buttons

- *Frame Control Counter:*

fig 81 *Frame Control Counter*

- Start and End define the start and end frame of the animation range (corresponding to the range defined in the Render Properties tab);
- Frame is the number of the current frame and allows you to jump directly to the typed frame;
- The playback buttons allow you to start, stop and move through the animation. From left to right: jump to the beginning; Fast backward; play backward; play / pause (ALT + A) ; Fast forward; jump to the end.

fig 82 the *playback buttons*

- The *Sync Mode* dropdown menu defines the sync mode (*AV-Sync; Frame Dropping; No Sync*).

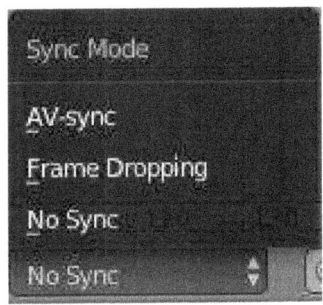

fig 83 *Sync Mode* dropdown menu

fig 84 *Keyframe Control buttons*

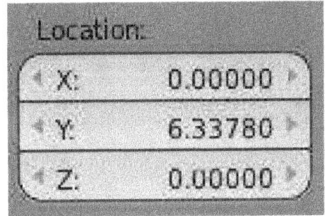

fig 85 *location* counters turning yellow when the *I* key is pressed

- *Keyframe Control* buttons help to manage the keyframes. *Keyframes* record a specific information in the selected frameand playback it during the animation. In Blender you can *keyframe* almost any button, counter or value. To add a keyframe to a frame from a specific info, just type the *I* key with your mouse pointer on the selected value. The color of the box or the button will turn yellow and a yellow keyframe will then appear on the *Timeline* as a vertical bar.

- *Record* (the red dot button) enables/disables the automatic keyframe insertion for Objects and Bones;
- Auto Keying insertion allows you to automatically insert new keyframes according to the selected *Auto Keying Set*.

All animation functions and tools will be discussed in detail in the following chapters, with tutorials and exercises.

2.2.6. The *Outliner* editor

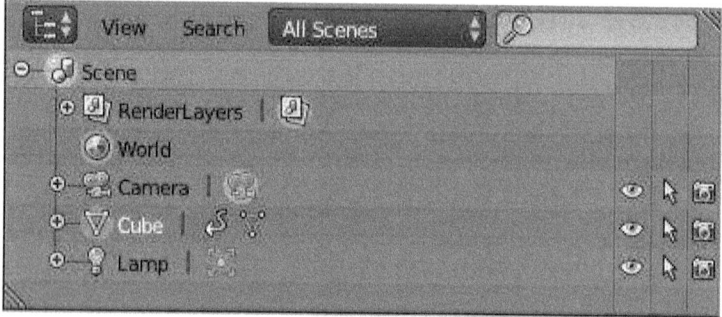

fig 86 the *Outliner* editor

The *Outliner editor* (or *Outliner window*) contains the set of objects, their properties and relations.

The *Outliner* is divided into two parts: the *header*, at the top by default, and the main area in the lower part.

Let's now analyze the main working area and the way it is organized.

The structure of the *Outliner* has a "tree" organization.

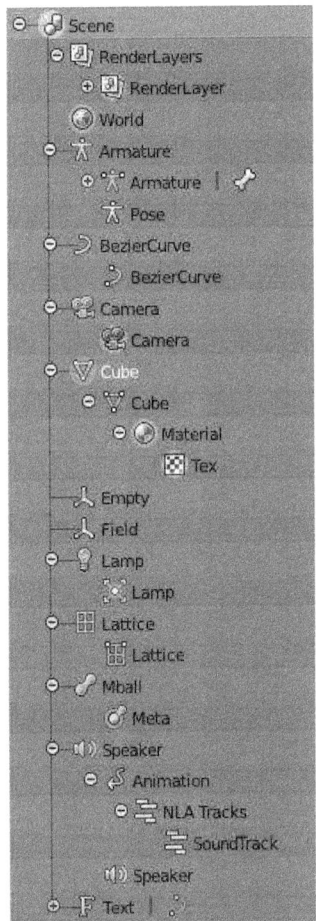

fig 87 *Outliner* tree structure

The *Scene* has a general *World* and a rendering system organized in *Render Layer* (as we shall see further on). Organizing a scene indifferent layers (such as in some other photo editing software) allows to gain a more precise control on the various aspects of the final render.

Some objects may be explored into their sublevels, going into the specifics of their geometry or properties, based on the object type.

The small "+" opens the root of an object, containing all data blocks referring to it, each one with its proper icon or symbol.

The *World* contains all the objects in the scene, each one listed in the *Outliner* tree and represented by a different icon, specific for each category, followed by its name.

The main root of an object corresponds to its *Object Mode*.

The selected object or the active one is displayed in the *Outliner* with white characters.

Right-clicking (RMB) on an item in the list opens a dropdown menu, called *Outliner Object Operation*, in which you can:

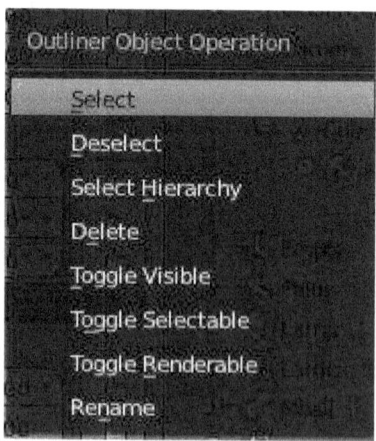

fig 88 main root object dropdown menu

a) for main root objects: *Select; Deselect; Select Hierarchy; Delete; Toggle Visible, Selectable and Renderable and Rename;*

b) for objects or properties in secondary level: *Unlink* (i.e. disconnecting the material from a mesh), *Make Local*; other secondary functions that we discuss elsewhere (*Make Single User, Add Fake user, Clear Fake user, Rename, Select Unlinked*).

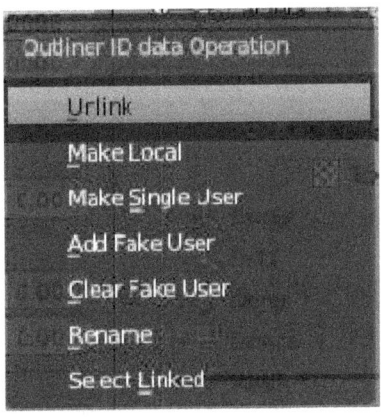

fig 89 second level object dropdown menu

Let's analyze now the *Header*'s options.

To the very right of the window type icon (a stylized flow chart), we find the *View* menu.

- *Sort Alphabetically* displays objects on the list in alphabetical order;
- *Show Column Restriction* enabled the three columns to the right of the objects list (with the icon of an eye, an arrow and a camera) – see details below;
- *Show Active* (. NUM) focuses the list on the active object in the 3D view;

- *Show/Hide One Level* shows the root and all the sub-levels of all the objects in the list;
- *Show Hierarchy* minimizes the list showing all main roots only;
- *Duplicate Area into New Window* duplicates the *Outliner* window in a new Blender window;
- *Toggle Maximize Area* (CTRL + UP ARROW) that maximizes the *Outliner* area into the Blender window (CTRL + DOWN ARROW to restore);
- *Toggle Fullscreen Area* (ALT + F10) that sets the *Outliner* window to full screen;

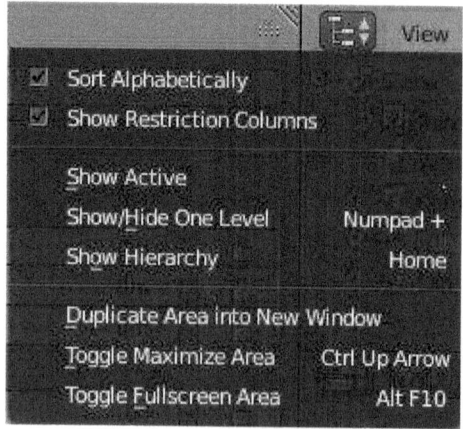

fig 90 the *View* menu of the *Outliner*

The *Search* menu contains two check boxes that will be explained in the following pages:

fig 91 the *Search* menu of the *Outliner*

- *Case Sensitive Marches Only;*
- *Complete Matches Only.*

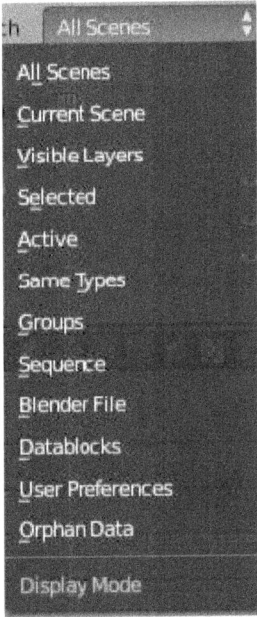

fig 92 thr *Display Mode* menu

The *Display Mode* is a filter for the objects displayed in the list, allowing you to sort i.e. *all the scenes*, the *current scene*, the *visible layers* , etc.

The *search* input box allows you to type your own filter option to easily find the object you want to select and view the list.

fig 93 the *search* input box

The three display icons (an eye, an arrow and a camera) respectively allow you to make the object:

- Visible/not visible in the 3D view;

- Selectable/not selectable in the 3D view;
- Renderable/not renderable.

fig 94 the display icons

2.2.7. The *Properties* editor

The *Properties* editor (not to be confused with the *Properties Bar*) allows you to manage the global properties of the whole project.

The *Properties* window is located By default below the *Outliner* and is divided into 12 *tabs*, each one symbolized by a different icon and all contained in the *Properties* window's *header*, right after the window type icon (a slider and a counter).

fig 95 the *header* of the *Properties editor*

To describe and to analyze all the functions in the *Properties* window at this stage would be counterproductive because many concepts and information we didn't explained so far would be required.

It is better to acquire all of the first introductory concepts on modeling, before going into the details of the *Properties* window.

We will then briefly review the content contained in the 12 *tabs*.

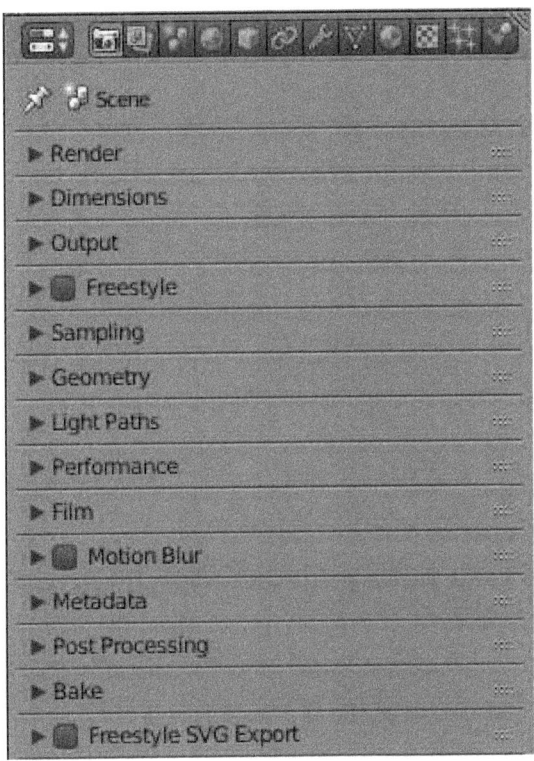

fig 96 Render Properties

- **Render** (camera icon) contains all the rendering settings for still images or animations. It contains the following panels (may change according to the used render engine): *Render* (with render buttons and details and graphic device settings); *Dimensions* (frame size and resolution settings); *Output* (output file settings); *Sampling* and *Volume Sampling* (rendered image sampling settings); *Light Path* (light controls and settings); *Motion Blur* (motion blur effect settings); *Film* (exposure and transparency settings); *Performance* (rendering process optimization according to the installed hardware); *Post Processing* (enable/disable internal post production passes of the rendered file); *Bake* (the parameters to create 2D bitmap images of a mesh object's rendered surface); *Freestyle* (hand drawing render effect settings).

- **Render Layer** contains all the render layers parameters and settings.

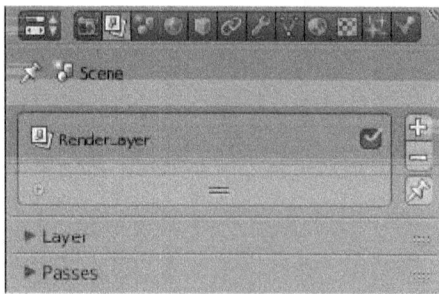

fig 97 *Render Layer Properties*

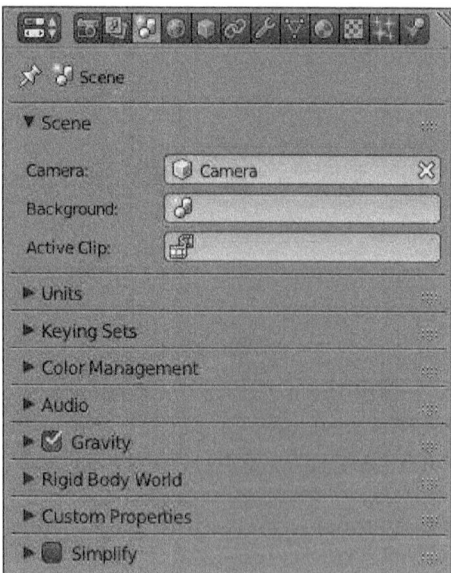

fig 98 *Scene Properties*

- **Scene** contains the current scene settings divided in the following panels: *Scene* (Camera and background information); *Units* (unit systems settings); *Keying Sets* (keyframing settings); *Color Management* (color settings); *Audio* (audio settings); *Gravity* (gravity simulation settings);*Rigid Body World* (settings about rigid bodies physical environment simulation);

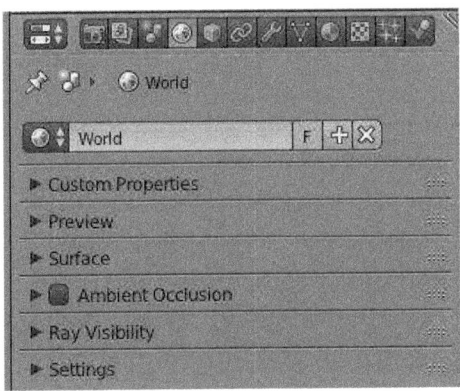

fig 98 *World Properties*

- **World** contains all the settings about the environment and background of the 3D scene: *Preview* (provides a preview of the background); *Surface* (background settings); *Ambient Occlusion* (ambient occlusion effect settings); *Ray visibility* (information and settings on the visibility and the effects of light in the scene and rendering); *Settings* (general lighting and background settings).
- **Object** shows the general properties of the selected object: the name of the object, *Transform* (position, rotation and scaling of the object); *Relations* (possible relationships with other objects); *Delta Transform* (difference in position, rotate and scale after a transformation compared to starting values); *Transform Locks* (enable/disable transformations locks); *Groups* (groups settings); *Duplication* (object duplication method settings); *Relations Extras* (parent and

camera tracking settings); *Motion Paths* (details and settings on the paths assigned to the movement); *Motion Blur* (settings on the trail left by the rapid movement).

fig 99 *Object Properties*

- **Constraints** lets you assign to an object concatenation relationships with other objects, paths, forces, etc. Some examples, especially about camera movement and animations, will be deeply discuss in the following pages. With a drop-down menu you can choose the type of constraints among *Motion Tracking, Transform, Tracking* and *Relationship*.

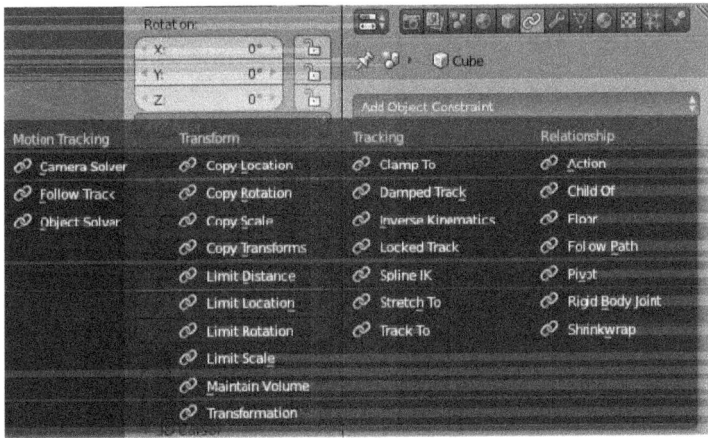

fig 100 *Constraints Properties*

- **Modifiers** contains the most useful, common and powerful tools of all the modeling environment Blender. *Modifiers* add algorithms to the selected object to deform the geometry according to specific parameters and functions. The modifiers will be deeply discuss into the dedicated chapter, detailed one by one, with several practical examples.
- **Data** allows to manage the internal geometry data of the selected object. With a mesh selected, you can manage groups of selected geometry elements (such as vertices), to assign them colors, effects, specific behavior or particles; or with curves you can for example set their shape, thickness etc. The tab icon may change depending on the selected object type.

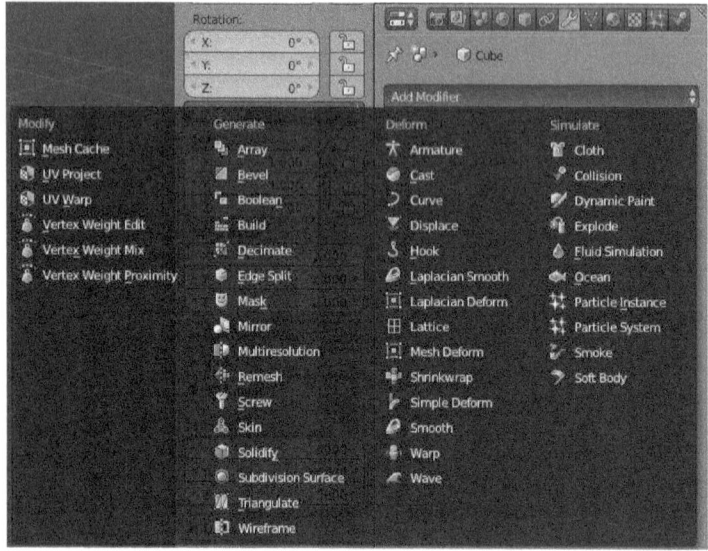

fig 100 *Modifiers Properties*

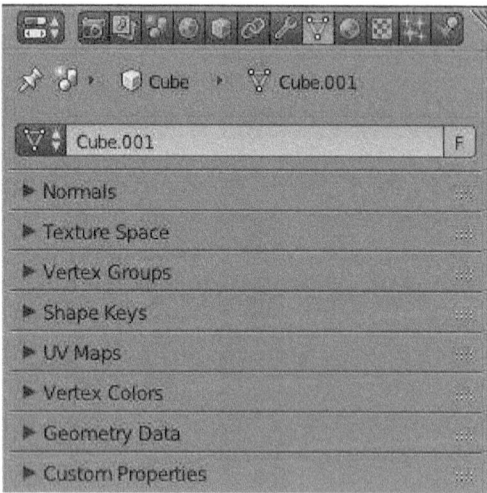

fig 102 *Data Properties*

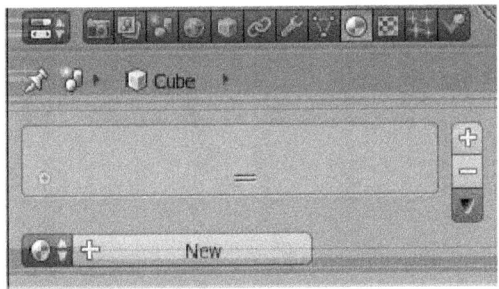

fig 103 *Material Properties*

- **Material** (another topic we'll deeply discuss in the following pages) assigns a material to an object, and manages its properties.

- **Texture** allows you to manage all used textures and add new ones to the mesh and/or some of the modifiers; textures could be procedural (generated by specific mathematical algorithms) or external bitmap files.

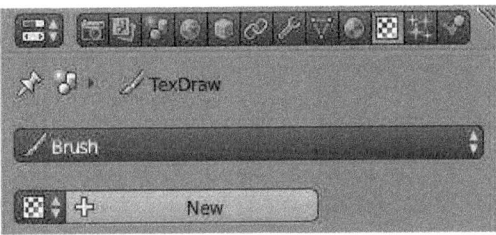

fig 104 *Texture Properties*

- **Particles** allows to manage particle systems applied to amesh, which are useful to simulate hair, grass strands, fur or emission simulations. This topic will be deeply discuss in the following pages.

113

fig 104 *Particles Properties*

- **Physics** finally enables physic components to objects or to the environment. The list of available components may change according to the selected object. I.e. with a mesh selected the following are available: *Force Field* (external forces such as wind, vortex, magnetism, etc.); *Collision* (makes an object subject to collision with another belonging to the physical system); *Cloth* (simulates the behavior of a fabric, when applied to a mesh); *Dynamic Paint* (allows you to assign specific influences on the physical system by *painting* vertex directly on the mesh); *Soft Body* (assigns *elastic* behavior to a mesh); *Fluid* (allows to manage fluid simulations); *Smoke* (simulates smoke and flames); *Rigid Body* (applies rigid bodies dynamics to a mesh, which becomes subject to gravity, collision and breakage); *Rigid Body Constraint* (sets the influences of physics with other parameters). It is finally interesting to note how the various physical components can interact with each other and with the particle systems, such as the wind can simulate the waving of a flag or mess up hairs. We will discuss the *Physics* in detail in the following chapters.

114

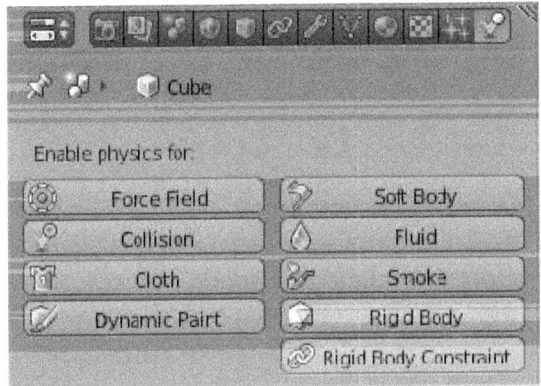

fig 106 *Physics Properties*

2.3. Keyboard shortcuts

The keyboard shortcuts commands are simply obtained by pushing a button or with a combination of keys on your keyboard; it helps you to speed up work operations.

Using shortcuts to avoid looking for commands and tools in the menu is the best way to save your time and optimize your workflow.

You must then accept (but you'll soon agree) the idea that working with two hands is the best approach and that you need to learn at least the more frequently used shortcuts we'll gradually know and use.

In any case, all commands can be run either from the specific menu (or button) in the Blender windows or by its own shortcut .

fig 107 the shortcuts customization in the *User Preferences* window

116

As previously shown in the introduction, you can customize your shortcuts the *Input* tab of the *User Preferences* window (CTRL + A + U), although we highly recommend to use the default settings, for compatibility reasons with other courses or tutorial.

All available commands are organized by groups and functions.

 NOTE: You can find a lot of shortcuts schemes online.

2.4. Mouse and keyboard navigation system

As previously mentioned, the use of the keyboard and shortcut is essential, but the mouse is the primary tool to navigate the 3D view, to select objects and elements and to make any transformation. You can select, move, or orbiting a scene with it.

Let's see the main mouse functions in the table below:

LBM (RMB by default)	Select objects or elements
RMB (LMB by default)	Pace the 3D Cursor
MMB and dragging	Orbit the view (pivot point is specified in the *Interface* tab of the *User Preferences*)
WM	Zoom in or out
SHIFT + MMB	Browse freely in the 3D view (*pan*)
CTRL + MMB	Dragging the mouse up and down to zoom in or out
SHIFT + WM	Pan up/down
CTRL + WM	Pan right/left
ALT + WM	Scroll forward/backward the current frame

These are the main shortcuts that let you quickly switch through the predefined views in the 3D view:

7 NUM	Top view
CTRL + 7 NUM	Bottom view
1 NUM	Front view
CTRL + 1 NUM	Rear view
3 NUM	Right view
CTRL + 3 NUM	Left view
5 NUM	Split from orthographic to perspective and vice versa

4, 6 NUM	horizontal rotations of 5 ° of the view
2, 8 NUM	vertical rotations of 5 ° of the view
0 NUM	Active Camera view
CTRL + 0	Set object as Active Camera
CTRL + ALT + 0	Set the current view as camera view

2.5. Selection

As shown before, you can select objects in different ways.

We quickly sum up the main methods and their shortcut:

a) *Selection* with LMB (RMB by default);
b) *Multiple* selection with SHIFT + LMB (SHIFT + RMB by default);
c) *Border* selection with B
d) *Circle* selection with C (ESC or ENTER to confirm);
e) *Lasso* selection with CTRL + RMB (CTRL + LMB by default);
f) Select/deselect all with A;
g) *Invert* selection with I;
h) *Random* selection from the *Select* drop down menu in the 3Dview.

> **NOTE: These selection methods are valid in either mode Object Mode and Edit Mode.**

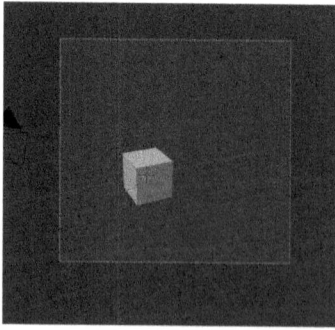

fig 108 *Border* selection (B)

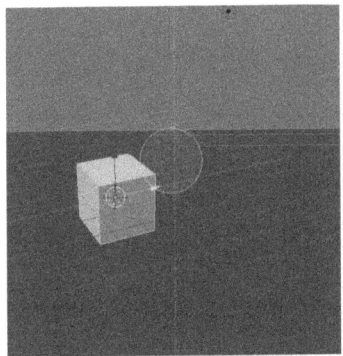

fig 109 *Circle* selection (C)

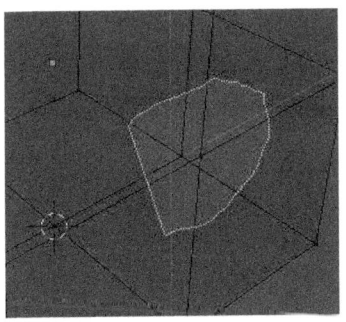

fig 110 *Lasso* selection (CTRL + RMB)

2.6. 3D Cursor and Origin (Pivot)

The *3D Cursor* is an uncommon tool in almost all 3D modeling software; actually it can be said that Blender is the only software to use it among the most important ones.

It is displayed as a white and red sight.

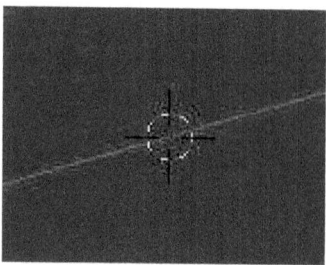

fig 111 the *3D Cursor*

Apparently hard to understand, the *3D Cursor* is fundamental because it allows you to operate in many different ways on objects or in the 3D view.

First of all the *3D Cursor* is the exact point in the 3D space where a new object is added, or more precisely where the *Origin* of the new object will be placed.

Managing *3D Cursor* and *Origin* together you will be able to modify the mass origin of objects, set the center of rotation or scale, snap objects and other important operations.

To move the *3D Cursor* you can simply click anywhere in the working area of the 3D view with RMB (LMB by default), or type the coordinates in the *3D Cursor* panel of the *Properties Bar*.

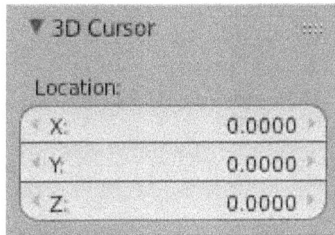

fig 112 *3D Cursor* coordinates

You can also assign to the *3D Cursor* and *Origin* a specific position in relation to other elements of the scene with SHIFT + S.

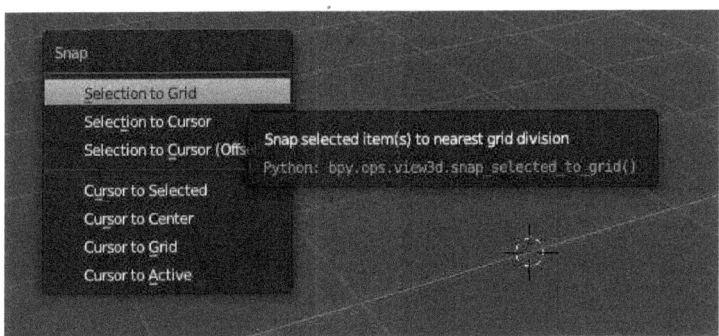

fig 113 advanced placement options for *3D Cursor* with SHIFT + S

The *Snap* drop-down menu (SHIFT + S) options are:

- move the object's *Origin* to the closest grid point (*Selection to Grid*);
- move the object's *Origin* in *Object Mode* or an element or group of elements in *Edit Mode* on the 3D Cursor (*Selection to Cursor*);
- move the *3D Cursor* to the active object's *Origin* in Object Mode or to the selected element or group of elements in *Edit Mode* (*Cursor to Selected*);
- move the *3D Cursor* to the 3D world's origin (*Cursor to Center*)

123

- move the *3D Cursor* to the closest grid point (*Cursor to Grid*);
- move the 3D Cursor to the active object's *Origin* (*Cursor to Active*).

Similarly, you can assign the object's *Origin* a specific position in relation to other elements or the 3D Cursor himself from the *Set Origin* menu (SHIFT + CTRL + ALT + C) in the *Tool* tab of the *Tool*.

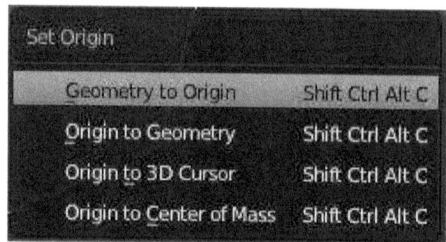

fig 114 *Set Origin menu*

From this menu you can choose where to place the *Origin:*

- *Geometry to Origin* moves the mesh geometry around its *Origin*;
- *Origin to Geometry* moves the object's *Origin* to the geometric center of an object's;
- *Origin to 3D Cursor* moves the object's *Origin* to the *3D Cursor*;
- *Origin to Center of Mass* moves the object's *Origin* to the center of mass of the object.

EXERCISE n. 1: PLACE THE 3D CURSOR ON THE ORIGIN AND VICE VERSA

Let's try to place the *3D cursor* on the *Origin* and vice versa with a simple exercise.

Insert a cube and type the G X 3 sequence (we shall see later the meaning), to move it along the X axis by 3 meters.

Now type SHIFT + S and set *Cursor to Selected*. The 3D Cursor will be placed at the origin of the cube.

Undo the last two steps by typing twice Ctrl + Z. The cube will return to the axis origin (original insertion point) while the cursor will not move.

With the cube selected Type R to rotate it. Moving the mouse it will rotate around its origin, which is placed exactly in its center of gravity.

Press ESC to cancel the operation.

Now type SHIFT + CTRL + ALT + C and choose the option *Origin to 3DCursor* . The *Origin* will be placed to the *3D Cursor*.

Now lel's try to freely rotate the cube in the 3D space by simply typing R and moving the mouse.

The cube will rotate around its origin placed this time outside of its center of gravity.

Press ESC to cancel.

With this simple exercise we have seen how the interaction between the *3D Cursor* and the *Origin* is important to get different results, depending on the case.

3
INSERT OBJECTS

3.1. Graphic card settings

Before you start modelling and inserting objects into the scene, it is important to set your preferences so that Blender is better configured depending on your hardware and operating system.

Open the preferences window (CTRL + ALT + U), enter the *System* section and set the *Compute Device*, i.e. the logical drive that will perform *render* calculations.

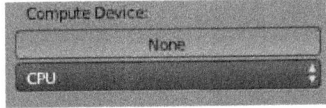

Fig. 115 setting CPU as *Compute Device*

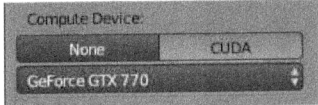

Fig. 11 6 setting GPU as *Compute Device*

If you have a graphics card with *Cuda Core* logical, set the GPU *Device* , otherwlse set CPU.

The panel where you adjust these settings *(Performances)* is located in the *Render* panel of the Preferences window.

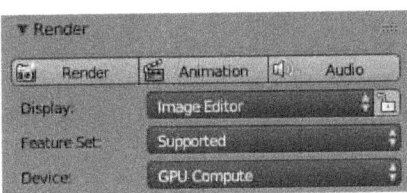

Fig. 117 *device* setting in the *Render* Panel

129

If a *CUDA* technology graphics card is available, evaluating the *performances* resulting from the number of logical processors *(Cuda Core)* available will be required. The economic cards are not well suited, while 3D *gaming* ones (Nvidia GTX technology) are more than acceptable, as those of the Nvidia Quadro group.

Performances could change a lot depending on the number of the *Cuda Cores* and graphics cards with this technology aren't always more performance than the CPU.

To give you an approximate idea, use GPU device for rendering operations if it has at least 1200 *Cuda Core* and not less than 3 GB of dedicated RAM.

With lower values, probably CPU will give better feedback and will be even faster.

Finally, it will be important also adjust the dimensions of *Tiles,* in the *Performances* panel, which is the small image areas that will be simultaneously rendered by the compute device.

Studies and experiments allow us to skip the tedious and hard *tests,* setting the X and Y values 64 when using the CPU, 256 if you use the GPU.

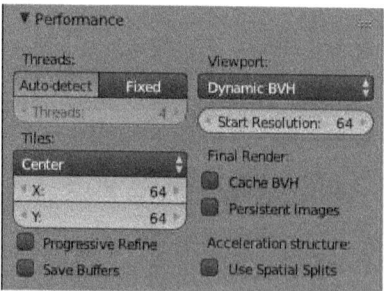

Fig. 11 8 *Tiles* setting in the *Performances* with CPU compute device

We recommend saving these settings as *Startup file* for all the next Blender sessions by typing CTRL + U or by selecting *Save Startup File* in the *File* menu of the info window and then confirm.

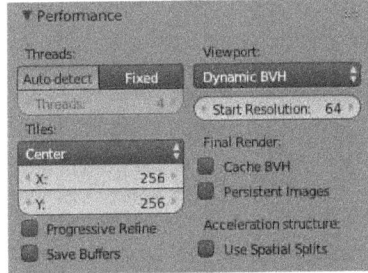

Fig. 11 9 *Tiles* setting in the *Performances* with GPU compute device

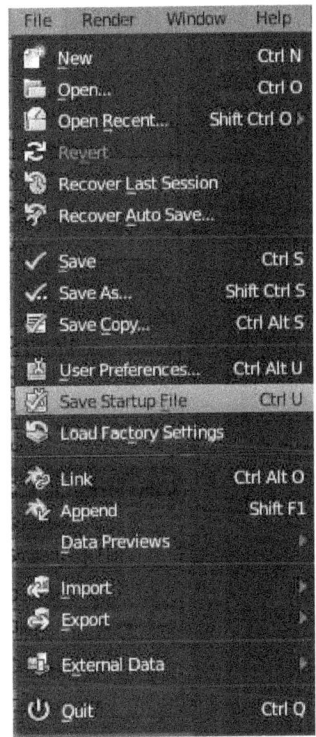

Fig. 120 *Save Startup File*

131

3.1.1. Set the file units and the project scale

Another very important topic to be defined before you start working is the units and scale one.

Enter a numeric value that defines a geometry might not be enough to represent a three-dimensional object. Even for more advanced features such as mapping or 3D printing, Blender has to know the real object units and its dimensions.

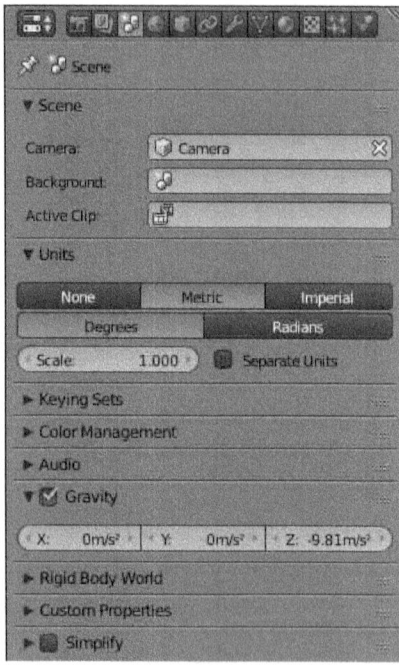

Fig. 121 project unit and scale settings

To set the units you must enter the *Scenes* tab in the *Properties* window. We recommend to use *Metric* system and *Degrees* notation for the angles.

The *Scale* parameter will define, within the chosen system, the proportion between the typed values and the system default value.

132

By *default*, 1 in metric system stands for 1 meter. If you want your numerical inputs stand for centimeters, you will need to set the scale with the value 0.01.

Mind that any decimal value will be compared to the scale setting.

For example, thinking in meters *(Scale = 1)* and inserting the value 0. 03, Blender will automatically interpret the value and display the string *3 cm.*

3.2. Placing objects

At this point, we possess sufficient knowledge to start inserting objects into the scene and edit them.

Blender divides the objects into groups.

there are three ways to insert any object into the scene:

a) Open the *Add* menu in the 3D View *header* and choose the type of object from the available ones;

b) With the mouse pointer in the work area of the 3D view type SHIFT + A and select the item from the drop down menu that will open;

c) Choose the object to be included in the second *tab* starting from the top *(Create)* the *Tools Shelf.*

You can add more objects and instruments, activating them from the *Addons* tab in the *Preferences* window or loading from Blender browser the specific *.py file from an external source, after clicking on the *Install from File* button.

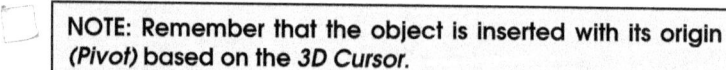

NOTE: Remember that the object is inserted with its origin *(Pivot)* based on the *3D Cursor.*

To delete any object or group of objects, even if of a different category, simply select it and type Del or X, then confirm the operation.

You can cancel the entries by typing CTRL + Z *(undo)* or restore operation with SHIFT + CTRL + Z *(Redo).*

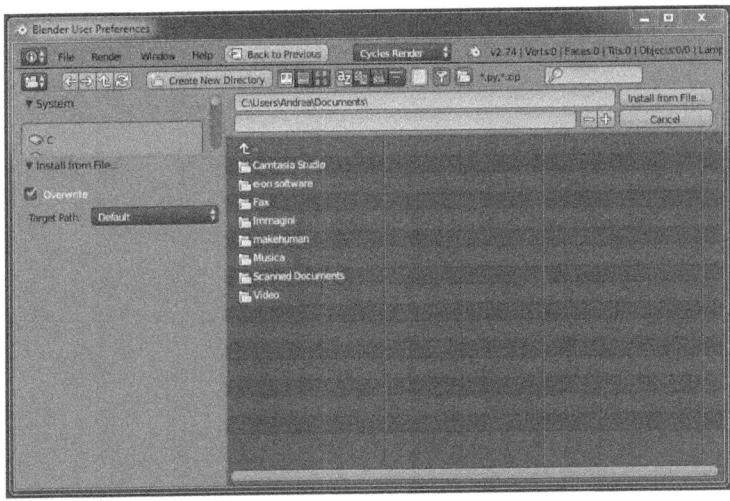

Fig. 122 importing a new *Addon*

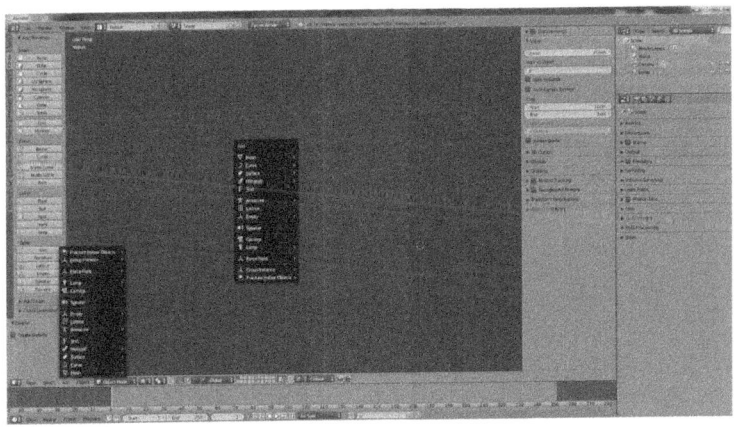

Fig. 123 methods for objects insertion

3.2.1. Mesh

The first group of objects that we analyze is called *Mesh*, literally *point cloud*.

 As the word says, a *mesh* is a set of points (the minimum geometric units), eventually connected to each other with edges and faces that define a polyhedral object.

These geometric elements *(vertices, edges,* and *faces)* are the three basic geometries from which to create and model an object.

 EXERCISE N. 2: ADDING A MESH IN 3D VIEW

After starting Blender, we first delete all the objects in the scene.

We type A to select them all, then X to remove them and confirm the operation.

The *3D Cursor* is n the axis origin. We click with RMB anywhere in the work area to move the *3D Cursor*.

Let's type SHIFT + A and then we choose *Mesh*, and *Cube* from the drop down menu.

The cube is placed with its origin (the center of gravity by *default*) placed on the *3D Cursor*.

 Now try to insert other types of mesh in the scene.

You can choose from: *Plane, Cube, Circle, UV Sphere, Ico Sphere, Cylinder, Cone, Torus, Grid* and *Monkey,* which are called **primitives.**

The *primitives* will be described below this exercise.

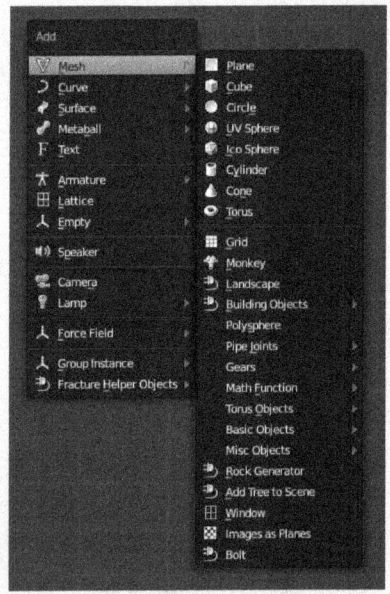

Fig. 12 4 adding a *mesh*

Finally, try to select and deselect *mesh* with the tools you already know, especially using the rectangle, circle and lasso methods of selection.

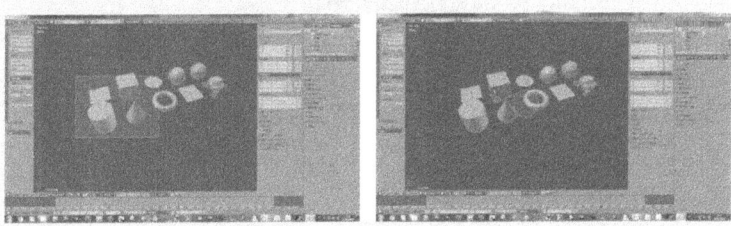

Fig. 12 5 multiple selection of *mesh*

You also insert objects from the **Create** *tab* in the *Tools Shelf.*

All new objects can be immediately edited, resized and accurately positioned by setting the parameters shown in the bottom region in the *Tools Shelf.*

In menus and counters you can enter information on the number of vertices, the position, rotation and sizing. These parameters may change depending on the type of inserted *mesh.*

As soon as you click inside the 3D view, these parameters can no longer be modified in that region, but it will be necessary to act in the *Properties Bar.*

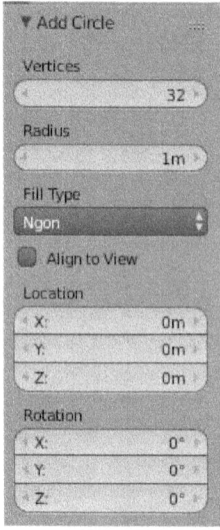

Fig. 12 6 Adding settings of a *mesh* (in the example *Circle*)

Let's look briefly at what the *primitives* are and their basic characteristics.

Plane add a square with a default dimensions of 2 x 2 into the scene;

Cube adds a *cube,* better called *icosahedron,* into the scene with 6 faces, 12 vertices and 8 edges and measuring 2 x 2 x 2.

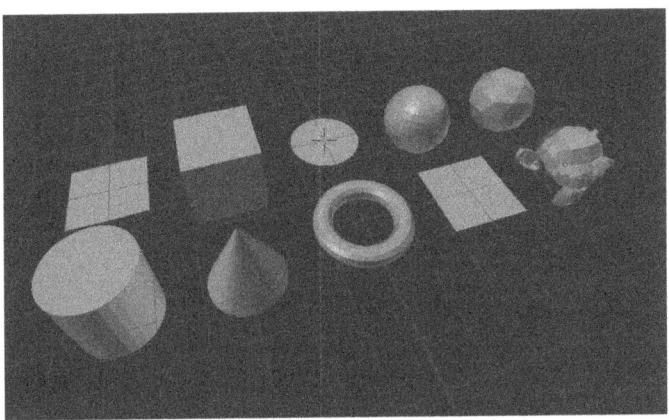

Fig. 12 *7 primitive mesh*

Circle adds the perimeter of a *Ngon,* with a radius of 2 and 32 segments by *default,* that make it similar to a circumference. Technically it is a regular polygon with 32 sides, that can be redefined in order to make it less or more detailed acting in the bottom of the *Tools Shelf* region, within the *Vertices* counter. You can also make it a surface by setting *Ngon* in the *Fill Type* menu. It is also possible to add an hexagon for example by adding a circle and setting 6 vertices.

Sphere adds a *mesh* that simulates the appearance of a sphere. This *mesh* is composed of quadrangular faces except for those at the poles that are triangular and are joined at a point. As well as for *Circle,* also for Sphere it is possible to set the radius, the number of vertices (and, actually, on the meridians and parallels), as well as on the position.

Icoshpere adds a spherical solid, but made of all triangular faces.

Cylinder inserts a solid similar to a cylinder, by default made of 32 vertical faces and two 32-side parallel polygons at each cap. Even in this case, details and size parameters can be redefined.

Cone inserts a solid made of a 32 segments polygon base and a body of triangular faces which merge into a single point at the top. To define the dimensional parameters also in this case you must act in the *Tools Shelf* region.

Torus inserts a toroidal shape, a solid created by the rotation of a *circle* around the object origin.

Grid adds a plane of 2 x 2 total size, more detailed than a default *Plane*, as it is divided both in the *x and y direction* by a network of *n* segments, the number of which is adjustable in the *Tools Shelf* region.

Monkey finally adds a medium definition polygonal *mesh* representing the head of a monkey, the Blender "mascotte" named *Suzanne*. It has no specific function but to be a *test* for some operations.

Fig. 128 Suzanne

3.2.2. *Curve*

Like the mesh insertion system, you can place in the 3D space also curves.

The curves, in contrast to the mesh which simulate a solid by detail approximation, are two-dimensional objects and relate to geometric and mathematical models to define a path in space. This implies that are composed of an infinite number of consecutive points.

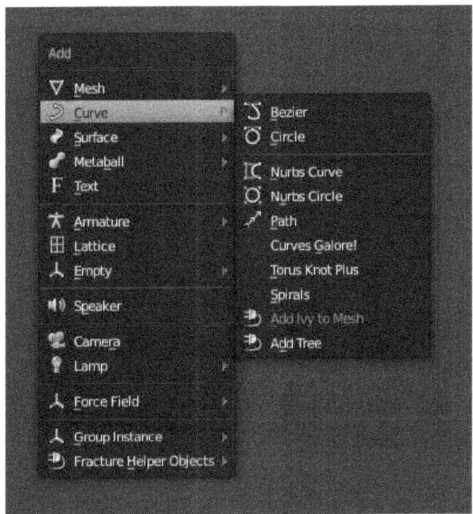

Fig. 12 9 the *Curve* menu

Two types of curves are available:

a)   ***Bezier* curves,** defined by a few key points with handles. In the menu you can choose from:

1.   *Bezier,* a basic curve with two control points;

2.   Circle, a circumference with four control points.

b)   ***NURBS*** (acronym of *Non Uniform Rational B-Spline*), instead defined by key points that are controlled by other points outside of the curve. In the menu you can choose from:

1.   *NURBS curves,* a basic curve with two control points;

2.   *NURBS Circle,* a circumference with four control points;

3. *Path* a simple segment with two control points.

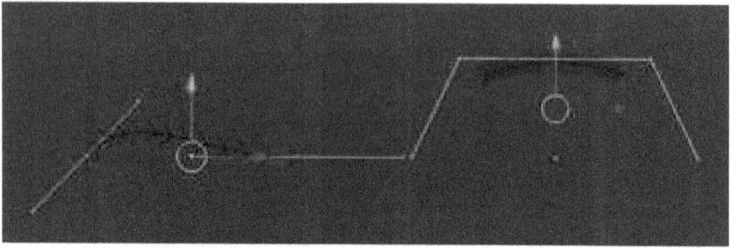

Fig. 130 Curve *Bezier* and *NURBS*

By moving in space the curve key points, you can define curves in space, not to be confused with the surfaces.

3.2.3. Surface

The surfaces are three-dimensional objects defined by two or more curves definable, as for the curves, through key points and handles.

The following choices are available:

a)   **NURBS curves;**

b)   **NURBS Circle;**

c)   **NURBS Surface;**

d)   **NURBS Cylinder;**

e)   **NURBS Sphere;**

f)   **NURBS Torus.**

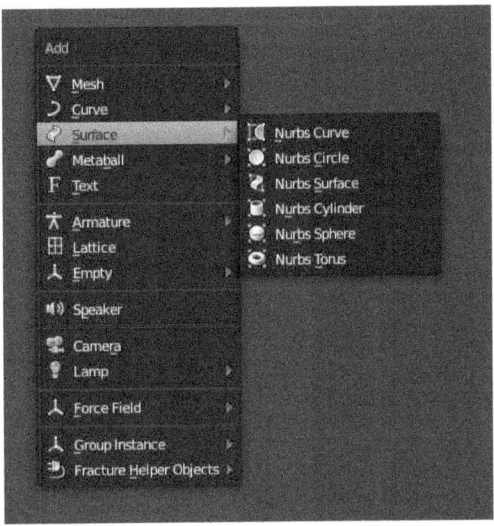

Fig. 131 surface insertion

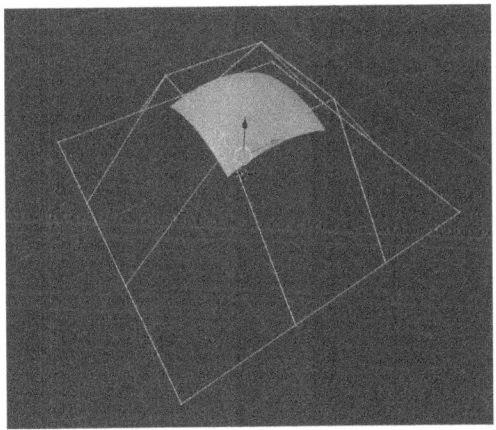

Fig. 132 surface insertion

143

3.2.4. *Metaballs*

Unlike other objects, the *Metaballs* are surfaces that are shaped through the attraction with other nearby *Metaballs*.

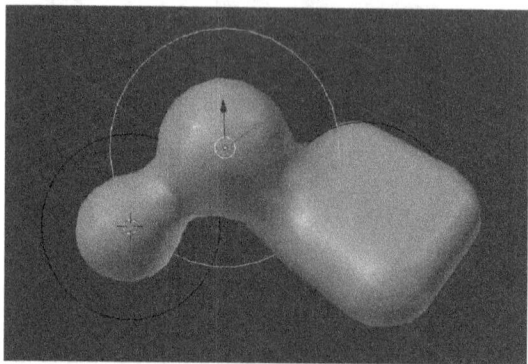

Fig. 133 three Metaballs

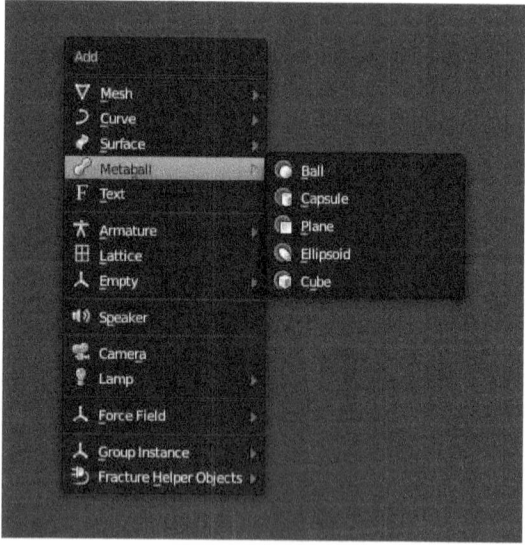

Fig. 134 inserting *Metaballs*

The following *Metaballs* are available:

144

a) **Ball;**

b) **capsules;**

c) **Plane;**

d) **ellipsoid;**

is) **Cube.**

The circle around a *Metaball* indicates its influence on the other ones.

As well as for *meshes, curves* and *surfaces,* you can change settings from the *Tools Shelf* region.

3.2.5. *Text*

Text allows you to enter text objects. We will see in the foregoing how to type text and change its font and style.

You can access all the *fonts* available for your operating system.

Fig. 135 text

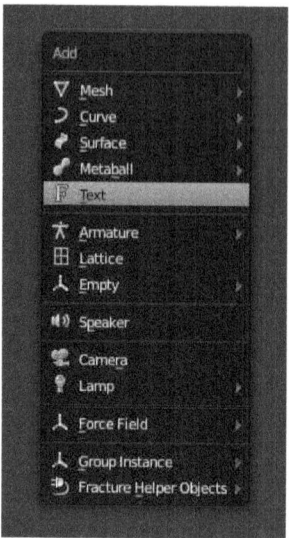

Fig. 136 text inclusion

3.2.6. *Empty*

The *Empty* object is dimensionless and may not even be rendered.

Its use is very common when you want to focus the camera on a precise point, or as a rotation and transformation centre when applied to the *modifiers,* as we will see later.

The *Empty,* ultimately, is an empty object, simply a *target* of a certain operation.

It can be optionally displayed in the 3D view as an axis system, a *circle,* a *sphere,* an *arrow,* etc. and, as well as other objects, it can be moved, rotated and scaled.

146

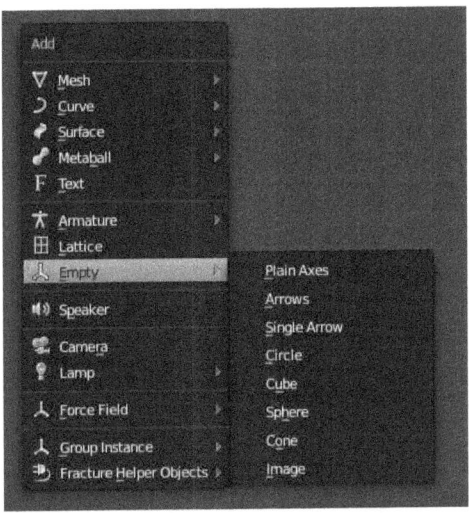

Fig. 137 insertion of an Empty object

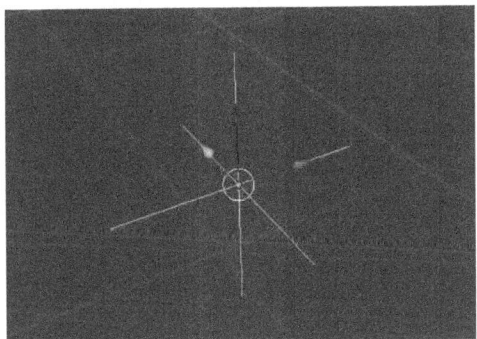

Fig. 138 *Empty* object

3.2.7. *Camera*

Concerning the camera it is convenient to spend more words.

It is the tool defining the framing of the objects in the scene, heart and main goal of the entire modelling process.

When you start Blender, besides a cube and a light, a camera is also present.

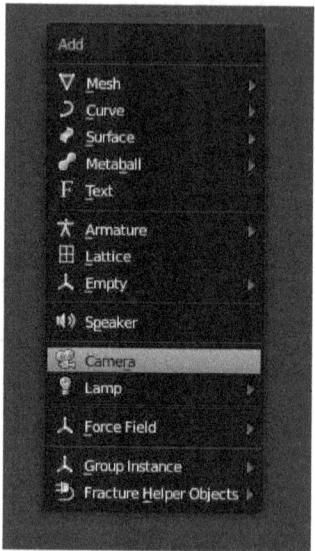

Fig. 139 camera insertion

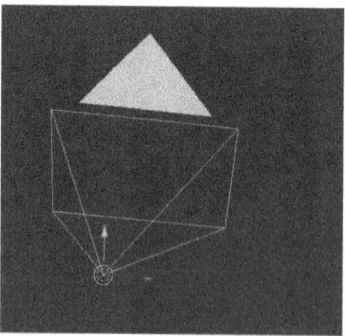

Fig. 140 the *Camera* object in the 3D view

Within a scene you can enter several cameras, keeping in mind that the **active** one will be the one framing the scene.

To determine which should be the active camera, simply enter the *View* menu of the 3D view and select *Set Active Object as Camera* in the *Cameras* submenu, or type the *shortcut* CTRL + 0 NUM.

The visualization of active camera shot can be readily recalled by pressing the 0 NUM key, or by choosing the option *Active Camera* in the *View / Cameras* menu.

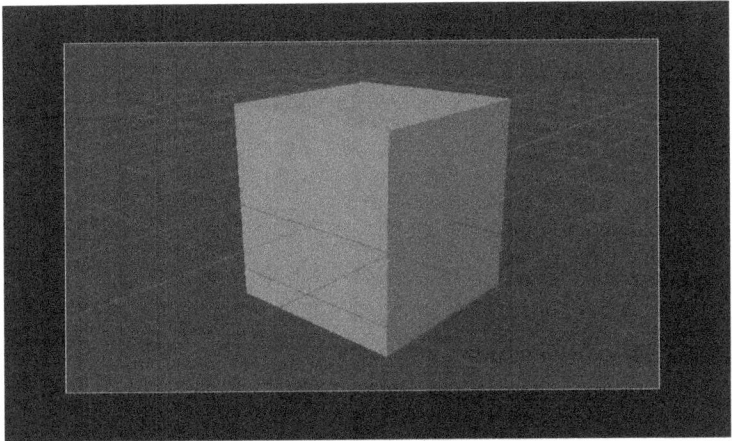

Fig. 1 41 shot of the active camera (CTRL + 0 NUM)

As well as for any other object, once the camera has been added with *SHIFT + A*, you can readily change some properties of the camera in the *Tools Shelf* region dedicated, in particular, its position and rotation.

Other settings regarding the visualization and the current camera can be found in the **View panel** of the *Properties Bar*.

In particular:

- *Lens* defines the lens of the 3D view in the 3D view;

- *Lock to Object* sets the view of a selected object;

- The check *Lock to Cursor* sets the view on the *3D Cursor;*

- *Lock Camera to View,* in camera view (0 NUM) enter inside the camera shot and allows you to modify it. Remove the check mark at the end;

- *Clip* sets a limit near and far for the view. Beyond that range the image is clipped, i.e. the elements outside the assigned margin are cut;

- *Local Camera* displays the local camera;

- *Render Border* renders within the margins of a region set with CTRL + B.

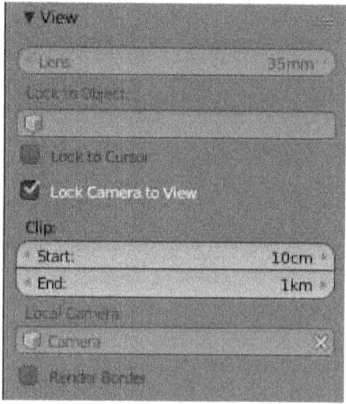

Fig. 142 the *View* panel of the *Properties Bar* with *Lock Camera to View* checked

In the *Properties* window, you can get and enter further information about the camera and the view.

In particular in the **Dimensions** panel of the **Render** *tab,* you can define the frame size in pixels, or in the drop-down menu *Render Presets* define default formats such as PAL, while in the *Film* panel set the exposure.

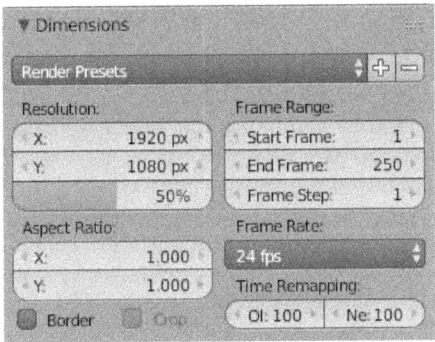

Fig. 143 The *View* panel

Fig. 14 4 The *Film* Panel

Moreover, the camera selection activate settings related to it in the **Data** tab of the Properties window, whose icon takes the form of a camera.

In the *tab*, from top to bottom we find different panels.

- The camera icon selects the choice of the current camera;

- *Lens* panel contains the parameters and information concerning the lens typology, choosing from three main views:

    • *Perpective*;

    • *Orthographic* (isometric projection);

    • *Panoramic* (panoramic, with choice between *Fisheye* and *equirectangular*).

- *Focal Length,* expressed in millimeters defines the camera focal length;

- *Shift* allows to translate in a horizontal direction *(x)* or vertical *(y)* a frame without image deformation and displacement of the vanishing points;

- *Clipping* has the same function of homonymous 3D view function;

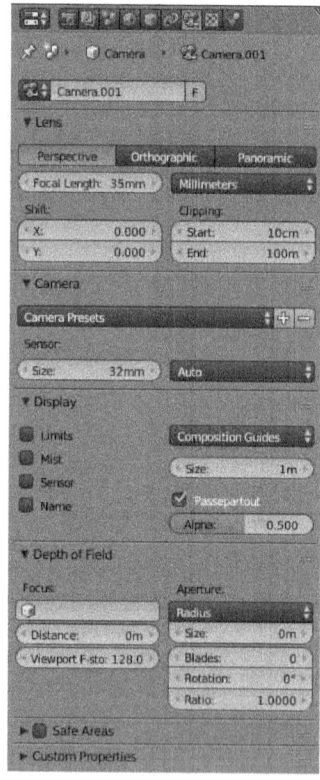

Fig. 145 *Data* property of the *Camera*

- *The House panel sets the camera* physical characteristics:

- *Preset Camera menu* lets you choose a camera defined in the settings according to commercial models in use;

- *Sensor* defines the size in millimeters of the camera sensor;

- Display defines what should be displayed and rendered:

  - *Limits (limits); Mist (fog and mist when activated); Sensor (data on the sensor), Name (the camera name);*

  - *Composition Guide* is a drop-down menu that allows you to view (but not render) some guidelines, useful and used in photography for a correct framing;

  - *The line size;*

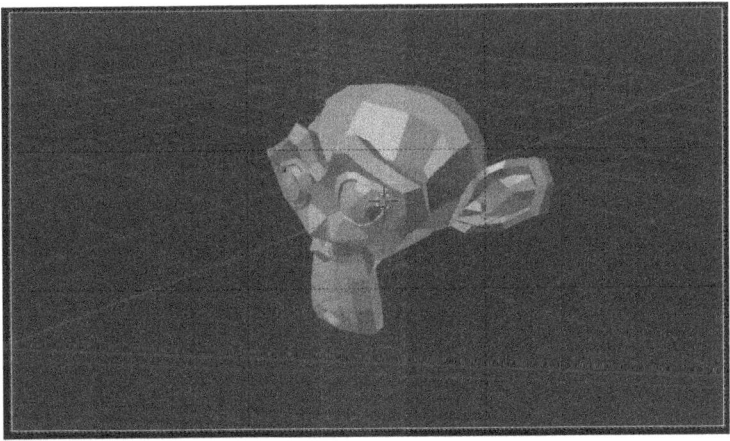

Fig. 146 the guidelines (in the picture: the middle third method)

  - *Passpartout* and its Alpha value as a percentage, make darker the external part of the frame making it more visible.

- The *Depth of Field* panel contains all data on the focus of the camera and the lens aperture:

- *Focus* allows you to enter as focus target an object, chosen from the list of those present in the scene in the drop-down menu (for example, an empty object);

- *Distance,* the focusing distance;

- *Aperture Type,* expressed either with the distance radius (in meters) or F-Stop value (e.g. 5.6);

- *The aperture value;*

- *Blades* indicates the number of blades in the objective lens;

- *Rotation* the number of rotation degrees of the blades;

- *Ratio* the distortion simulating the anamorphic effect of the blades (with parameter from 1 to 2);

- The *Safe Area* panel defines the safe shooting area, beyond which the image or video will be displayed in any case even if the support format were different. For example 14:9 instead of 16:9.

Finally, more information about the *Camera* object, as well as for all the other objects, are included in the **Object** tab of the *Properties* window, in particular the name, position, rotation and scaling.

3.2.8. Lamp

You can insert, for the sake of illuminating the scene, type *Lamp* objects, namely lamps.

There are 5 different types of lamps, each represented by a specific icon:

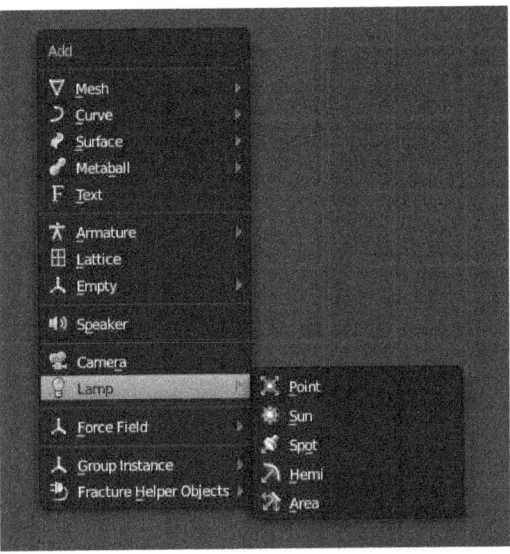

Fig. 147 insertion of a *Lamp* object

- *Point* places a point light, omnidirectional;

- *Sun* inserts a strongly directional light, with parallel beams, similar to sunlight;

- *Spot* insert a light that mimics the effect of a spotlight, point wise at the origin and circular to the edge, complete with a cone of light;

- *Hemi* reproduces a umbrella reflective panel, similar to those used in photographic studios;

- *Area* insert a panel emitting a light source, producing a diffuse light and soft shadows.

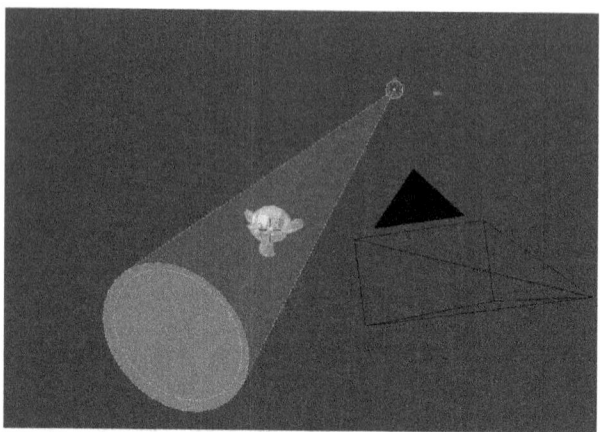

Fig. A 148 *Spot* type lamp

The characteristics of these lights can be set in the Data tab, whose icon, in the present case, will take the same form as the type of selected lamp.

Fig. 149 properties of the 5 different *Lamp* types

In these properties you can visualize the lamp *Preview*; the typology *(Point, Sun, Spot, Hemi, Area)* and the colour and intensity (in the *Nodes* panel, which will be widely considered in the foregoing).

In the *Sun* and *Spot* lamp typologies two other panels can be found, respectively:

156

- *Geographical Sun* (where the sunlight will simulate that indicated in the geographical coordinates, in the time and day);

- *Spot Shape,* which will define the shape and the definition of the light cone.

- Finally, you can define the behaviour of the shadow produced by *Lamp,* acting on the parameters:

- *Size,* for which low values will produce a sharper shadow, whereas high values a more soft and diffuse one;

 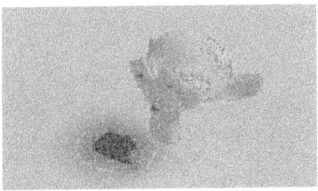

fig. 150 and 151 sharp and soft depending on the *Size* parameter (resp. 0 and 30 cm)

- *Max Bounces* the maximum number of bounces of the light;

- *Cast Shadow,* if the option is checked, objects will cast shadows, if not checked, they will not cast shadow;

- *Multiple Importance* reduces the light noise and makes reflections sharper, resulting in a heavier *rendering* process.

Finally, in the case of Area-type Lamp, it is possible to define if the emitting surface is a rectangle or a square, and the dimensions.

3.2.9. Other object types

There are other object types, the use of which will be the subject of subsequent chapters.

For now we will limit ourselves to list them summarily.

157

- **Armor** inserts a bone object, necessary for animation and *rigging;*

- **Latex,** will be highlighted in the chapter of modifiers. Create a low-density cage that serves to control high-definition polygon *meshes* with few points;

- **Speaker** introduces a sound source into the scene;

- **Force Field** inserted into the scene objects simulating the physical forces of nature such as wind, the vortex, the magnetism, alternating current, the harmonic motion, turbulence and others, which will interact with the other objects causing animations and stunning realism effects.

Other objects can be placed into the scene, choosing them among the *Addons* or downloading them in *Internet* (installing from the Blender preference panel).

4
BASE MODELING

4.1. Environments and work organization

We now finally face the heart of object modeling and work organization.

For work organization we mean to have clearly in mind what we want to represent concerning one or more objects in a scene, the level of detail (fundamental parameter for the geometry definition), the distance and the setting type.

Having clearly fixed in mind those choices will allow you to get a proper control of the 3D object modeling in their environment and a detail level appropriated to what will be possible to be felt and appreciated.

Moreover, using more scenes in the same project will allow you, in addition to separately manage different framings and specific illuminations, to play on different effects, colors, variants and detail levels.

4.1.1. *Object Mode* and *Edit Mode*

As we have already mentioned, without deeply analyzing it, in this first part of the volume, Blender offers several working modalities on an object.

In particular now we will analyze the *Object Mode* and *Edit Mode*.

These represent the two main modalities (or environments) of the modeling phase.

In the first modality, *Object Mode*, the 3D object is considered in its entirety and not in its intrinsic geometry. It will be possible to globally transform and modify it, without specifically considering its vertices, edges and faces, in the case of a mesh, or its key points and handles, in the case of a curve.

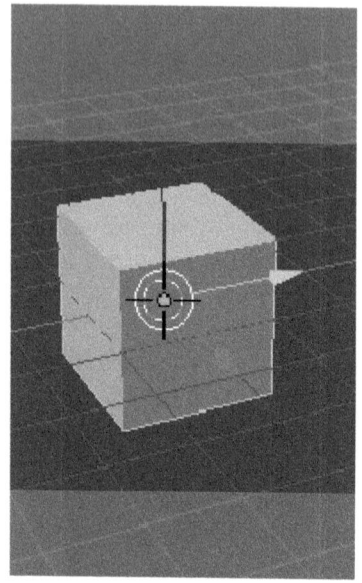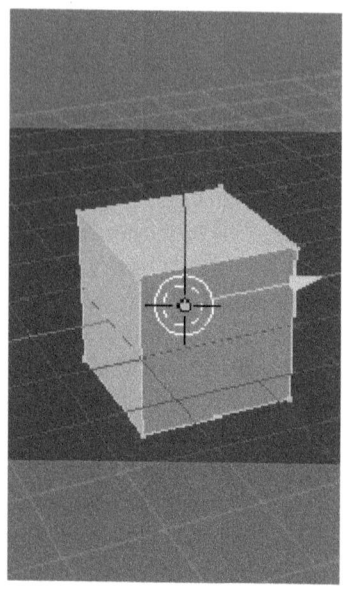

figg. 152 and 153 a *mesh* (cube) in *Object Mode* (on the left) and in *Edit Mode* (on the right)

To switch from the *Object* to *Edit* modality and vice versa click on the *Mode* menu of the 3D view header or, more quickly, press the TAB key.

Switching from a modality to another one, you will have certainly noticed that the menus and commands in the editors and *sidebars* will partially change. This is because some functions will be active and will have a meaning in a modality instead of the other one.

4.1.2. *Pie Menu*

An *Addon* exists, named *Pie Menu* (which must be activated from the preferences by typing "*Pie Menu*" in the search and activating it with a flag), allowing you to switch from a modality to the other one, using a graphical interface.

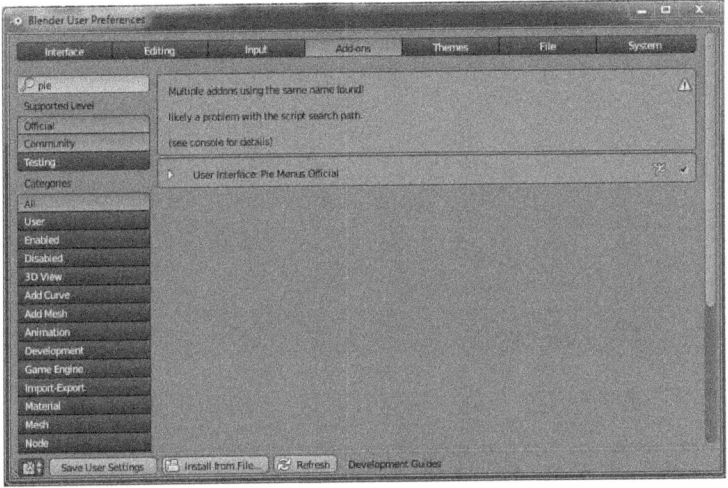

fig. 154 activation of the *Pie Menu* from the preferences

Pie Menu allows you to select any of the possible modalities. Just press the TAB key and click with the LMB (or type the corresponding number) on the desired modality and the latter will appear in the overlaid circular menu.
To cancel, simply press ESC.

Analogously the *Pie Menu* allows you, with the same system and the same circular menu typology, to select one of the visualization modalities (*Shade*), such as, for example, *Wireframe*, *Solid*, *Texture...* etc., pressing the Z key.
The use of the *Pie Menu* is obviously personal.

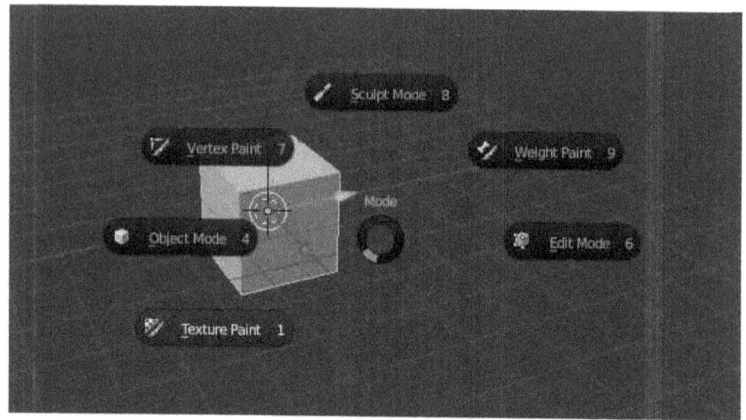

fig. 155 *Pie Menu: Mode*

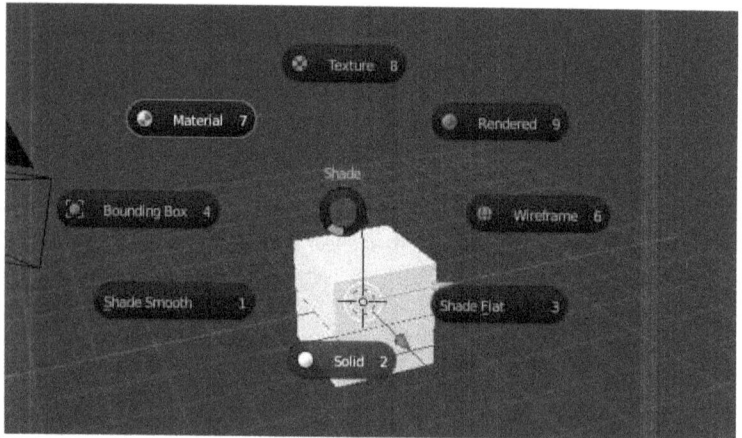

fig. 156 *Pie Menu: Shade*

4.1.3. Command search

 If you forget about the position or the shortcut of a command, just press the SPACEBAR in the 3D view and make a search by name in the box with the magnifying glass, placed above the menu that will appear.

4.2. The transformers (Grab, Rotate, Scale)

Even if the transformers are the most basic commands of the modeling, they are very effective.

They allow you to transform the object with respect to its position, rotation and dimensions (and consequently the scale).

 The transformation can be applied both in _Object Mode_ (and thus on the whole object), and in _Edit Mode_ (and thus on the object geometry elements: vertices, edges and faces).

The transformation can act on the whole object or element, or specifically along an axis _x_, _y_ or _z_ or, finally, according to a defined direction.

It is possible, for example, to freely shift the cube in the space, or in the _x_ direction, leaving unchanged the _y_ and _z_ coordinates.

The transformers are then: **Displacement** (_Grab_), **Rotation** (_Rotate_) and **Scaling** (_Scale_).

There are several methods for performing one of these three transformation operations on an object.

First of all the transformation can be applied only on the selected objects, active and not active, for example an object multiple selection, even of different nature.
After selecting the object (or the objects) or the element (or the elements) in _Edit Mode_, you will be able to:

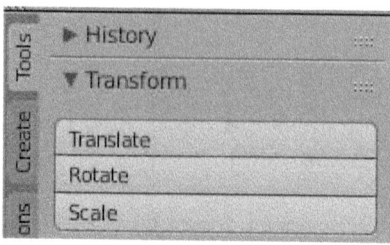

fig. 157 transformation commands in the *Tools Shelf*

- Click on one of the buttons *Translate, Rotate* or *Scale* in the *Transform* panel, in the *tab Tools,* inside the *Tools Shelf.* With these buttons you will be able to freely transform the object, without the possibility of inserting numerical values of specific directions unless, immediately or after pressing the button, you specify with the X, Y and Z keys the direction and possibly after the numerical value, even negative. For example, clicking the *Translate* button and then typing X, and then the value – 2 (or 2 –), the object will shift along *x* of 2 units in negative direction;

- Numerically insert the displacement values (*Location*), rotation (*Rotation*) or the exact dimensions (*Dimension*), and/or as a consequence the scale (*Scale*) along the three axes. In this way the absolute values of the transformations will be defined.

- Performing the same operation as the point 2) in the *Transform* panel, placed inside the *tab Object* of the *Properties* editor;

- Choose the transformation among the options *Transform* of the *Object* menu of the 3D view header: *Grab/Move* for the displacement, *Rotate* for the rotation, *Scale* for the scaling, suitably followed, like for the other cases, by the *x, y, z* direction and by the numerical value;

166

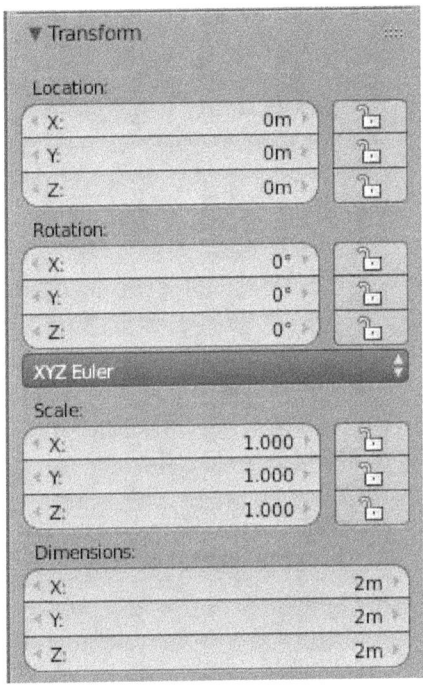

fig. 158 the *Transform* panel of the *Properties Bar*

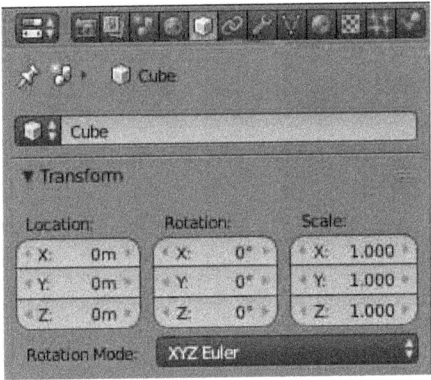

fig. 159 the *Transform* panel inside the *tab Object* of the *Properties* editor

167

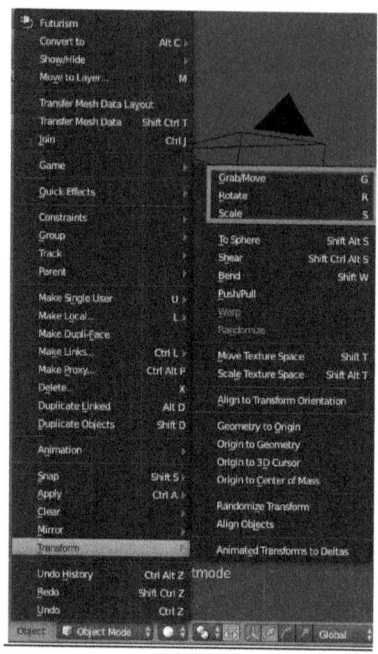

fig. 160 the *Object*/Transform menu of the 3D view header

- Manually using the manipulators, which can be activated from the menu placed in the 3D view header. They allow you, by clicking on the suitable colored symbol (arrow, circle or square respectively for the displacement, rotation and scaling) to make a transformation along the desired direction (red along or around the *x* axis; green along or around the *y* axis; blue along or around the *z* axis). On the other hand, by clicking on the white circle of the manipulator, the transformation will not be related to any axis. Like for the other cases, the displacement, rotation or scaling axis will be highlighted by Blender with a brighter color.

168

fig. 161 activation and choice of the manipulators

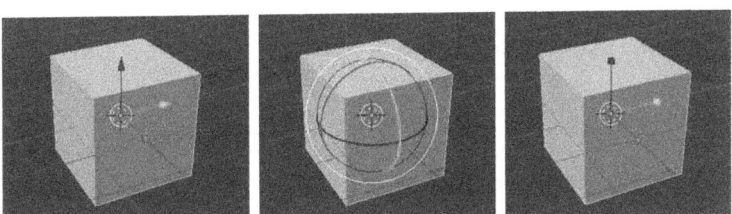

fig. 162 the three geometry manipulators

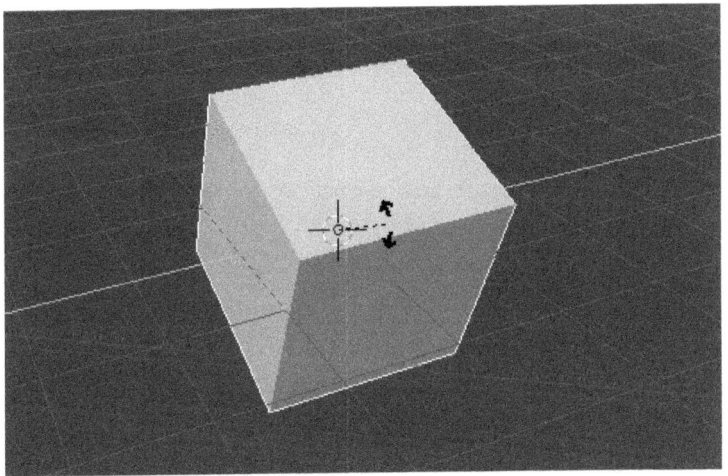

fig. 163 rotation by means of manipulator around the y axis

- The last but not the least method is the one using *shortcuts*. We greatly recommend this method, since it is quicker and more straight. You only need, in fact, to type **G** (*Grab*, for translating); **R** (*Rotate*, for rotating); **S** (*Scale*, for scaling), possibly followed by the letter X, Y or Z (indicating the axis) and by the numerical value, even negative. For example, to

169

half an object height you only need to type the sequence: S, Z and .5.

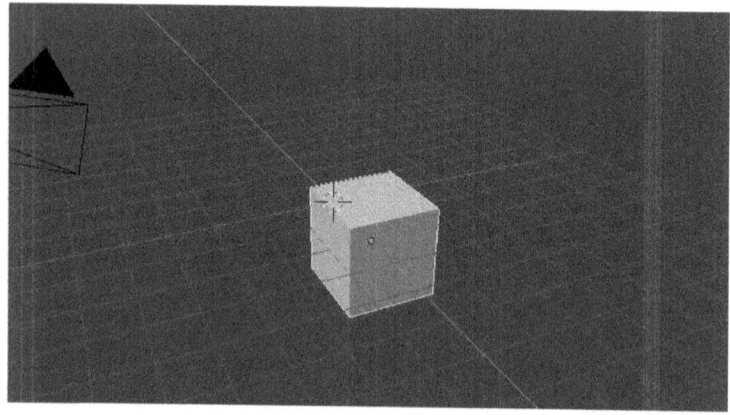

fig. 164 trasformations using *shortcuts*, in the example in the figure along the *x* axis

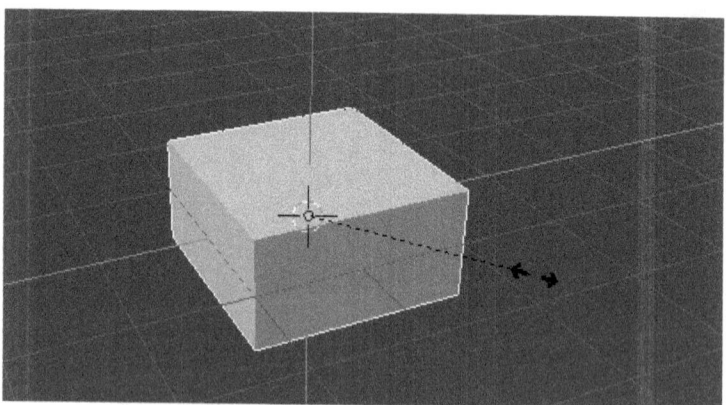

fig. 165 cube vertical scaling

NOTE: The scaling can be also used for quickly mirroring an object or some elements typing the negative value −1 to the mirroring direction. For example, for mirroring an object with respect to the *y* axis you only need to select it and type the sequence S, Y, −1.

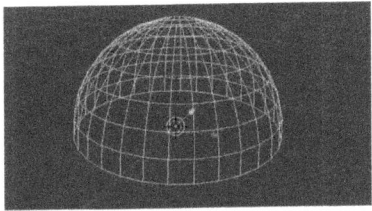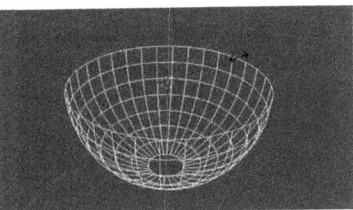

fig. 166 mirroring using the -1 scaling along an axis

NOTE: The scaling i also used to align elements (usually vertices) on the same plane. For example, if you want to equalize the *z* coordinate of a vertex group, you must select them in *Edit Mode* and type the sequence S, Z, 0. The vertices will be aligned on the same *z* coordinate, in correspondence to the mean among the *z* coordinates of all the vertices.

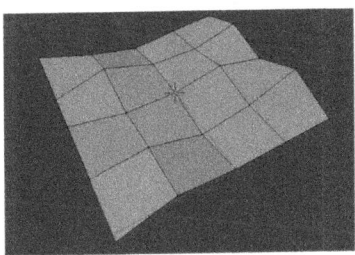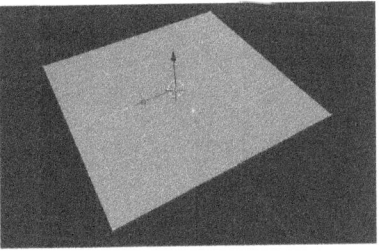

fig. 167 alignment of the mesh vertices: scaling by 0 on *z*

4.2.1. Apply (reset) the transformations

It is worth highlighting a fundamental concept which, if left out, could affect the success of subsequent modifications: the transformation reset.

After a transformation Blender always leaves the possibility of restoring the shape and position of the transformed object. In fact, after the object has been modified, in the *Transform* panel of the *sidebar Properties Bar*, the values relevant to the transformations will remain highlighted (with respect to the starting values 0 for position and rotation and 1 for scaling).

However, once you are sure about the transformation effect, it is recommended you make the changes definitive, by applying the transformations themselves and resetting the values, as the modified objects had been inserted with those *default* values.

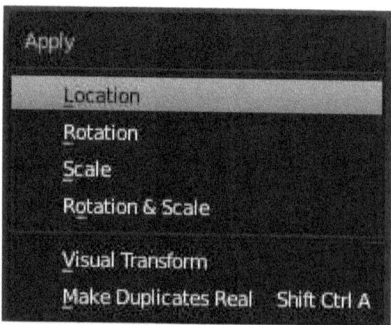

fig. 168 the operation of application (or reset) of the transformation (CTRL + A)

In doing so, the values relevant to *Location* and *Rotation* will be reset, whereas those relevant to *Scale* will be equal to 1, with the dimensions (*Dimension*) due to the transformation being definitive.

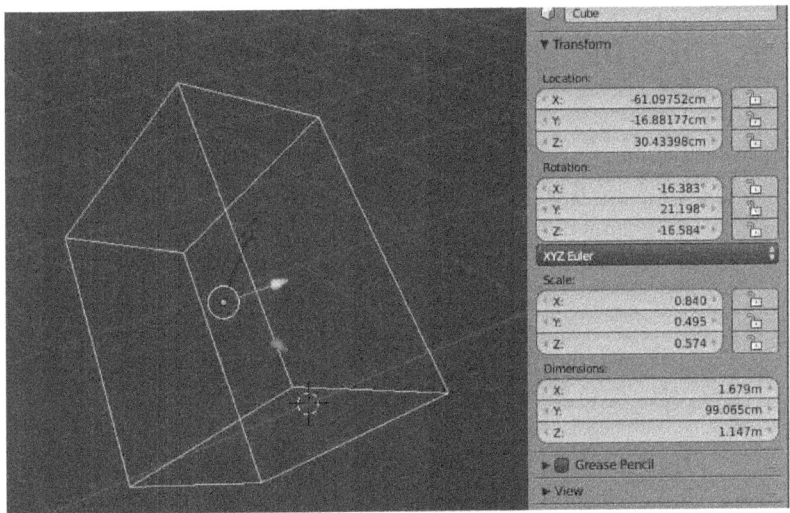

fig. 169 the transformed cube (note the values of the *Transform* panel)

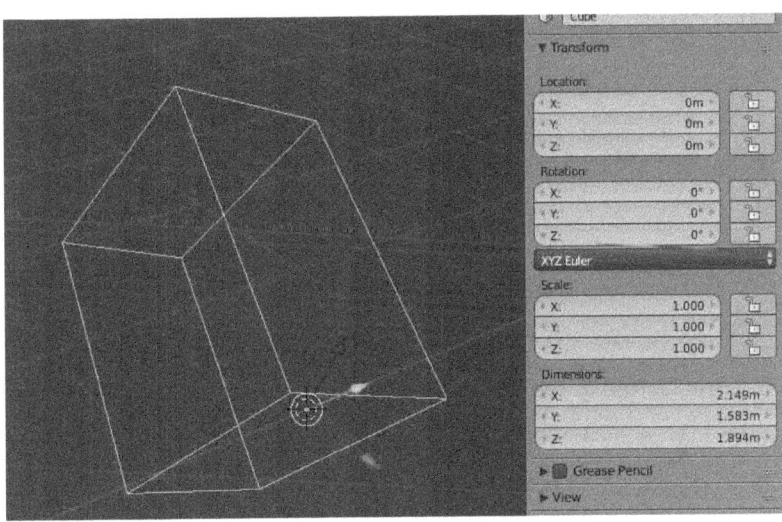

fig. 170 the effect of the transformation application

173

In order to apply the transformations you only need to type CTRL + A and choose one or more options among *Location, Rotation, Scale, Rotation + Scale.*

4.2.2. Use of the transformers with the *Proportional Editing*

The *Proportional Editing* is a powerful and useful tool allowing you to apply some transformations to objects and, in particular, to geometry elements (vertices, edges and faces) such as to influence in the transformation also the neighboring ones, inside a certain *range* (or influence area).

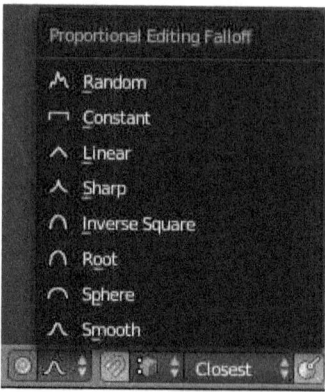

fig. 171 the *Proportional Editing* menu

For activating the *Proportional Editing* you only need to activate the button in the 3D view header. Once activated (the dot will become blue), a drop-down menu will appear in which you can choose to proportional effect, i.e.:

- *Random*: the influence on the elements close to the selected one (ones) will be random. This function is useful for creating non-flat surfaces, mountain ranges, rippled water;

174

- *Constant*: the influence on the elements close to the selected one (ones) will be constant;

- *Linear*: the influence on the elements close to the selected one (ones) will be linear;

- *Sharp*: the influence on the elements close to the selected one (ones) will follow a parabolic behavior, creating a sort of cusp;

- *Inverse Square*: the influence on the elements close to the selected one (ones) will have a behavior similar of a parabola, but with a cusp on the selected elements;

- *Root*: the influence on the elements close to the selected one (ones) will exhibit a pure parabolic behavior;

- *Sphere*: the influence on the elements close to the selected one (ones) will be spherical;

- *Smooth*: the influence on the elements close to the selected one (ones) will be smoothened, such as to create a gaussian behavior.

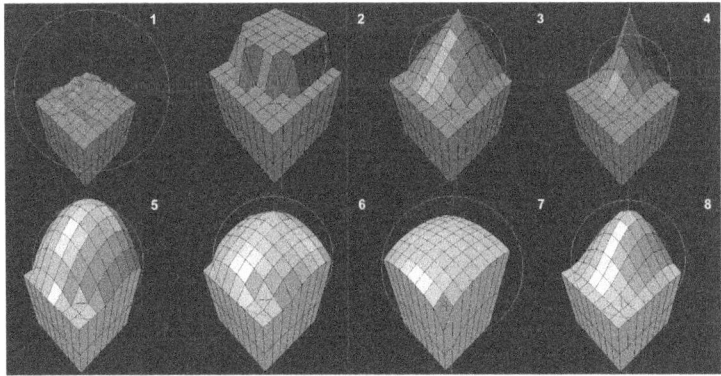

fig. 172 the effects of different *Falloff* of the *Proportional Editing*

4.2.3. Use of the transformers with the *Snap*

The *Snap*, usually used with the *3D Cursor* and the *Pivot* is a fundamental tool for precisely modeling and placing the objects in the space, snapping them through chosen vertices, edges, faces or other elements.

The two commands *Snap* (SHIFT + S), allowing you to place the cursor depending on an object (and vice versa), and *Set Origin* (SHIFT + CTRL + ALT + C), allowing you to determine the origin position (*Pivot*) of a selected object, managed together with the three commands *Snap during Transform* (button with the magnet), *Snap Element* and *Snap Target*, allow you to snap any object or element to any other one.

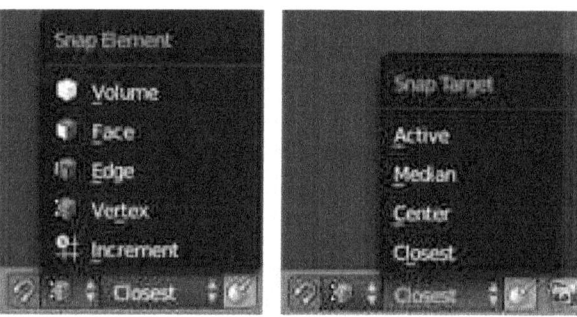

fig. 173 the commands relevant to the *Snap* to a element

The *Snap Element* menu allows you to determine the place the selected object or element will snap to: incremental method, to the closest vertex, to the closest edge, to the closest face, to the volume, i.e. the closest whole object.

The *Snap Target* menu, on the other hand, will determine the way the magnet will act on the closest element relevant to the *Snap Element*, i.e.: on the closest (*Closet*); on the object or element center or on a group (*Center*); on the mean point

176

(*Median*) or on the active object or element of a selection (*Active*).

To better clarify the topic let's make an example.

EXERCISE n. 3: SNAP A CUBE VERTEX TO A POINT OF A SPHERE

Insert a cube and a sphere in the scene with SHIFT + A and separate themselves in the space with G.

By *default* both the objects will have their origin (*Pivot*) in their center of gravity.

Select the cube and, with TAB, enter in *Edit Mode*. Select then a vertex like in the figure.

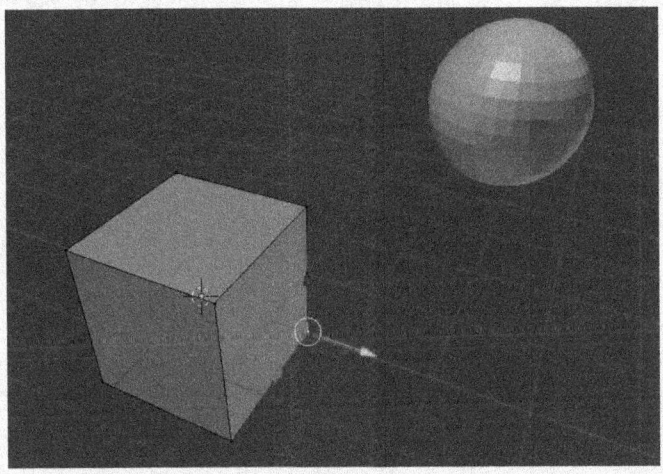

fig. 174 the two objects in the scene with the cube in *Edit Mode*

Press now SHIFT + S and choose the option *Cursor to Selected*. The *3D Cursor* will be placed on the selected vertex.

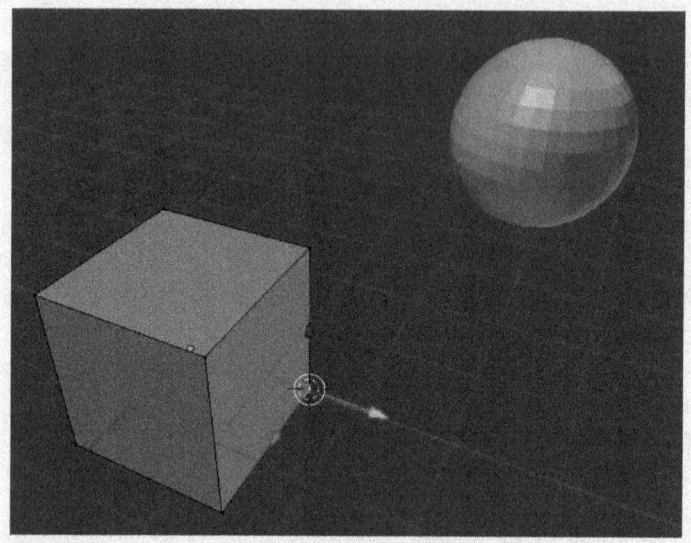

fig. 175 placement of the *3D Cursor* on the selected vertex

Return in *Object Mode* and press SHIFT + CTRL + ALT + C and choose the option *Origin to 3D Cursor*. The origin will be now placed on the vertex.

If you try to make with R a rotation, you can see that the cube will rotate not anymore around its center of the gravity, but around the selected vertex.

Now, you must activate the button with the magnet (which will be visualized in colors) and set the *Snap Element* on *Vertex* and the *Snap Target* as *Closet*, such as the closest elements will snap to themselves.

With the cube selected, press G and move close to the sphere. The cube will instantaneously snap to the closest vertex (which will appear circled). Until you will not confirm with the LMB you will be able to choose the desired vertex.

fig. 176 placement of the origin on the vertex

fig. 177 *snap* of the cube vertex to the sphere vertex

NOTE: Instead of activating the magnet button we recommend, after having chosen the transformation type (for example pressing G = *grab*), to hold CTRL pressed until the snap. This method is advisable because during the transformation you can choose in real time when using the *snap* and when not, holding pressed or releasing CTRL.

4.3. Tools and object modify in Object Mode

In this section all the tools applied to an object in *Object Mode* will be analyzed in detail. Let us start analyzing the panels of the *tab Tools* of the *Tools Shelf*.

4.3.1. the *Transform* panel

In the *Transform* panel of the *Tools Shelf*, three items are available, with the corresponding three buttons.

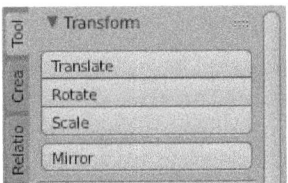

fig. 178 the *Transform* buttons

The first three (*Translate*, *Rotate* and *Scale*) have been already deeply described.

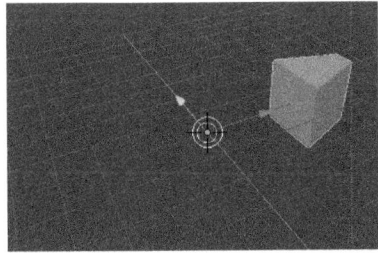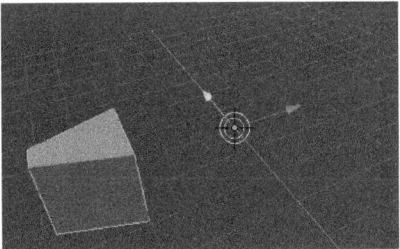

fig. 179 effect of the mirroring with respect to the x axis and the origin

The fourth button (*Mirror*) mirror the selected object with respect to its origin and a selected axis.

In order to apply the *Mirror* transformation you only need to select the object, click on the *Mirror* button (or the combination CTRL + M), followed by the choice X, Y or Z (depending on the specified mirroring direction).

4.3.2. the *Edit* panel

In the same *tab*, just under the *Transform* panel, you can find the *Edit* panel.

fig. 180 the Edit panel

In this panel you can find some very important tools:

- *Duplicate* (SHIFT + D) duplicates the selected object or objects creating identical copies with the same parameters, dimensions, materials, but totally independent from themselves and the originals;
- *Duplicate Linked* (ALT + D) creates duplicate linked of the originals. The substantial difference is that any geometry

182

modify (*Edit Mode*) made on the original, will be automatically applied also to the duplicate linked;
- *Delete* (X or CANC), followed by the confirm, cancel what has been selected;
- *Join* (CTRL + J) joins two or more *meshes* into a single *mesh*.

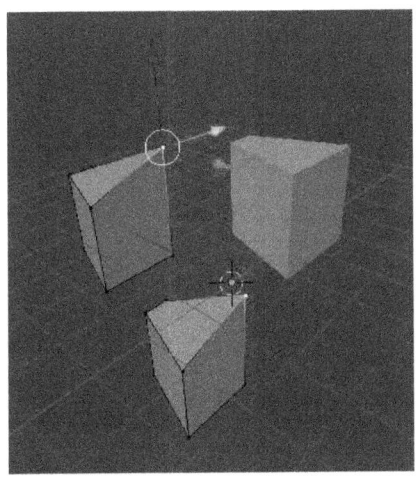

fig. 181 copy and duplicate linked of the *mesh*: the duplicate linked is automatically modified together with the original. The *Set Origin* menu recalls the commands on the *Pivot*, as already seen by the combination SHIFT + CTRL + ALT + C.

The switches *Smooth* / *Flat* alternate a smoothened shading effect in the selected mesh.

This smoothing effect of the faces can result nice in case of curved surfaces, but not on the flat faces.

This effect is normally applied for further rounding a surface, together with the modifiers *Subdivision Surface* and *Edge Split* which we will analyze in the foregoing.

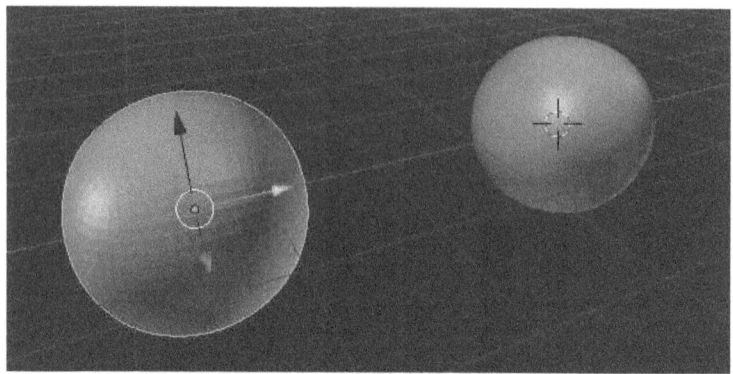

fig. 182 two *meshes* under *Flat* effect (on the left) and *Smooth* (on the right)

The switches *Data Transfer* (SHIFT + CTRL + T) and *Data Layout* transfer from the active mesh to the selected ones the *layers* and *layouts* data.

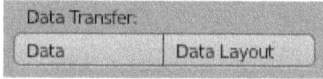

fig. 183 Data Transfer

The buttons open a drop-down menu from which you can choose the data type to the transferred.

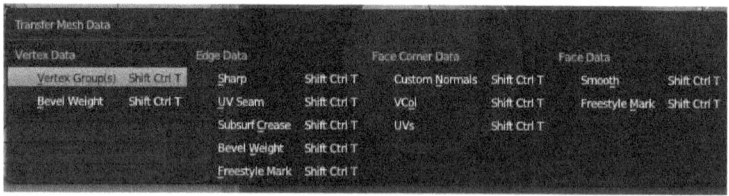

fig. 184 drop-down menu Transfer Mesh Data

4.3.3. the *History* panel

We finally highlight the **History** panel allowing you to jump to previous or next operations or *Undo*.

4.4. Tools and object modify in Edit Mode

In **Edit Mode** some commands remain unchanged, whereas others have been added, relevant to the geometry modify.

We recommend to add from the properties the **Loop Tools** addon.

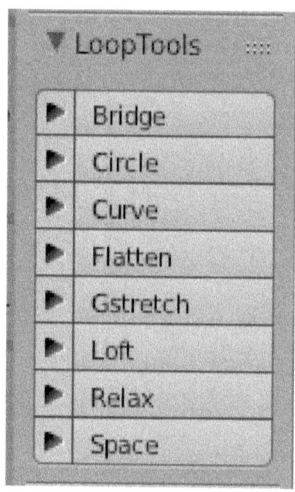

fig. 185 the *Loop Tools* menu

In the foregoing we will analyze the commands and tools in *Edit Mode* for the *meshes,* the *curves,* the *surfaces,* the *Metaballs* and the *texts.*

- **TRANSFORM**

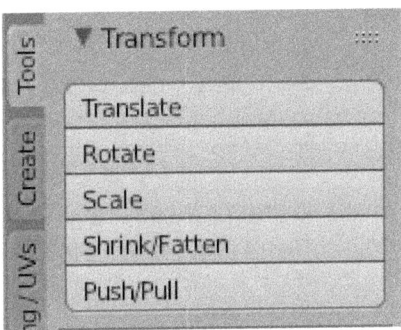

fig. 186 *the Transform* menu in *Edit Mode*

In the *Transform* panel the main three transformers are present (*Translate*, *Rotate* and *Scale* having in *Edit Mode* exactly the same behavior and functionalities than in *Object Mode*.

It is possible to move, rotate and scale vertices, edges and faces, sensibly modifying the geometric structure of the *mesh*.

In addition to these transformers, other two modifying tools are present: *Shrink/Fatten* and *Push/Pull*

- **Shrink/Fatten**: this *tool* allows you to translate all the mesh vertices along its normal, such as to shrink (for negative values) or fatten (for positive values) the figure. It is necessary to pay attention not to use too large in modulus negative values to avoid interference between the faces;

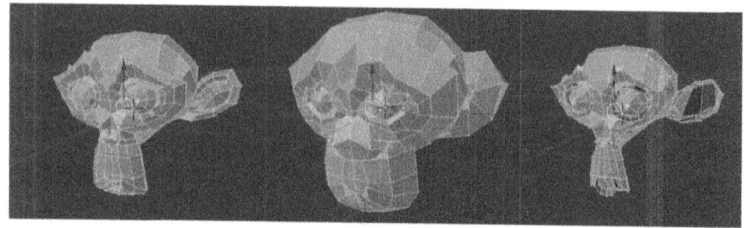

fig. 187 *Shrink/Fatten.* From left to right: original *mesh, Fatten* effect; *Shrink* effect

- **Push/Pull** is similar to the previous one, but fattens or shrinks the *mesh* vertices along the directions obtained joining the vertices to the center. For positive values the *mesh* is inflated, for negative values is shrinked.

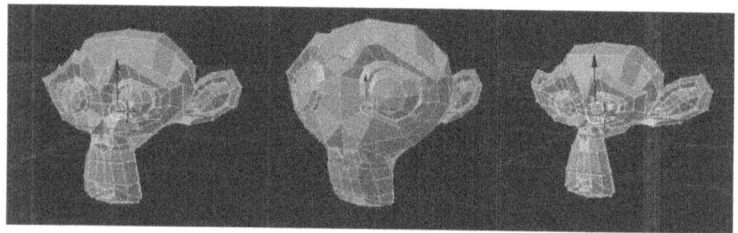

fig. 188 *Push/Pull.* From left to right: original *mesh, Pull* effect; *Push* effect

4.4.1. The Loops

Before describing the next *tools,* let us introduce a new concept, the one concerning *loops.*

 A *loop* is a sequence of vertices, edges or faces easily visible, representing a geometry, though complex, clear and manageable.

The *loop* control, thanks to the tools dedicated to it (see, for example, *Loop Tools*) and to the selection commands, allows you to model in a simple and clear way.

Let's see which are the loop selection methods.

- select a *loop* by a selected vertex, edge or face: select one of the three elements and, holding pressed ALT, click on the neighboring element above which is part of the *loop*. For example, by selecting a vertex, the edge starting from that vertex and being part of the loop should be selected;

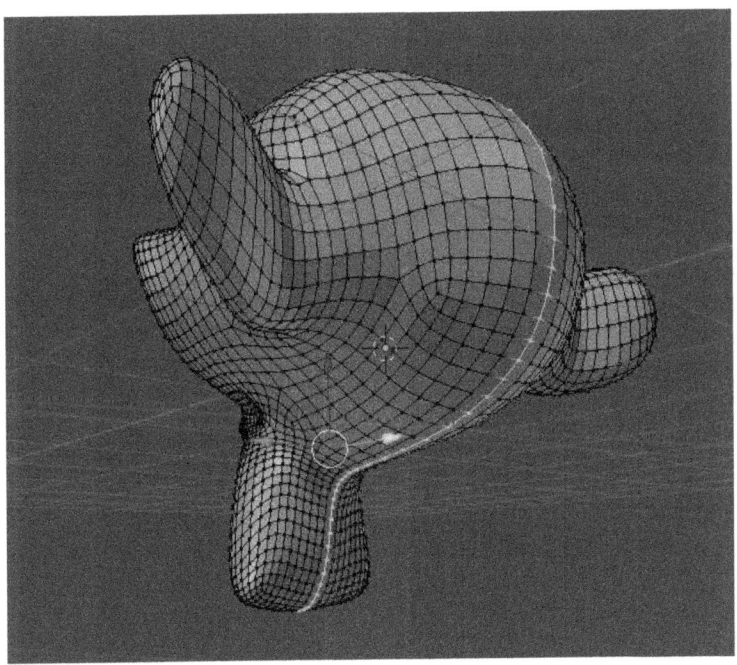

fig. 189 a selected *loop* in light orange

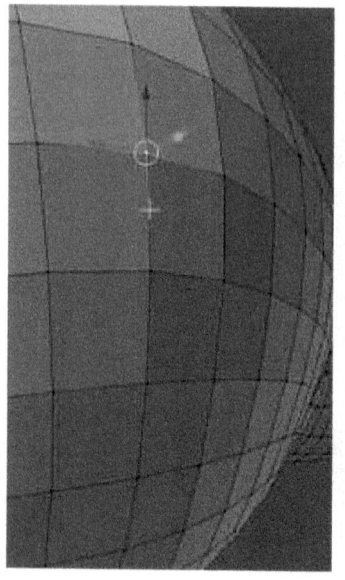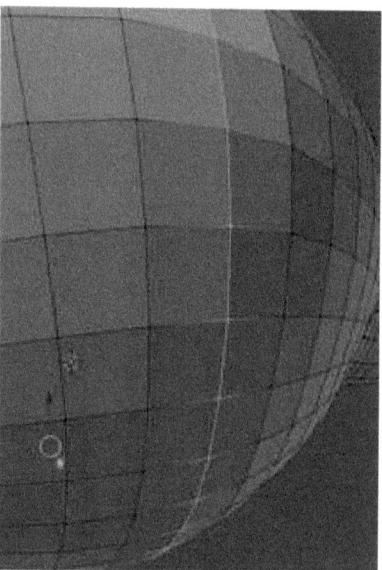

fig. 190 *loop* selection with ALT + LMB

- select point by point or with the rectangular selection (B) or circular (C): like in *Object Mode*, also the elements, and thus the *loops* of a *mesh* can be selected vertex by vertex, edge by edge, or face to face) with SHIFT pressed;
- selection of a next *loop*: holding pressed both ALT and CTRL and clicking with the LMB on the edge perpendicular to the *loop*, the next loop parallel to the previously selected one can be in turn selected;
- multiple loop selection: it is possible to continue the loop selection holding pressed SHIFT + CTRL + ALT and clicking with the LMB on an edge perpendicular to the loops;
- selection of a *loop* perpendicular to the selected one: you only need to click with the LMB on an edge perpendicular to the selected *loop* holding pressed SHIFT + ALT.

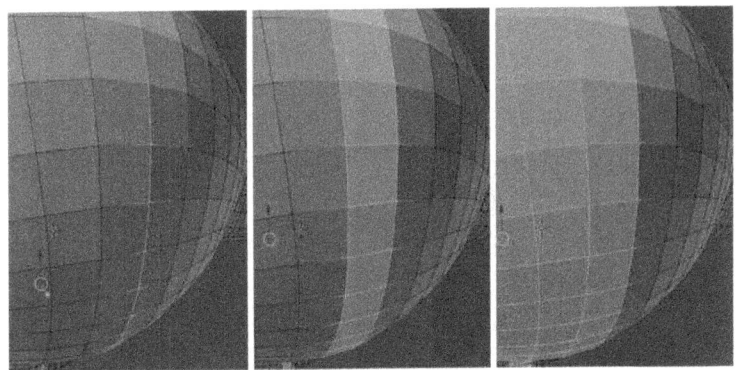

fig. 191 selection of a loop, of the next loop, and of a *loop series*

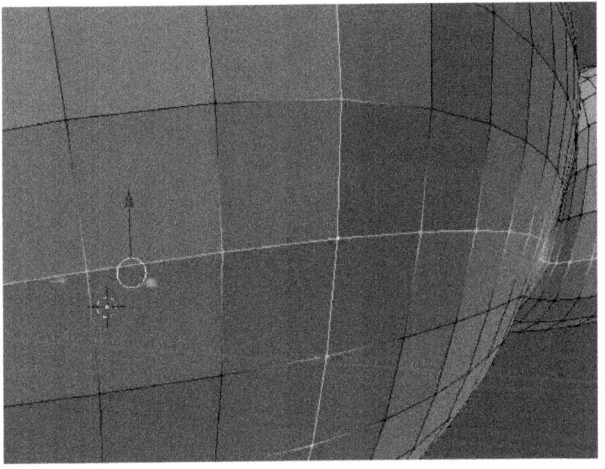

fig. 192 selection of a perpendicular *loop*

For inserting one or more loops dividing the mesh surfaces or edges you only need to type the combination CTRL + R (or press the button **Loop Cut and Slide**) in the *Tools Shelf* and place the mouse pointer in correspondence of the edge perpendicular to the loop, then, with the mouse wheel, to increase or decrease the loop number (and thus the subdivision number), to confirm with LMB, then possibly to place the loop/s along the perpendicular edge. Finally, confirm again with the LMB.

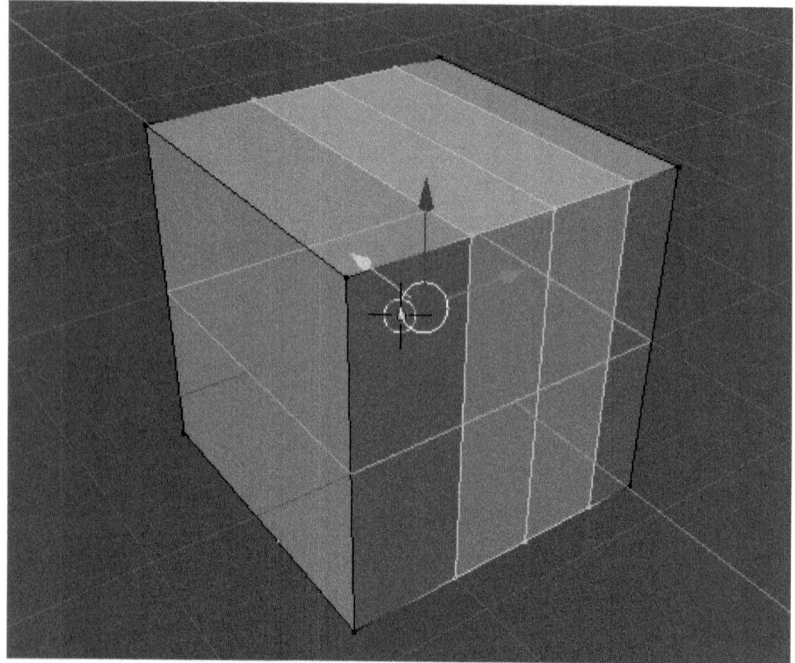

fig. 192 *loop* insertion

- **MESH TOOLS**

The *Mesh Tools* panel contains a large number of tools, grouped in four panels.

1) The first section (**Deform**) contains *tools* tending to deform the selected objects.

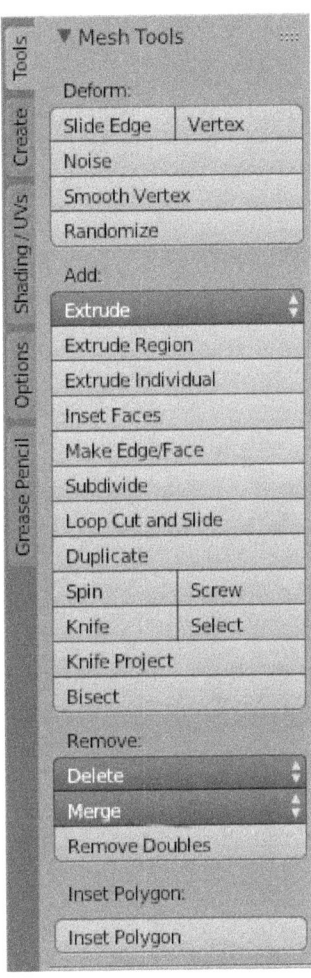

fig. 194 the *Mesh Tools* panel

- **Slide Edge** makes a selected *loop* sliding perpendicularly along the *mesh*. The function can be activated also pressing twice the G key;

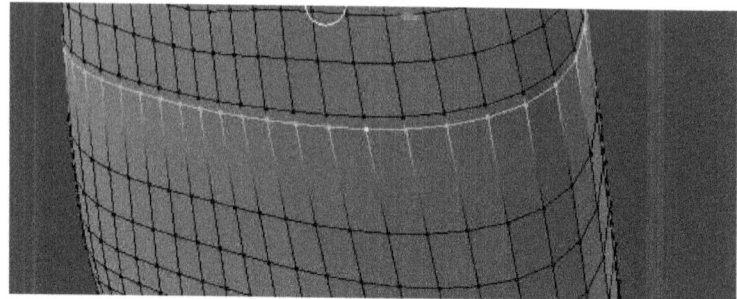

fig. 195 *Slide Edge* (G + G)

Vertex (SHIFT + V) makes a loop or a vertex group sliding along the direction selected in yellow;

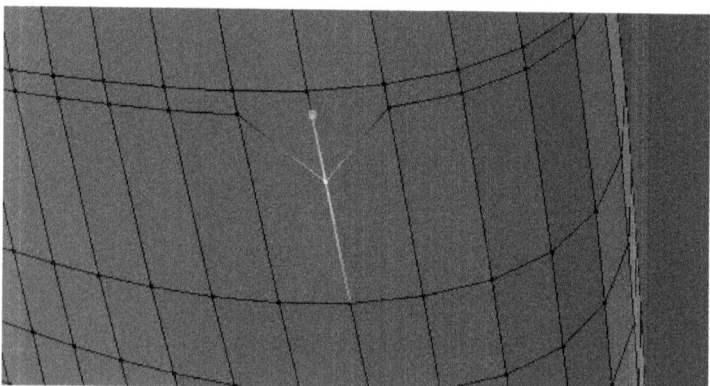

fig. 196 *Vertex*

- **Noise** *adds some noise to a group of selected vertices; the noise is regulated by an assigned texture (see in the foregoing) of a parameter* defined in the cursor placed in the underlying region (from 0 to 1);

fig. 197 the *Noise* cursor

- **Smooth Vertex** rounds and smooths the mesh selected vertices, according to the *Smooth Vertex* parameters in the underlying region. These parameters define the quantity (cursor *Smooth* from 0 to 1), the number of the rounding steps (*Repeat*) and the direction (flags on the *x*, *y* and *z* axes);

fig. 198 the *Smooth Vertex* panel

- **Randomize** generates a noise in the position of the selected vertices, achieving an outcome much similar to that of the *Proportional Edit* set to *Random*. The parameters can be found in the underlying region and regulate: the point offset with respect to the original position (Amount); the deformation uniformity (*Uniform* from 0 to 1); the offset

195

alignment with respect to the normals (*Normal* from 0 to 1); several random configurations (*Random Seed*);

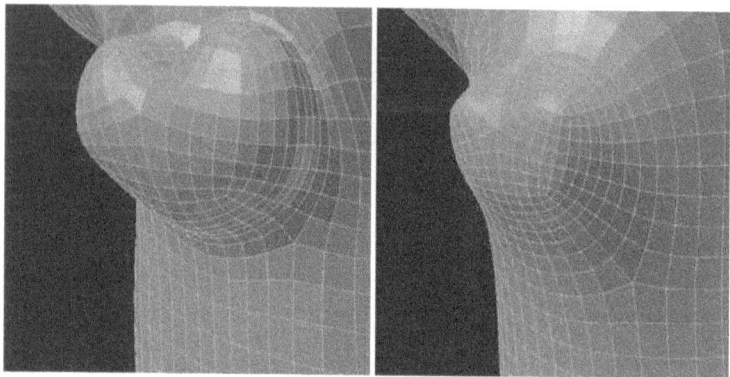

fig. 199 the *Smooth Vertex* effect (on the right)

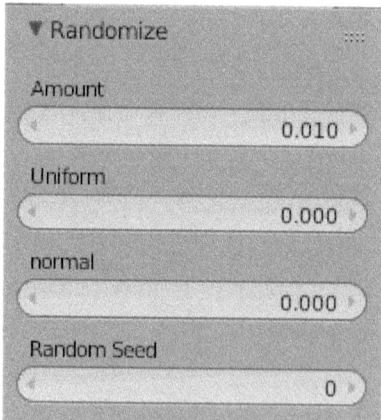

fig. 200 the *Randomize* panel

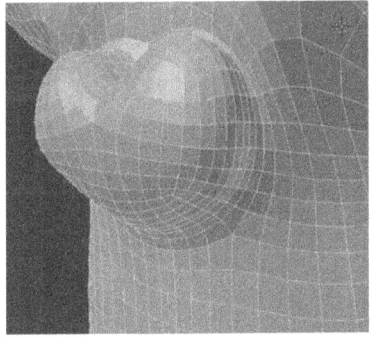 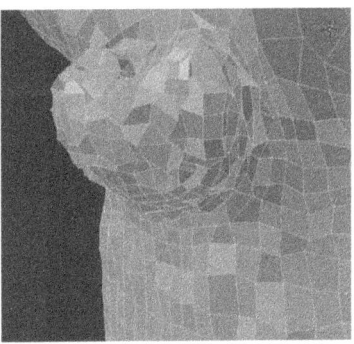

fig. 201 the *tool Randomize* effect (on the right)

The second group (**Add**) contains the tools adding geometry to the *mesh*.

2) Add

Among the tools contained in the Add section, the one perhaps most used in the modeling and most important is the **extrusion**.

- The extrusion (**Extrude**) allows you to add new elements starting from the selected ones.

 More specifically:

    a) from a vertex extrusion an edge is obtained;

    b) from an edge extrusion a face is obtained;

    c) from a face extrusion a solid is obtained.

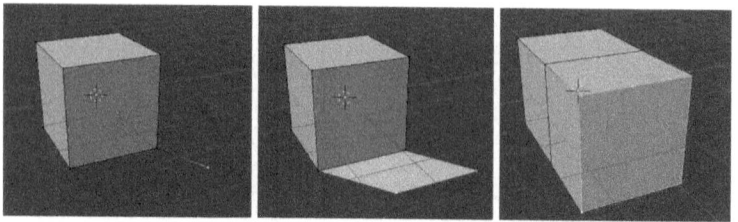

fig. 202 vertex, edge and face extrusion

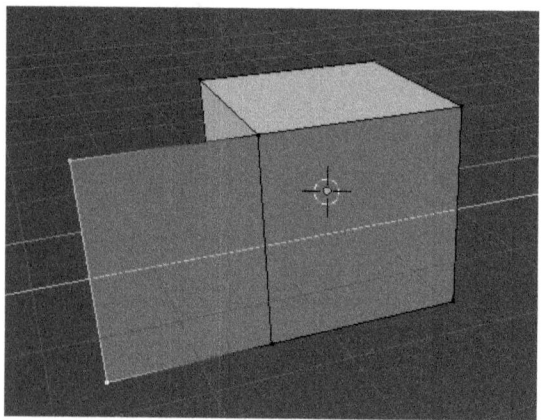

fig. 203 edge extrusion along *y* (the *y* axis is highlighted in green)

The extrusion can freely occur in the space or according a specific direction *x, y* or *z*. Blender will highlight the specified direction by coloring the relevant axis (red for *x*, green for *y* and blue for *z*).

For extruding one or more elements you only need to select them and press E, possibly followed by the extrusion axis (X, Y or Z key) and by the value, positive or negative, of the extrusion.

For example a mesh face can be inward extruded of 2 centimeters, by selecting it and typing E, X, .2 -.

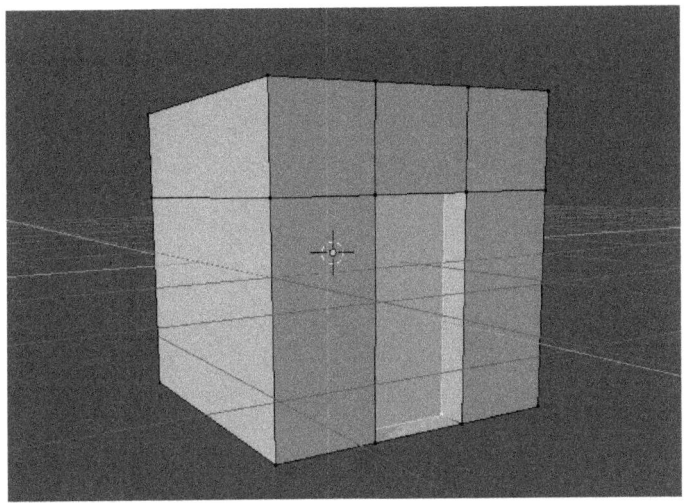

fig. 204 mesh face inward extrusion

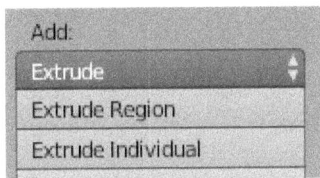

fig. 205 extrusion commands in the *Tools Shelf*

The extrusion commands is present in the *Tools Shelf*, together with more specific commands like:

a) *Extrude Region* (normal extrusion of a previously described selection;

b) *Extrude Individual* (extrusion of different elements according to their specific normal). It applies to vertices, edges and faces depending on what has been highlighted in the *Edge Select*.

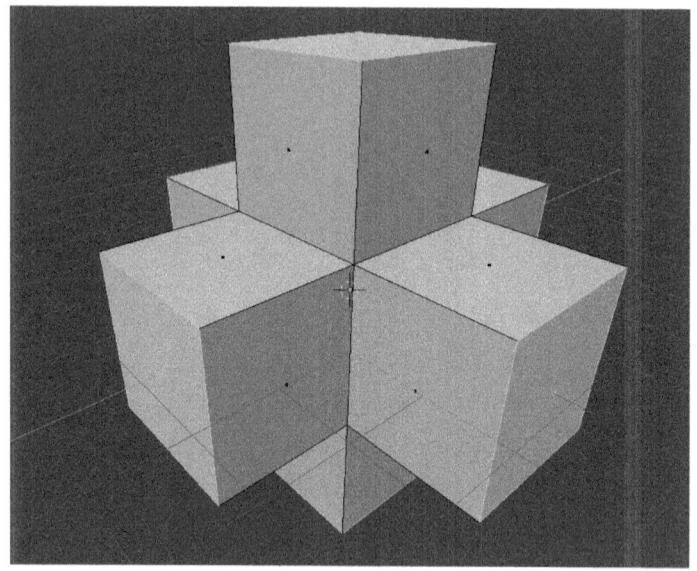

fig. 206 Extrude Individual of the cube faces

Moreover, specific extrusions can be chosen in the drop-down menu *Extrude*, such as:

1) *Region* (E), i.e. standard object extrusion (previously seen);

2) *Region (Vertex Normals)*: extrusion along the normals of the selected vertices;

3) *Individual Faces*: face extrusion along the corresponding individual normals (previously seen);

4) *Edges Only*: extrusion only of the selected edges;

5) *Vertices Only*: extrusion only of the selected vertices.

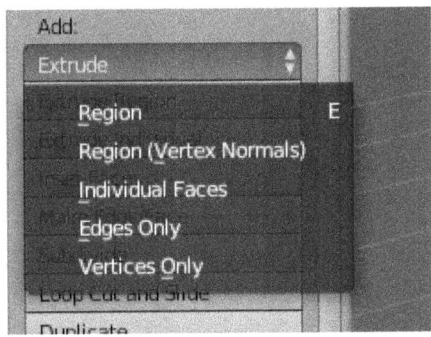

fig. 207 the drop-down menu *Extrude*

Now we are already able to start modeling a quite complex object, using the most known tools: transformation, extrusion and *loop*.

 EXERCISE n. 4: MODELING A SMALL HOUSE

For modeling a small house you can start from a square.
Select all the objects present in the scene with A, then cancel them with X or CANC and confirm. Finally, insert a plane with SHIFT + A, MESH, PLANE.

Don't worry about dimensions. It's only an example. With the plane selected, enter with TAB in *Edit Mode*, being sure to have selected each element comprising it and extrude it by 2 units in *z* direction, typing E, Z, 2.

The plane is transformed into a cube. Obviously you could insert a cube from the beginning.

fig. 208 plane extrusion

Insert now a *loop* with CTRL + R at the center of the *xz* face placing the mouse pointer close to one of the two horizontal edges.

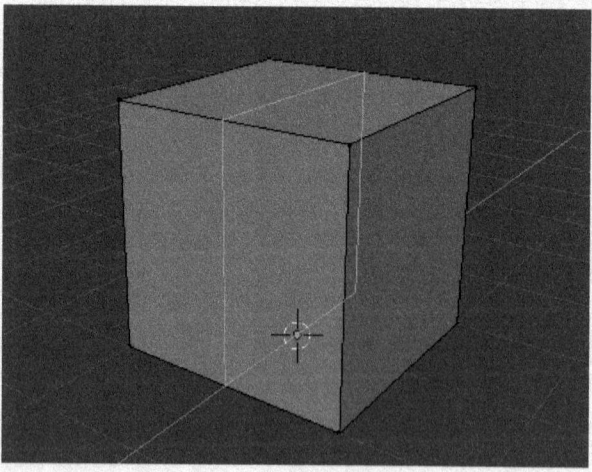

fig. 209 *loop* insertion

Confirm, then, upon selecting the edge of the mesh top face, lift it of 1 unit typing G, Z, 1.

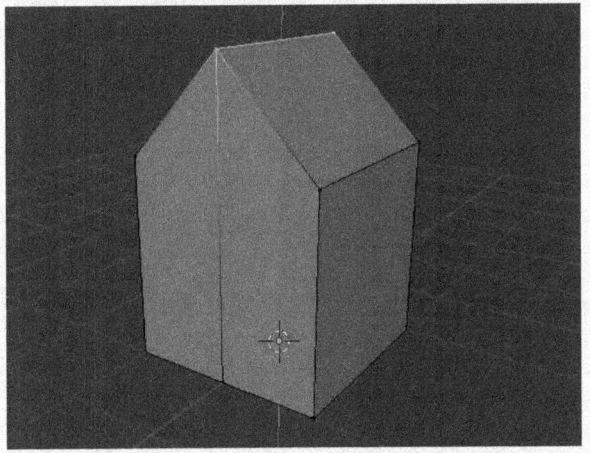

fig. 210 top edge lift and creation of the pitched roof

You have obtained the pitched roof.

Create now an horizontal *loop* and place it such as it is coinciding with the edges comprising the pitched roof. Then, without unselecting the new *loop*, lower it of 0,1 units typing G, Z, .1-.

You have now given a thickness to the pitched roof.

You now need to create the object of the pitched roof itself.

Select the opposite faces representing the thickness of the pitched roof and extrude outward them with *Extrude Individual* of 0.2.

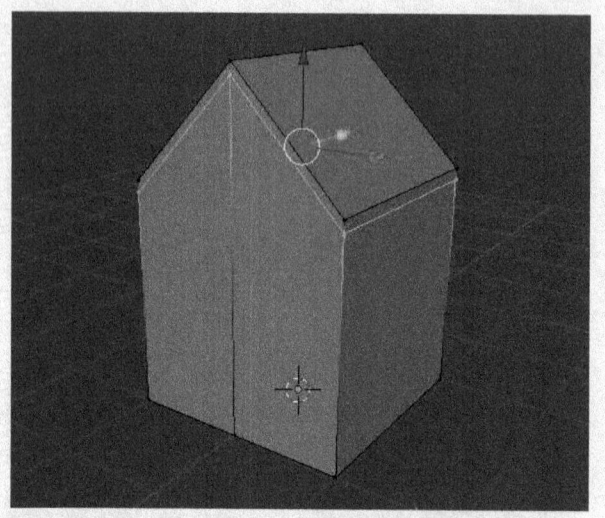

fig. 211 roof thickness with a *loop*

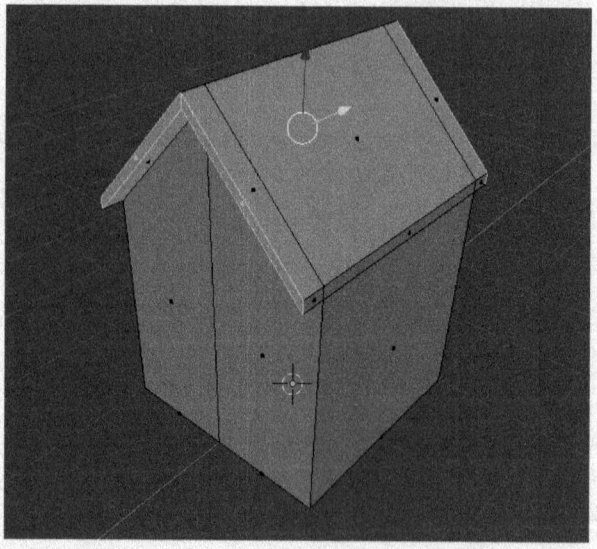

fig. 212 extrusion of the pitched roof thicknesses and creation of the objects

Execute the same operation with the six opposite faces comprising the thicknesses in the other two pitched roof sides. The faces will be horizontally extruded. Then you will have to lower them by hand, first passing in front view (1 PAD) and then typing G, Z until the slopes of the pitched roof will be aligned.

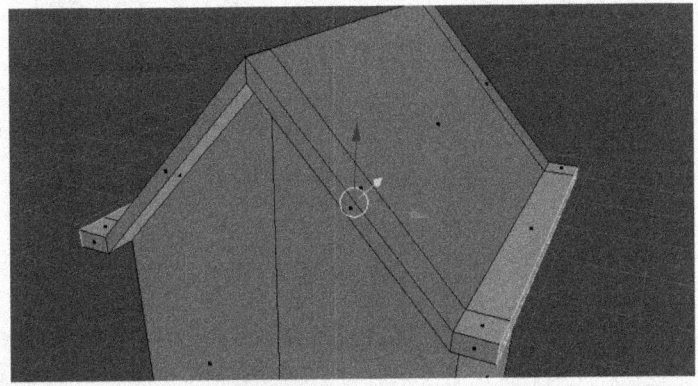

fig. 213 extrusion of the opposite sides

fig. 214 manual alignment of the pitched roof slopes

Now you can create windows and doors, by generating loops *and* extruding inward the generated faces, finally getting a model similar to this one.

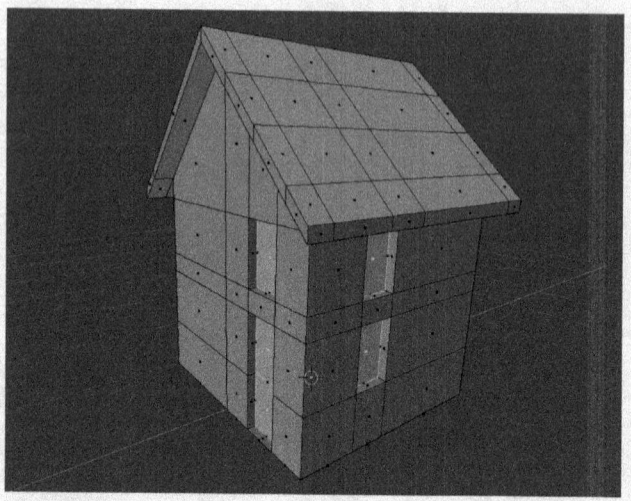

fig. 215 generation of windows and doors by using loops *and inward* extrusion of the mesh

Try to improve your model, by adding the chimney, the balcony, railings and other items.

Remember that for aligning the vertices of a selection (for example if you want to flatten the chimney top) you only need to scale with respect to z of 0, typing S, Z, 0 and confirming the operation.

Let us go on describing the other tools of Add type.

- The command **Inset Faces** (I key) is useful to subdivide a face, by inward extruding the perimetric vertices and edges of a defined constant amount.

fig. 216 the *Inset Faces* command

By selecting a face and pressing I, the latter will be subdivided in other faces which can be in turn deformed or extruded.

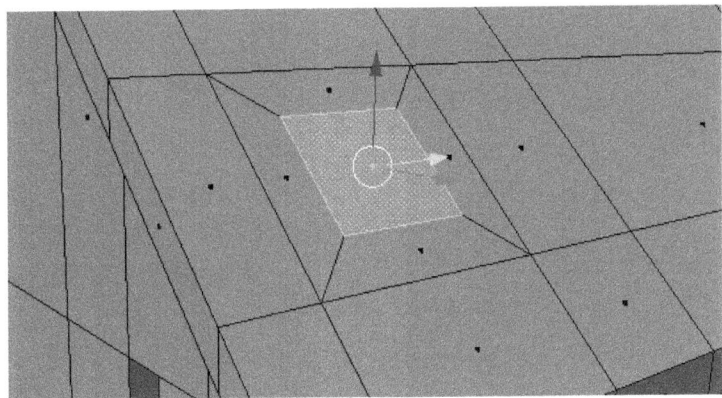

fig. 217 *Inset* of a face

- **Make Edge/Face** (*shortcut* F, standing for *fill*) is a function creating an edge between two or more selected edges or a face between two or more selected vertices/edges. It is a very useful tool to fill surfaces.

fig. 218 the *Make Edge/Face* command

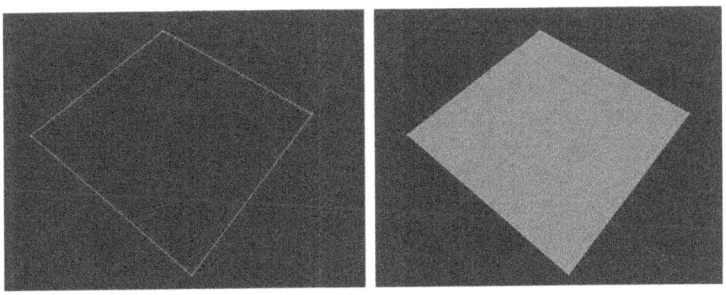

fig. 219 the function *fill* (F) applied to a rectangle assigns to the latter a surface

- **Subdivide** is a very useful tool for proportionally subdividing the selected faces of a mesh. It can be recalled even with the W key, choosing *Subdivide* from the drop-down menu.

fig. 220 the *Subdivide* command

From the specific panel related to it in the *Tools Shelf* you can define:

- *Number of* Cuts: the number of subdivisions;

- *Smoothness*: the subdivisions smoothing factor in tridimensional ambient;

- *Quad/Tri Mode*: if checked, reduces the occurrence or multi subdivisions, preferring the quadrangular ones;

- *Quad Corner Type:* opens a drop-down menu in which you can choose the way the mesh subdivision will be operated;

- *Fractal*: determines a fractal subdivision parameter;

- *Along Normal*: applies to the fractal subdivision a vertex relief along the normals;

- *Random Seed*: allows you to get *random* subdivisions numbered from 0 to infinity.

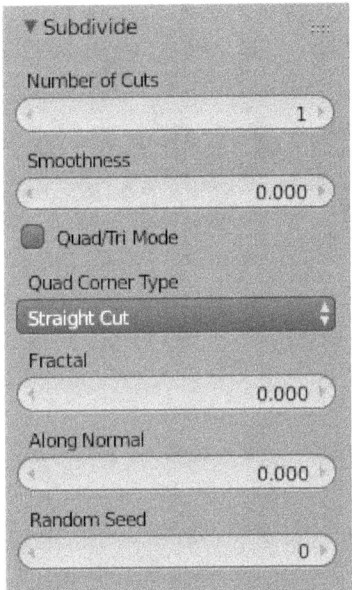

fig. 221 the *Subdivide* panel

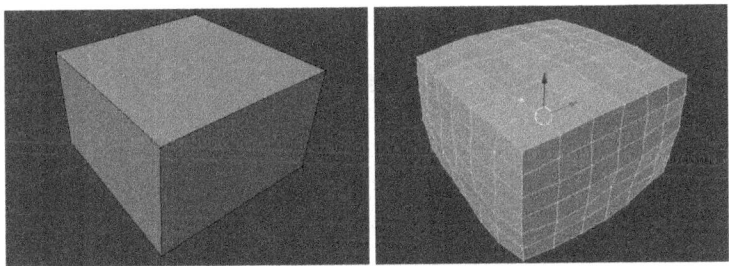

fig. 222 subdivision in 5 sides of a parallelepiped with the *Smoothing* and fractal system activated

In the same manner also a segment can be subdivided. You only need to select it and apply the subdivision.

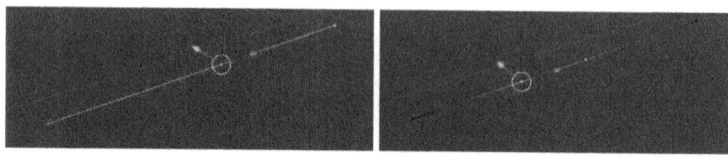

fig. 223 segment subdivision. A vertex is introduced between the two ends which can be shifted along the segment itself by pressing twice the G key

- ***Loop Cut and Slide*** is, as previously seen, the tool allowing you to insert a *loop*. The key combination is CTRL + R.

fig. 224 the *Loop Cut and Slide* command

- **Duplicate** is the tool (like the same one in *Object Mode*) allowing you to duplicate selected objects, like vertices, edges and faces. Once the elements have been selected, pressing the *Duplicate* button or the key combination SHIFT + D, a copy of the selected elements will be achieved, which can be arbitrarily placed in the space.

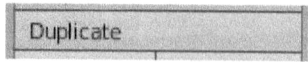

fig. 225 the *Duplicate* command

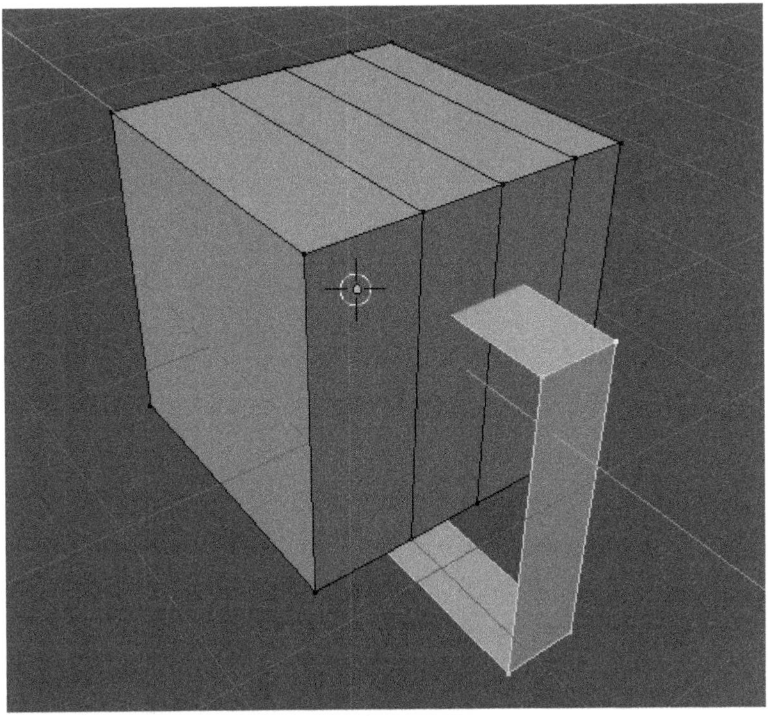

fig. 226 with the duplication of two loops an exact copy of four faces is achieved

- **Spin** allows you to create a rotation solid around one or more axes starting from a selected mesh.

fig. 227 the *Spin* command

By pressing *Spin* or typing the key combination (shortcut) ALT + R a specific panel is opened in *Tools Shelf* where you can define:

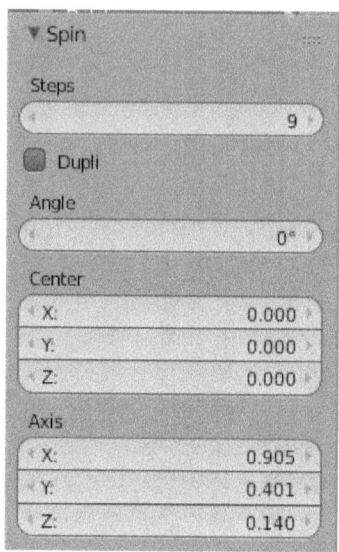

fig. 228 the *Spin* panel

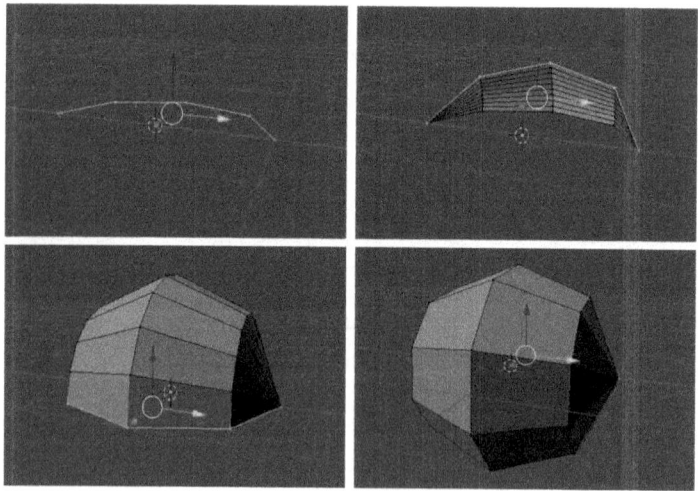

fig. 229 rotation of a half sphere with 4 segments, around the *y* axis of 0°, 30°, 180° and 360° with 9 divisions

- *Steps*: the number of repetitions related to the original *mesh*;

- *Dupli*: if checked, creates a duplicate;

- *Angle*: the number of rotation degrees of the mesh;

- *Center*: allows you to shift the rotation center with respect to the mesh pivot, along *x*, *y* and/or *z*;

- *Axis*: allows you to determine the mesh rotation axis.

- **Screw** tool screws a mesh around one or more rotation axes. It is very useful to achieve spiral effect or shells, coils, screws and twisted objects in general.

fig. 230 the *Screw* button

One the *mesh* has been selected in *Edit Mode*, by clicking the *Screw* button and optimizing the parameters, it is possible to achieve the desired effect.

Once the transformation has been applied which, as already mentioned, belongs to the *Add* tools adding a further geometry to the original, the *Screw* panel will be activated in the *Tools Shelf* where you can regulate the following parameters:

One the *mesh* has been selected in *Edit Mode*, by clicking the *Screw* button and optimizing the parameters, it is possible to achieve the desired effect.

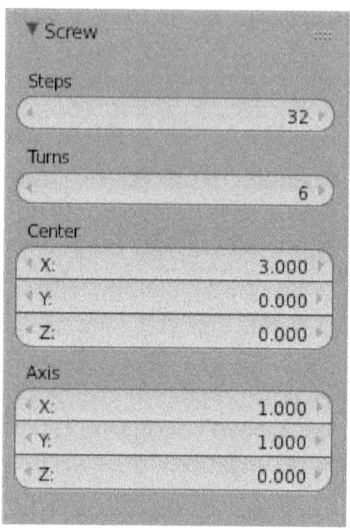

fig. 231 the *Screw* panel

Once the transformation has been applied which, as already mentioned, belongs to the *Add* tools adding a further geometry to the original, the *Screw* panel will be activated in the *Tools Shelf* where you can regulate the following parameters:

- Steps: the number of repetitions referred to the original mesh;

- *Turns*: the number of revolutions;

- *Center*: allows you to shift the rotation center with respect to the mesh pivot, along *x*, *y* and/or *z*;

- *Axis*: allows you to determine the mesh rotation axis.

For example, try to create a kind of shell starting from a semicircle.

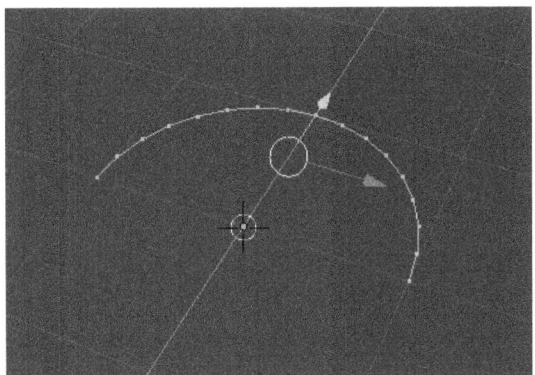

fig. 232 the starting mesh

Acting on the *X* and *Y* parameters of the axes (inserting the value 1), choosing the number of revolutions (6), setting 32 *steps* and shifting the center of 3 along *x*, you will achieve an outcome like that.

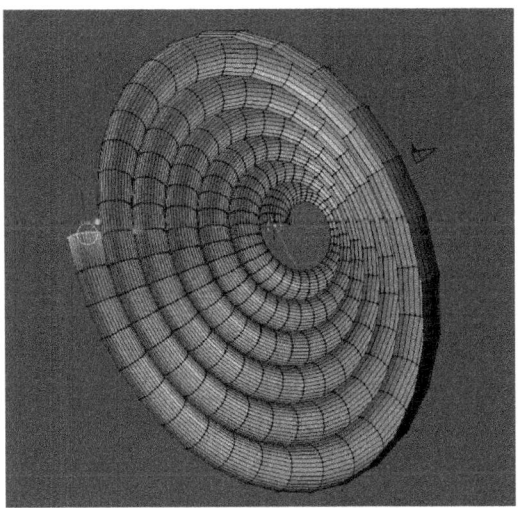

fig. 233 the modified mesh with 32 repetitions and 6 revolutions around the *x* and *y* axes

- **Knife**, which can be recalled also with the *K* key, allows you to cut a mesh thus getting new faces and new geometry.

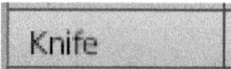

fig. 234 the *Knife* button

In edit mode clicking on *Knife* and approaching an edge, the first cutting vertex will be highlighted. Going toward a second vertex, a violet line will highlight the cutting line till the next vertex and so on until the operation is confirmed with the RMB.

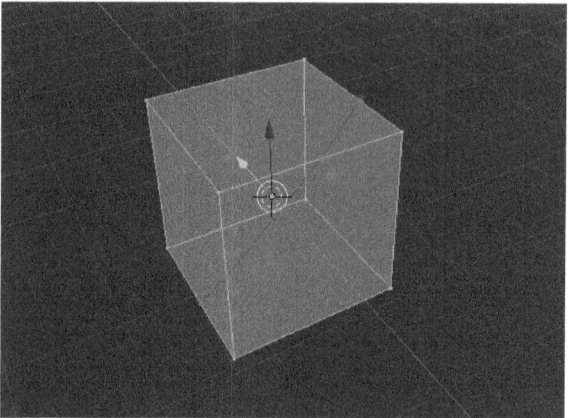

fig. 235 the outcome of a mesh cut with *Knife*

- **Select** (combination SHIFT + K) makes the previous cutting operation only on the selected faces of a mesh, creating further geometry, and leaving unchanged the others.

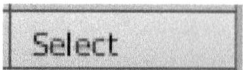

216

fig. 236 the *Select* button

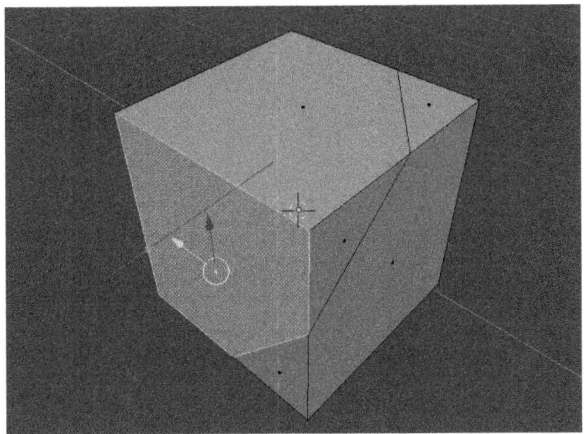

fig. 237 the outcome of the cut of a mesh face with *Select*

Once the cut has been made, confirm with ENTER.

- **Knife Project** allows you to project a mesh on parts of a second mesh.

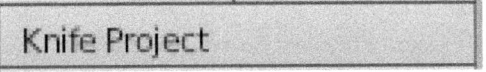

fig. 238 the *Knife Project* button

In order to achieve a mesh projection on another oneyou need, in *Object Mode*, first to select the *mesh* to be projected, and then, holding pressed SHIFT, the *mesh* on which you want to project.

Once the two meshes have been selected, the second one will be the active one (highlighted with the orange contour line).

fig. 239 projection of the number 8 on the sphere

After <u>placing the view in the projection direction</u>, you will need to enter in *Edit Mode* with TAB and press the *Knife Project* button.

Automatically the mesh will be projected on the active one, subdividing its geometry, like it were the shadow.

In the following example, the number 8 will be projected on a sphere obtaining the pool ball n. 8.

The view in the figure is the final outcome.

 The texts, like the curves, are not meshes and cannot be considered a point cloud. It is possible to transform a curve (or a text) into a mesh and vice versa by selecting it in *Object* Mode and typing the key combination ALT + C and choosing *Mesh from Curve* to transform the curve into a *mesh* or *Curve from Mesh* to execute the opposite operation.

fig. 240 ALT + C: for transforming a curve into a *mesh* and viceversa

- **Bisect** makes a manual cut on the faces selected in *Edit Mode*.

fig. 241 the *Bisect* button

You only need, once you have selected the faces and clicked the *Bisect* button, to draw a secant segment, by inserting with the LMB the starting and ending point of the segment, and then confirm.

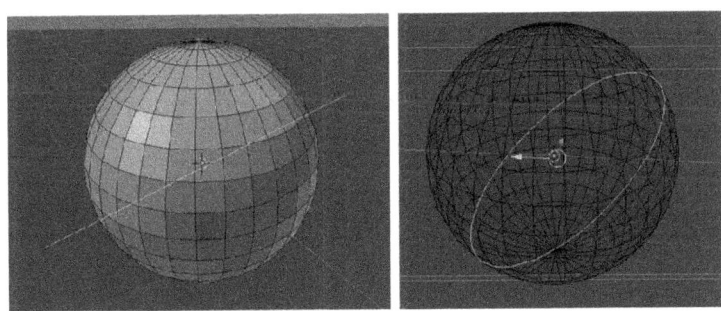

fig. 242 the outcome of the *Bisect* operation on a sphere

3) Remove

The group of the *Remove* tools allows you to cancel parts of the *mesh*, according to specific methods.

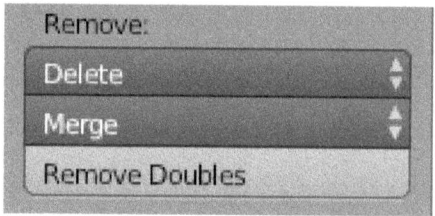

fig. 243 the tools of the *Remove* group

- **Delete** (X or CANC) is a drop-down menu allowing you to choose to cancel a selection of vertices (*Vertex*), edges (*Edges*), faces (*Faces*), only edges and faces (*Only Edges & Faces*), only faces, leaving unchanged vertices and edges (*Only Faces*).

Moreover, it is possible to dissolve selected vertices, without eliminating the edges and faces connected to them (*Dissolve Vertices*), to dissolve edges (*Dissolve Edges*), to dissolve faces (*Dissolve Faces*), to dissolve vertices and edges limited to the geometry limit angles (*Limited Dissolve*), to collapse vertices of full loops by joining together the closest elements (*Edge Collapse* and *Edge Loops*).

- **Merge** (ALT + M) activates a menu allowing you to merge together selected elements according to the methods:

  • *At First* (in correspondence of the first selected element);

  • at *Last* (in correspondence of the last selected element);

  • *At Center* (in the center of gravity of a selection);

  • *At Cursor* (in correspondence of the *3D Cursor* position);

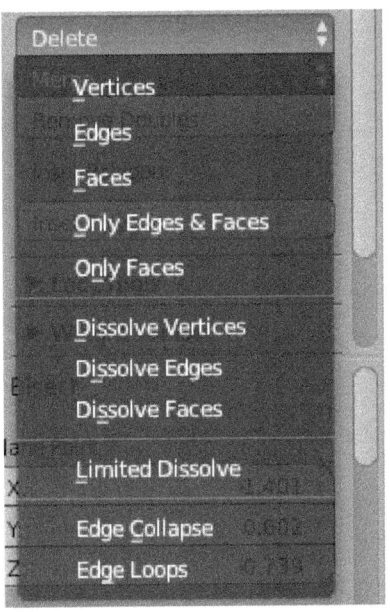

fig. 244 the *Delete* menu

Collapse (collapsing them on themselves).

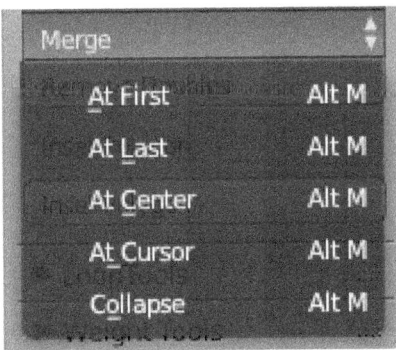

fig. 245 the *Merge* menu

221

- **Remove Doubles** is an essential function, to be used every time you make particular mesh transformations or modifications.

Nothing is worst for the modeling and final rendering than the presence of coincident or overlapped vertices, faces or edges.

The outcome contains ugly and annoying graphical artifacts.

We remind that a correct geometry, simple and well understandable, is essential to get a satisfying rendering engine response.

To solve the problem you only need to select with A all a mesh elements in *Edit Mode* and click the command *Remove Doubles*.

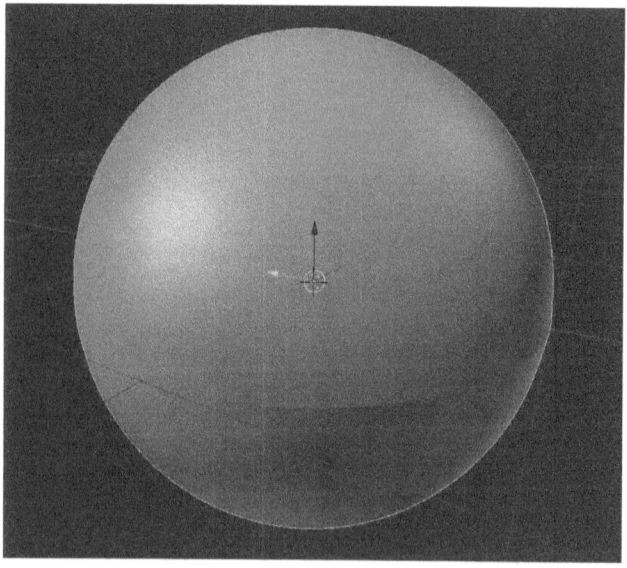

fig. 246 the sphere equator line is composed by overlapped vertices creating a visible graphical artifact

In the *header* of the info editor you will see a message reporting the number of eliminated double vertices.

fig. 247 the information concerning the removed vertices

4) Inset Polygon

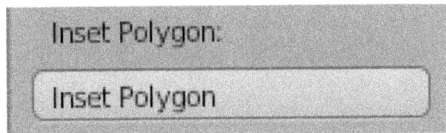

fig. 248 the *Inset Polygon* command

This command creates a polygon inside a selection.

- *LOOP TOOLS*

This panel, to be added from the *Addons* since not present in the default *user interface*, is very useful for managing the loops obtaining new geometries and connections.

The panel is in turn subdivided in 8 drop-down menus, each one with a specific function relevant to the loops.
In detail:

fig. 249 the *Loop Tools* panel

- **Bridge** allows you to create a new geometry connecting two separate loops (a bridge). The optimal condition is that the two loops have the same vertex number to be joined by faces and edges.

fig. 250 the *Bridge* menu

Among the parameters you can determine the connecting segment number (*Segm*), the segment percentage with lower edges in a loop, which have to be mixed into a single one; the

224

modality of interpolation between vertices (*Linear* or *Cubic*); the possibility of removing the connecting faces leaving the edges only (*Remove Faces*); the rotation of the connected vertices (*Twist*); the possibility to manually rotate the edge and face directions in the bridge (*Reverse*).

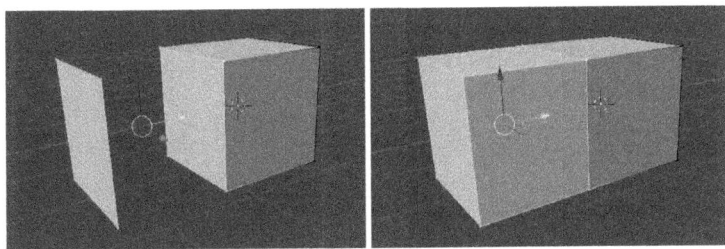

fig. 251 *Bridge* effect

- **Circle** places the vertices of a loop around a circumference, whose radius is computed according the loop maximum size.

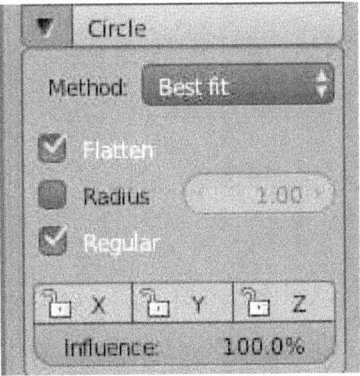

fig. 252 the *Circle* menu

The parameters allowing you to choose the operation method (*Method*); the possibility of aligning the transformed vertices on the same plane (*Flatten*); to force the radius (*Radius*); to place the vertices equally spaced on a regular circle (*Regular*) and to fix one or more axes for the shift.

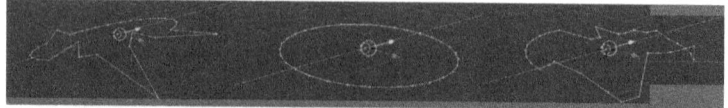

fig. 253 the *Circle* outcome with the *Flatten* parameter checked (second image) or unchecked (third image)

- **Curves** transforms a loop into a smoothened curve, acting on the interpolation parameters, possible restrictions, boundaries, possibility or making regular the curve and eventually fixing one or more axes.

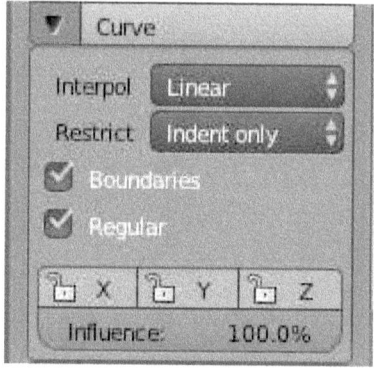

fig. 254 the *Curve* menu

- **Flatten** places all the vertices of a loop on a same plane. The plane choice is determined by the drop-down menu parameter *Plane* where you can choose if the vertices should be aligned automatically in the best possible way (*Best it*), according to the current view (*View*) or according to the normals (*Normal*). It is possible to force and fix one or more axes.

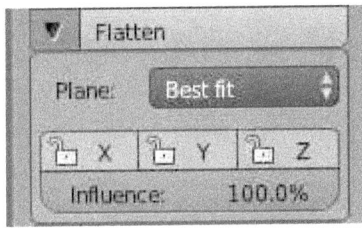

fig. 255 the *Flatten* menu

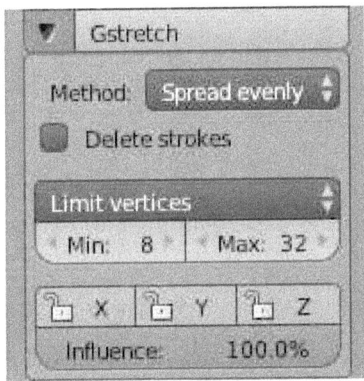

fig. 256 the *Gstretch* menu

- **Gstretch** stretch the vertices of a loop such that to follow the *Grease Pencil* line behavior (see in the foregoing). It is possible to define the vertex distribution method with respect to the *Grease Pencil* line (*method*) choosing between the options *Spread Evenly*, *Spread* and *Project*; choose if eliminating the line (*Delete Strokes*); choose if convert it into a piecewise linear function determining the minimum and maximum vertex number and of course fixing one or more axes.

227

- **Loft** connects together two *loops* (even having shape and vertex number quite different). The operation is much similar to *Bridge.*

fig. 257 the *Loft* menu

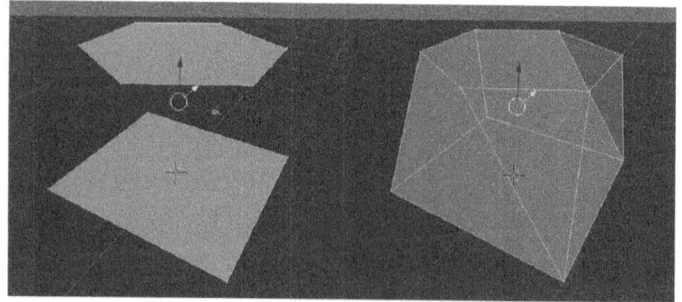

fig. 258 the outcome of the *Loft* command between a square and an exagon (*Circle*)

fig. 259 the *Relax* menu

- **Relax** rounds and smoothens a loop according to the chosen interpolation parameters (*Interpol*), the selected vertices (*Select*, i.e. if the selected or the parallel ones), the number of times the loop is subjected to relaxation (*Iteration*) and the possibility to make regular the new vertex distribution (*Regular*).

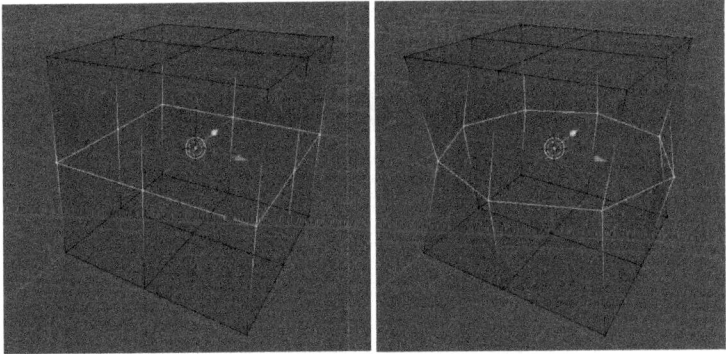

fig. 260 the outcome of the *Relax* command on the loop

- **Space** places in the space the selected vertices according to a regular distribution. The parameters are the interpolation method (*Interpol*), the selected vertices and eventually the possibility of blocking the transformation of one or more axes.

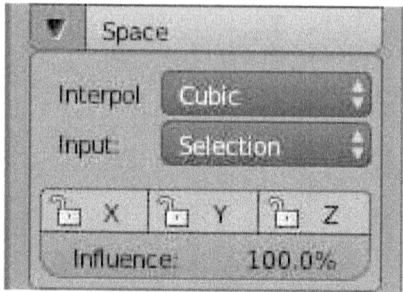

fig. 261 the *Space* menu

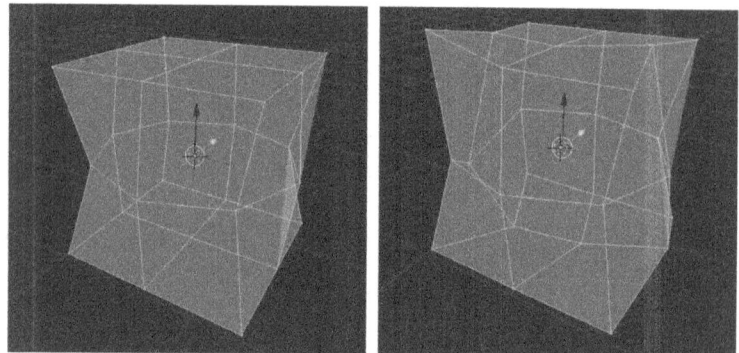

fig. 262 the outcome of the *Space* command on the selected loops

4.4.2. Normals

The normals represent a fundamental concept to be always kept in mind.

They represent the positive vector, i.e. the positive direction of a face, of a edge or also of a simple vertex.

Determining the positive direction of a element means to assign to the mesh a inner and an outer side.

This is of fundamental importance most of all while assigning a material, especially in the presence of a *texture*, and during the 3D print of an object, and in particular to avoid undesired effects of illumination and shading.

During the transformations, the extrusions, the *bridges*, the revolution solids and other commands adding or transforming the mesh geometry, it is often possible that the face normals be inverted or that new faces be created by the inverted normals.

We recommend, like for the case of duplicate and overlapped vertices, to check also the normals.

Three main methods are available:

- Visualization method: the reverted normals (negative) make a face darker than the faces with positive normals;

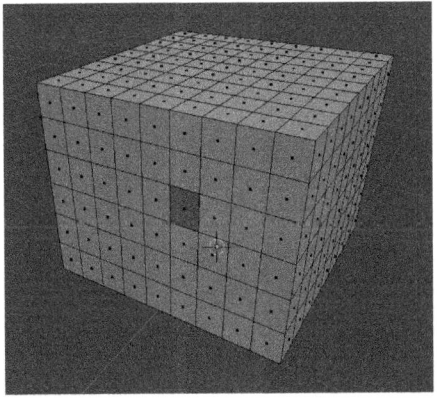

fig. 263 a face has inverted normal

- Use of *Normals* command in the *Mesh Display* panel of the *Properties Bar*. By selecting the desired button (vertex, edge, face or more than one) and the size of the dimensional arrow (*Size*), blue segments will appear at the element centers indicating the normal directions. A segment opposite directed will appear on the elements with inverted normals.

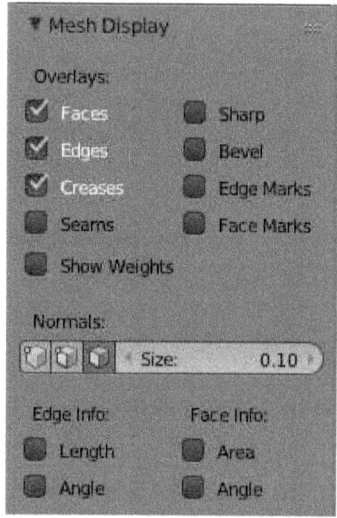

fig. 264 *Normals*

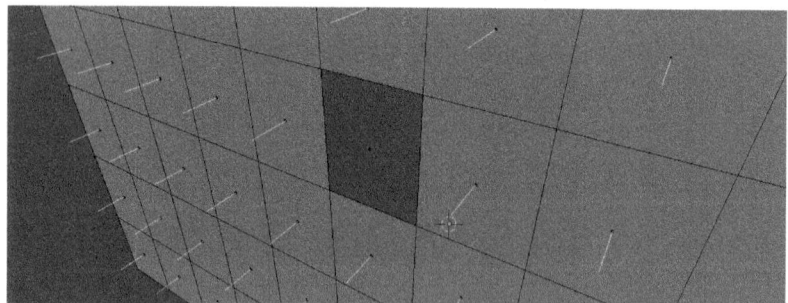

fig. 265 the blue segments indicating the normal directions

- Use of the *tab Shading/UV* in the *Tools Shelf* (third group) where the Normals item are visible in the *Shading* panel. In particular, it is possible to choose whether to try to automatically re compute the normals with the *Recalculate* button or to revert by hands the inverted normals with the *Flip Directions* button.

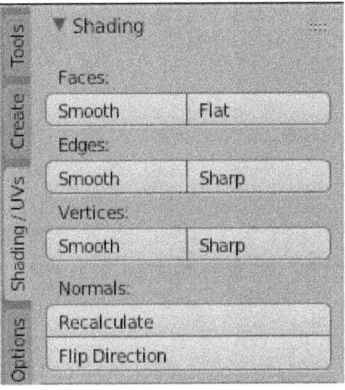

fig. 266 the *Recalculate* and *Flip Normals* buttons

4.4.3. Tab *Data*: object properties and *Vertex Group*

The *tab Data* in the *Properties* editor summarizes and allows you to handle the selected object geometry, in this case of the *meshes*.

The Icon corresponding to this *tab* changes depending on the selected object. Here are summarized the main ones.

fig. 267 the *Data* icons of the objects. From left to right: *Mesh, Curve, Surface, Metaball, Text, Armature, Lattice, Empty, Speaker, Camera, Lamp, Force Field*

Let us analyze now the *tab Data* referred to the *mesh*. The symbol depicts three vertices of a triangle joined by three edges. On the top you can find the *mesh* name.

a) The first panel (**Normals**) allows you to further manage the mesh element normals. *Auto Smooth* assigns a smoothing to the elements, by adapting the normals according to the indicated angle (Angle). *Double Sided*, on the other hand, if checked, makes a single face, without thickness, be considered as bi-facial.

b) the **Texture Space** panel collects the data and information relevant to the texturing, setting for example as texturing index the one of another mesh, chosen from the drop-down menu *Texture Mesh*, the possibility of automatically adopting a texture assigned in case of mesh modification (*Auto Texture Space*) or modifying the position and scaling of an assigned mesh.

c) the **Vertex Groups** panel is very important and much used. It simply groups the selected vertices of a group, which can be arbitrarily renamed. In order to group a vertex set, once the vertices have been selected, you only need to click on + (while – cancel an existing group) to create the group, then to click on the *Assign* button. On the other hand, the *Remove* button removes the vertices from the group, whereas *Select* and *Deselect* activate or deactivate the vertex selection of that group in the 3D view.

d) **Shape Keys** is a panel where you can manage the transformation of the shape of any object into another shape. There are two kinds of *Shape Keys*: *Absolute* (used to deform objects in time) and *Relative* (usually used for muscle and face animation and based on the original shape).

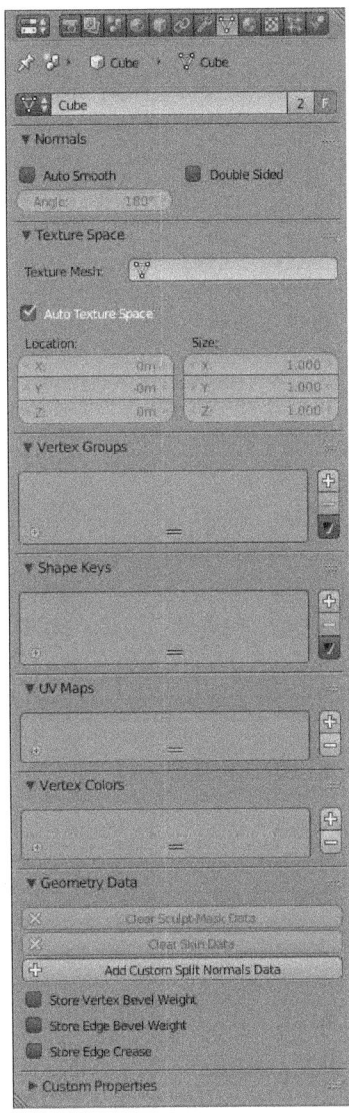

fig. 268 the *tab Data* panels relevant to the meshes

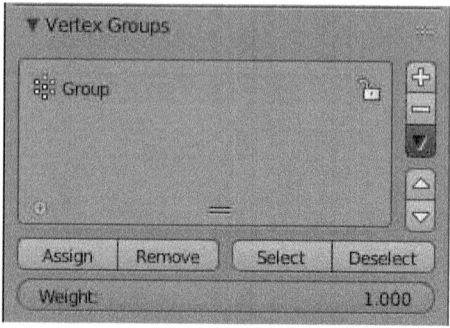

fig. 269 vertex assignment to the group

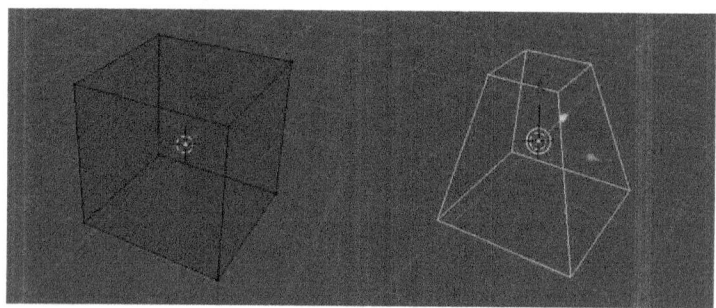

fig. 270 modification of the shape of the original mesh

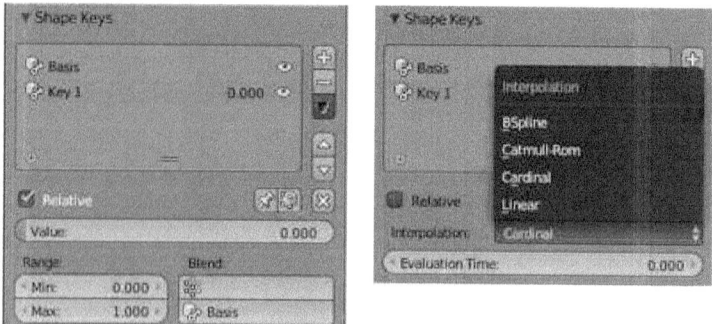

fig. 271 the *Shape Keys* panel in *Relative* modality (on the left) or *Absolute* (on the right)

236

ESERCISE n. 5: A FACE CHANGING EXPRESSION

In order to clarify the concept, we propose this example.
Insert a sphere, enter in *Edit Mode* and select the faces like in figure.

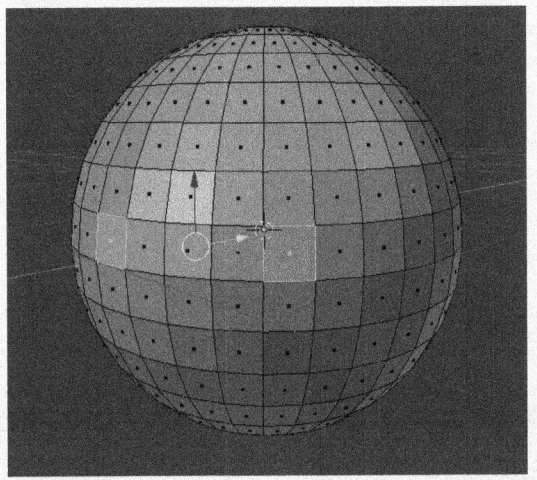

fig. 272 face selection in *Edit Mode*

Set the parameter *Individual Origins* in the 3D view header and extrude it with E inward.

fig. 273 *Individual Origins*

Select then some horizontal faces and, in lateral view (1 PAD), drag them inward with G Y direction.

237

We created a face with eyes and mouth.

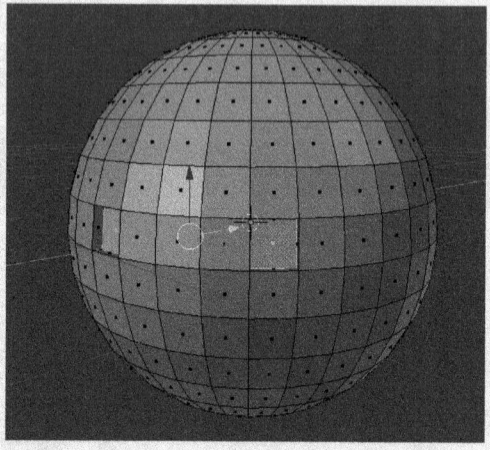

fig. 274 inward extrusion of the eyes

Now apply a modifier (which will be explained in the foregoing). For now don't ask questions about.

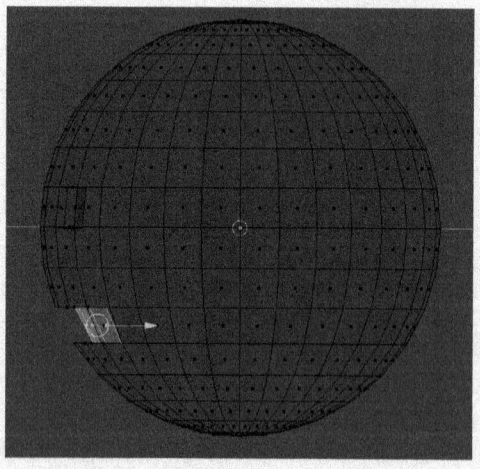

fig. 275 face shift in y direction inward

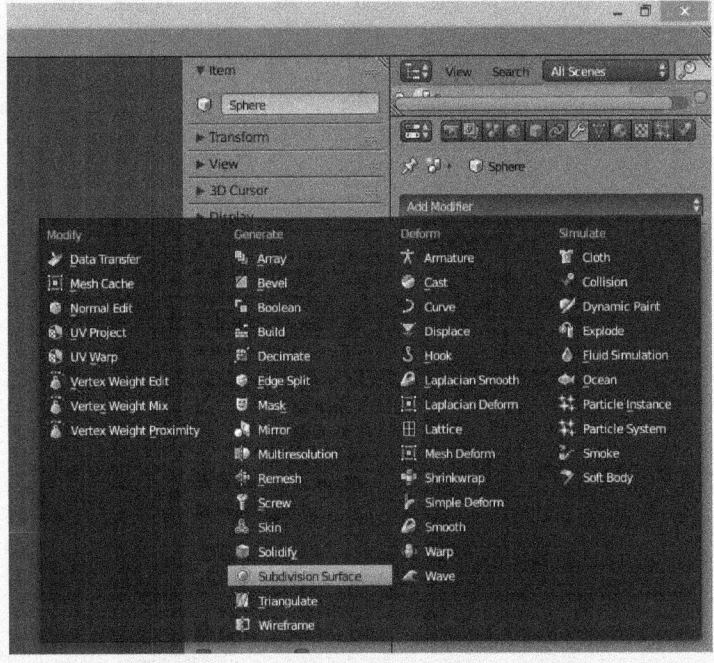

fig. 276 application of the modifier to the *mesh*

In the *Properties* editor of the *tab Modifiers* assign the *Subdivision Surface* modifier to the mesh, which will increase the mesh geometry and will smooth it at the same time. Set 3 subdivisions in the *View* and *Render* boxes. Finally apply the *Smooth*.

The *mesh* now appear rounded, smoothened, much more defined, with respect to the starting version.
Also the eyes and the mouth are less sharp.

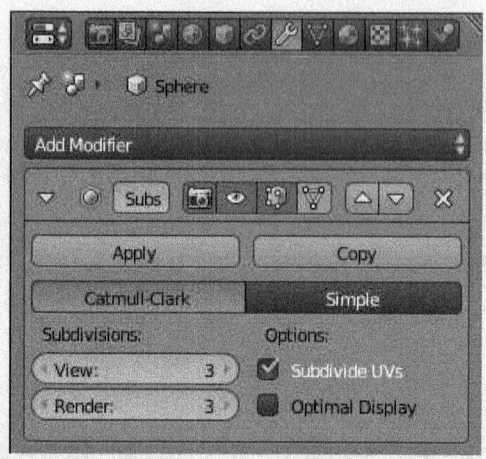

fig. 277 *Subdivision Surface*

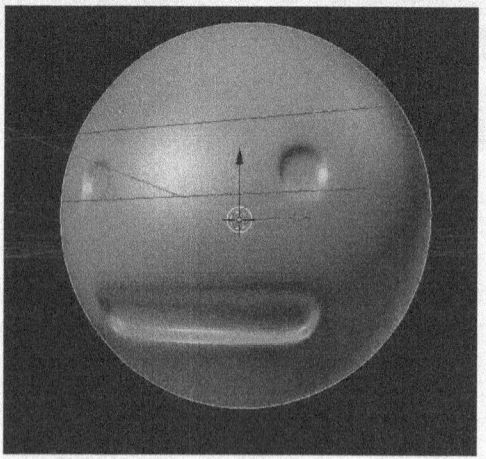

fig. 278 the face in greater detail

If you want you can better define the mesh details, by adding some loops. In fact, two close *loops* tend to reduce the rounding yielding an increased sharpness.

Select now the faces the faces comprising the inner part of the mouth and, with I, make an *Inset*.

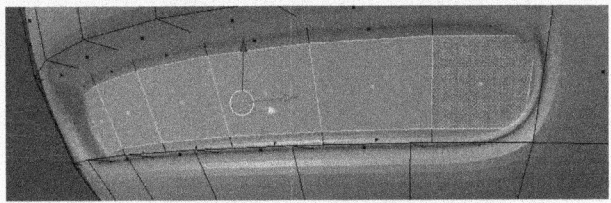

fig. 279 *Inset* of the mouth faces

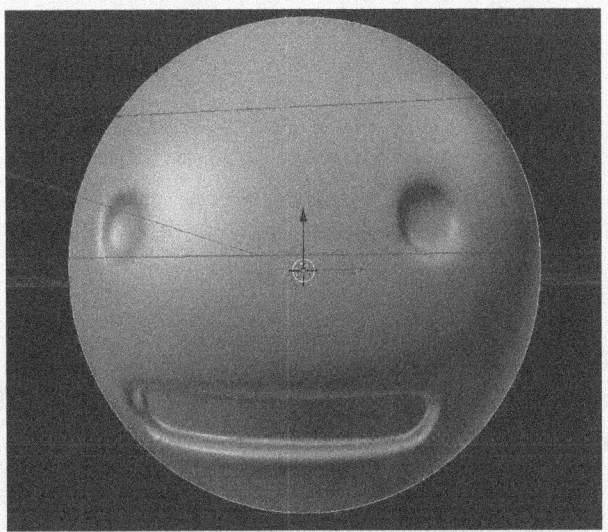

fig. 280 the mouth with sharp margins

Now enter the *Shape Keys* panel and click +, defining a key with the mesh shape automatically named *Basis*.

Click again + and create a new key which will be automatically named *key1*. You can rename it *smile* if you want.

fig. 281 insertion of two *keys*

Enter again in *Edit Mode*, temporarily switch off the modifier, clicking on the eye and modify the position of some vertices of the eyes and of the mouth, to make the face smiling.

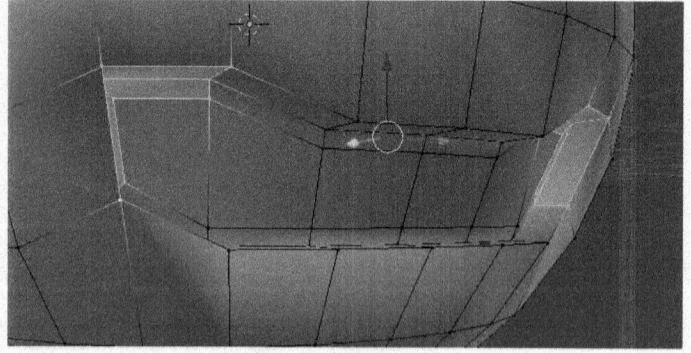

fig. 282 upward shift of the mouth boundary vertices

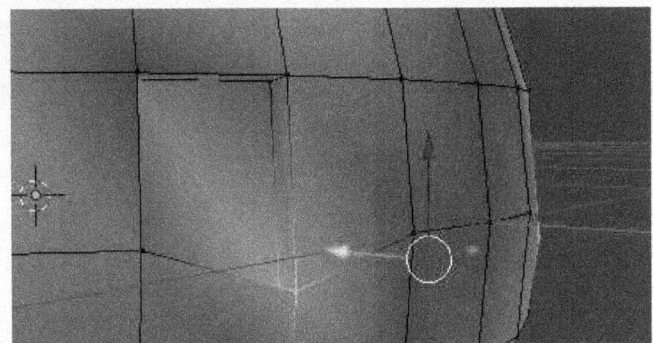

fig. 283 downward shift of the eye internal margins

Activate again the *Subdivision Surface*, clicking again on the eye and look to the outcome; the face has changed expression.

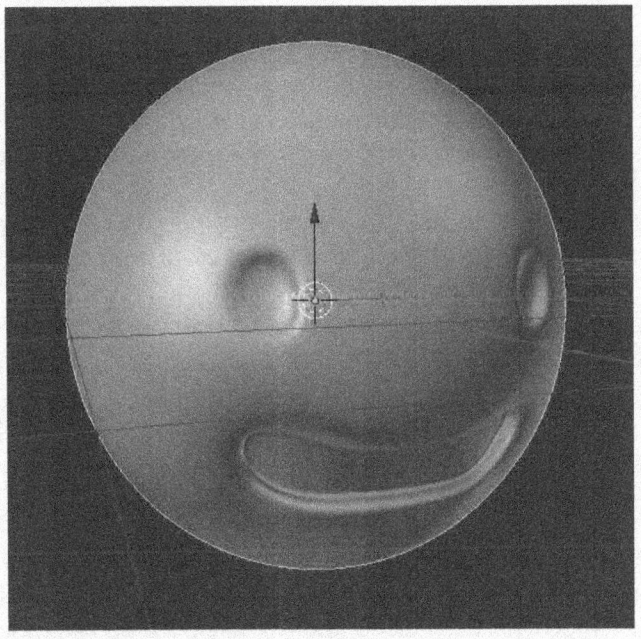

fig. 284 the face with smiling expression

By moving the *Value* cursor (with a value from 0 to 1), the face expression will change from neutral (value 0) to smiling (value 1).

Value: 0.347

fig. 285 the *Value* cursor

Of course it will be possible to make this face transformation automatic by creating an animation, but this will be explained in the foregoing.

e) **UV Maps** allows you to add to the selected vertices (and faces) a *UV Map*. This concept will be explained later.

f) **Vertex Colors** allows you to add a weight to the vertices, determined by a chromatic scale from red to blue, useful for some assignment functions like the *rigging* and the *Particle System*, which will be discussed in the foregoing.

g) **Geometry Data** contains some commands useful to add, modify and cancel the specific data assigned to the vertices (groups, masks in *Sculpt*, etc.).

CURVE

Also the geometry of curves and surfaces, likewise of the *meshes*, can be manipulated in *Edit Mode*.

The main difference between curves/surfaces and *meshes* is that the former are mathematical functions and cannot be represented by a point cloud approximating the curved shape.

Structurally curves and surfaces are composed of vertices, normals (element positive direction) and handles (control points) or tangent lines.

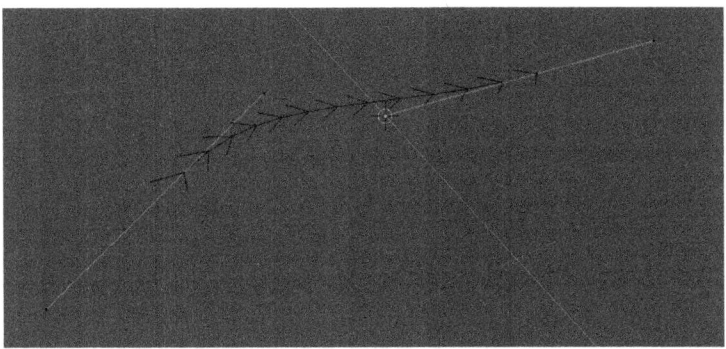

fig. 286 a *Bézier* curve in *Edit Mode*

As previously seen for the *meshes* also curves and surfaces can be manipulated and transformed by means of commands placed in the *tab Tools*. Let's analyze the one by one.

\- **TRANSFORM**

fig. 287 the *Transform* panel

The *Transform* panel contains essentially the same previously seen transformers (*Grab*, *Rotate*, *Scale* and *Shrink/Fatten*) and the new one *Tilt*, allowing you to twist a vertex around the tangent axis.

-    **CURVE TOOLS**

The most specific tools for the curves are contained in this specific panel.

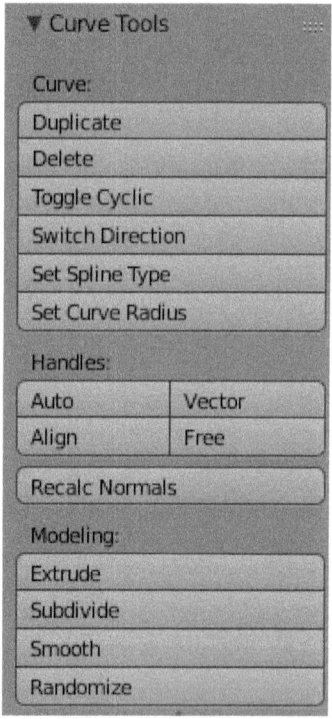

fig. 288 the *Curve Tools* panel

It is subdivided in three tool groups.

246

In the first group (**Curve**) the following tools can be found:

- **Duplicate** (SHIFT + D) duplicating the curve selected elements;
- **Delete** (X or CANC) canceling the selected elements;
- **Toggle Cyclic** linking and enclosing the selected elements into a closed figure;
- **Switch Direction** inverting the curve normals;
- **Set Spline Type** allowing you to transform the curve (or its selected elements) into a polyline (*Poly*), a *Bézier* curve or a *NURBS*;
- **Set Curve Radius** allowing you to set the radius which will be used for the *Bevel* curve thickening).

The second object group (**Handles**) contains the controls on the handles (*handles*) of each vertex. Each vertex is constrained by two handles (the pink segments with one end control vertex). The handles control the curvature of a curve or surface. The more they approach their reference vertex, the larger the curvature will be.

fig. 289 the handles affect the curvature

Blender offers 4 kind of handles, which can be selected from the panel.

Upon selecting the handle end point (and so the handle itself) the handle can be set as:

- **Auto** (automatic by *default*);

247

- **Vector**, such as to create cusps in correspondence of the vertex;
- **Allign**, such as the two handles controlling the vertex remain always aligned between each other;
- **Free**, such as the two handles be independent from each other.

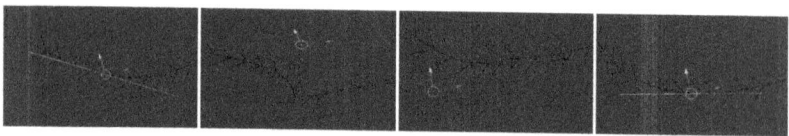

fig. 290 *handle* settings: *Auto, Vector, Free, Allign*

- The button **Recalc Normals**, allows you to automatically compute the normal direction.

The last section **Modeling**, finally, encloses 4 fundamental tools, useful for modeling and constructing shapes with the curves.

- **Extrude** (which can be simply recalled with E, after having selected a vertex) allows you to extrude a vertex, favoring the curve lengthening with the addition of the new vertices;

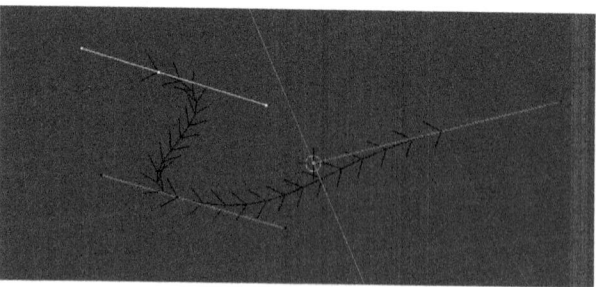

fig. 291 esxtrusion of a curve vertex

- **Subdivide** (which can be recalled with W after having selected two or more vertices) allows you to subdivide the

248

parts selected by the vertices into *n* segments, which can be defined from the *Subdivide* panel which will be activated by pressing the button, in the *Tools Shelf*;

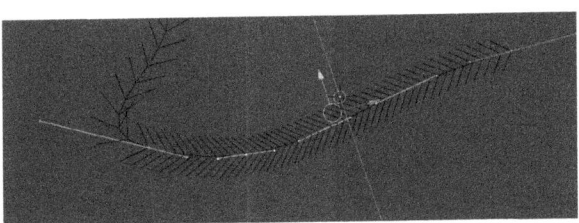

fig. 292 subdivision of a curve portion

- **Smooth**, upon selecting the curve or a part of it, click after click of the button, will decrease the curve curvature, making it smoother;
- **Randomize**, finally, will place, click after click of the button, the vertices randomly.

- **CURVE DISPLAY**

The **Curve Display** panel, placed in the *Properties Bar*, likewise the corresponding *Mesh Display* allows you to define the curve visualization style in *Edit Mode*, for example by showing or not (by means of the flags) the handles *(Handles)*, the normals *(Normals)* or by defining the graphical dimensions of the normals themselves.

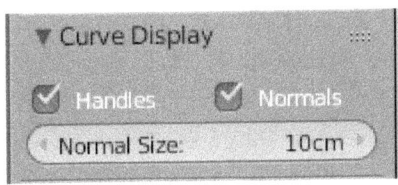

fig. 293 the *Curve Display* panel in the *Properties Bar*

249

4.4.4. Tab Data

As previously explained, by selecting an object in the 3D *view*, the corresponding *tab Data* will be activated in the *Properties* editor.
In the upper part the curve name is reported.

a) In the **Shape** panel you can set the curve thickening conditions for creating a solid, setting it as 2D or 3D. The **Resolution** values (in *Preview* and in *Render*) indicate the step number, i.e. the curve resolution in the space. For larger values the resolution will be higher. In the **Fill** menu you can choose the thickening type, depending from the *Bevel* and *Resolution* values placed in the *Geometry* panel, between *Half* (half section), *Front*, Back and Full (complete section). The flag on **Fill Deformed** allows you to close the section after the final application of the modifiers. The **Twisting** many defines the vertex twist modality and strength, such as to control possible geometry errors. The **Smooth** value controls the smoothing between the consecutive vertices near the tangents. The flags on **Radius, Stretch** and **Bounds Clamp** control, respectively, the behavior of the curve and the sections being deformed as a function of the curvature radius, the stretching and the mesh size for regulating the deformation.

b) the **Geometry** panel contains the information and parameters relevant to the curve geometry. In particular, **Bevel** has two options: **Depth** (the curve volumetric thickening dimensions defined in *Fill*) and *Resolution* (the section precision and rounding). **Offset** shifts the thickening with respect to the original curve whereas **Extrude** makes oval the section.

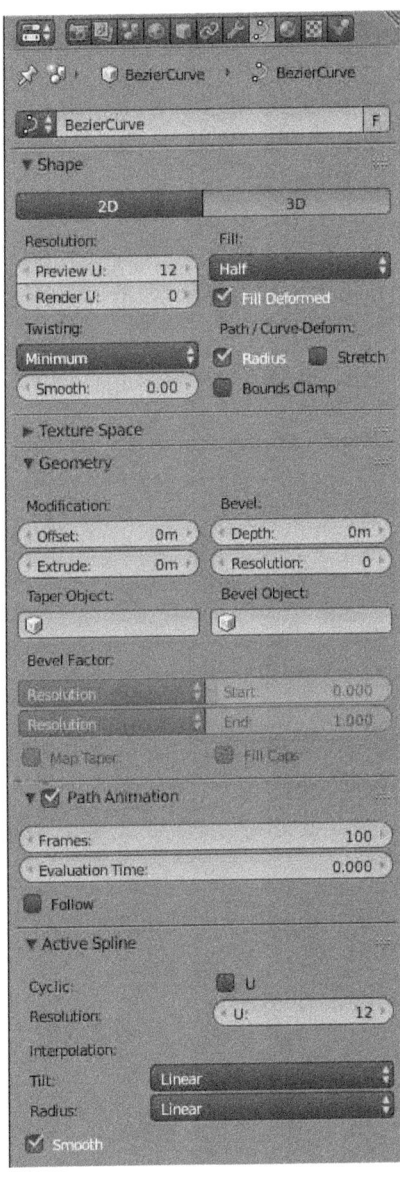

fig. 294 the *tab Data* relevant to the curves

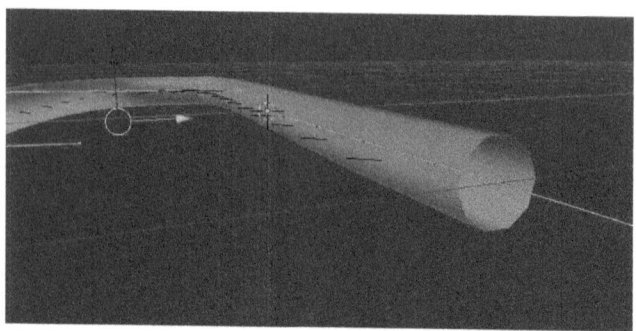

fig. 295 a curve thickened with the *Bevel*

It is possible to define a second shape (again of Curve type) as section of a 3D curve, setting it as **Bevel Object**, i.e. as thickening object of the main curve referred to as path. The **Start** and **End** values (of the path) define the transformation starting and ending points for the transformation of the curve into a 3D curve. In this way, making automatic these parameters, as we will see in the foregoing, animations of objects can be achieved, taking shape, lengthening and shortening.

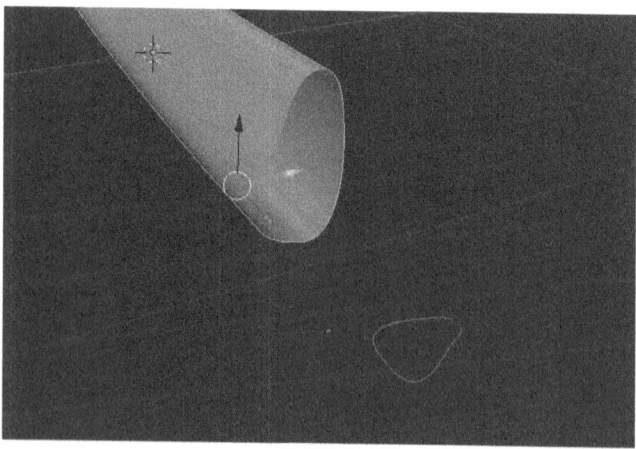

fig. 296 *Bevel Object*

Associating to the *Bevel Object* also the deformation tool **Taper Object** you can create an object with variable cross section according to the behavior of another curve. To make this, you need to insert the path curve, the section curve (for example a *Bézier* circle) and a deformation curve indicating to the path curve the amount (depending on the distance from the *x* axis) the section curve must be involved in the thickening operation. It is an effective methods for creating, for example, sinuous and tapered reptile tails.

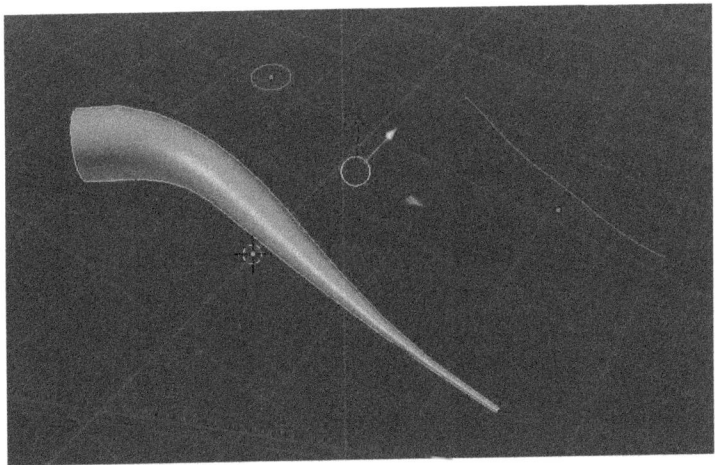

fig. 297 *Taper Object*

The flag on **Map Taper** controls the mapping on the *Taper* with respect to the present form, whereas **Fill Caps** closes the starting and ending section with a face.

c) the **Path Animation** panel controls the animation relative values, when the curve is set as animation path (for example the path of the camera or of a moving object). The frame number (*Frames*), set by *default* to 100 must be chosen depending on the Timeline frame number and the duration and execution velocity of the animation, whereas **Evaluation**

253

Time is a parametric value determining the position of the object associated to the curve along the path. By checking *Follow* the objects associated to the curve will follow the latter during the movement.

d) **Active Spline** summarizes the active curve behavior. A flag on **Cyclic U** makes it close, i.e. cyclic; **Resolution** determines the detail from piecewise to smooth; **Tilt**, **Radius** and **Smooth** control the torsion, the curvature radius and the rounding.

TEXTS

fig. 298 a text in *Edit Mode* with the typing cursor

The texts can be managed like 2D or 3D, modified, edited and finally transformed into a *mesh*, eventually distorted, extruded, colored, rotated etc.

Once a text is inserted (with written *Text* by *default*), entering in *Edit Mode* a text cursor will appear at the end. By canceling the text with BACKSPACE it is possible to insert, by typing it, a new text.

A) THE TEXT TOOLS PANEL

While in *Object* Mode, in the *Tools Shelf*, you can find the same curve base transformers (*Location*, *Rotation*, *Scale* and *Mirror*), in *Edit Mode* you can find only a reduced number of parameters: it is possible to increase and decrease the text dimensions with the **Upper To** and **Lower To** buttons and to choose the visualization style **Bold**, **Italic** and **Underline**.

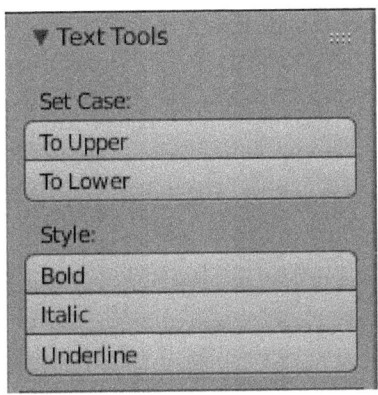

fig. 299 the *Text Tools* panel

4.4.5. Tab Data

Let's now consider the parameters present in the **tab Data** of the *Properties* editor.

In these panels, as we will see, you can modify the *font*, the style, the justification and the thickening of the inserted text.
As usual on the top you can find the name of the inserted text object.

Next, in the **Shape** panel, in the *Resolution* section, you can find the same parameters and functions for the curves, needed to

255

thicken the text and for creating a tridimensional text, smoothened and more or less defined in terms of resolution. These parameters are closely related to those contained in the **Geometry** panel, defining the dimensions and the thickening quality.

In the **Font** panel you can find all the data relevant to the character to be used and visualized. This character can be different depending on the styles *Bold*, *Italic* and of course *Regular* which can be recalled in the typical font folder of the operative system by clicking the folder icon at the right hand side of the text area of the defined character.

Size determines the character width, whereas *Shear* (value from -1 to 1) the writing angle.

It is possible to use objects like *fonts* and creating a writing with a deformed behavior depending on a curve, by inserting the latter as parameter inside *Text on Curve*.

The two parameters related to the *Underline* section, determine the distance of the underscore from the text (*Position*) and the line thickness (*Thickness*).

Small Caps makes the capital letters in the text as tall as the normal ones, whereas the flags on *Bold*, *Italic*, *Underline* and *Small Caps*, activated before entering the text in *Edit Mode*, define the style.

The **Paragraph** panel defines the text and parameter justification. You can choose a text justified on the right, on the left, centered or stretched up to the margins. You can also select the spacing between characters, words, lines and the offset, i.e. the distance from the text pivot, which can be shifted in *Object Mode* with the usual key combination SHIFT + CTRL + ALT + C.

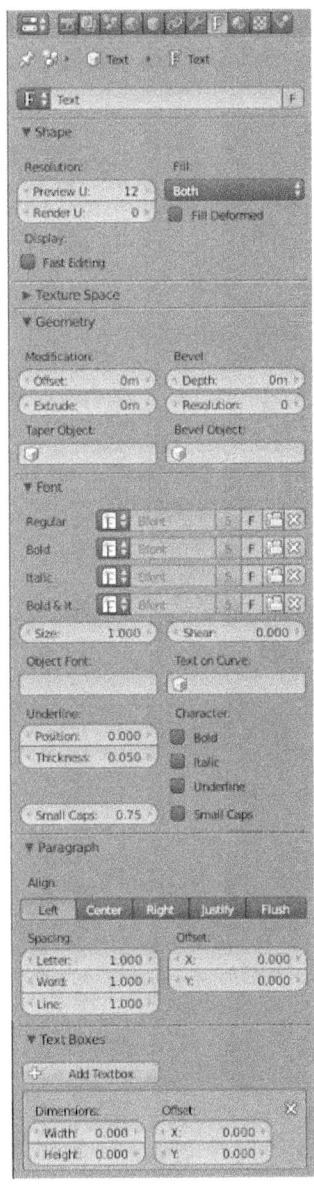

fig. 300 the *tab Data* relevant to text

257

The last panel, finally, **Text Boxes**, adds a text box where the selected text in inserted. This box can be freely sized using the *Width* and *Height* parameters. The text will adapt to the box.

fig. 301 text in 3D

fig. 302 the text inserted into a box and stretched till the margins with *Flush*

In *Tools Shelf* you can find the same tools relevant to the curves.
Also the parameters in *tab Data* of the *Properties* editor relevant
to the surfaces are essentially the same used for the curves.
The only difference is that the points comprising the surfaces are
uniformly places along the three axes.
For this reason, for example, the smoothening can be defined
independently along *U* and *V*.

NOTE: *U* and *V* are the vector variables corresponding to
x and *y*, but not necessarily related to the reference
Cartesian frame. Usually *UV* represents a mapping
coordinate system for a *texture*.

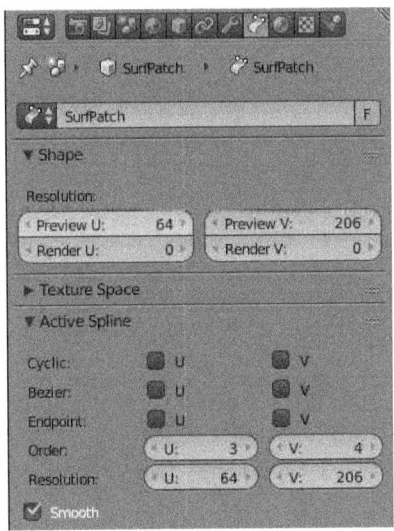

fig. 303 the *tab Data* panel relevant to the surfaces

Similarly, the cyclicity and resolution can be independently parameterized along *U* and *V*.

METABALL

Regarding the *Metaballs* not much is needed to be added to what has been previously said.

In *Edit Mode*, in the *Tools Shelf*, the only available transformation tools are *Translate*, *Rotate*, *Scale* and *Randomize*, whereas, in the *tab Data* of the *Properties* editor, you can find some parameters relevant to updates resolution and behavior, due to the attraction between different Metaballs.

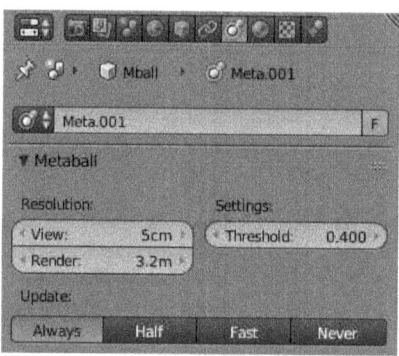

fig. 304 the *tab Data* panel relevant to the *Metaballs*

NOTE: In the next chapters, while discussing the other objects and topics more and more complex and specific, we will analyze the related *tab Data*.

4.5. Use of the reference images in background or blueprint

The white sheet has always been a problem for everyone.
Often, starting from zero in drawing something (or, in our case, modeling) can be counter-productive.

Copying, having a reference for starting, can be very helpful to achieve a satisfying and truthful outcome.

For this reason, when you have to create a model, we recommend you to look for drawings, pictures, technical sheets or references on internet, finding the proper reference image to be used for starting. Then you will have time to freely modify and personalize what you have created.

The trick is than *tracing*.

The best solution is to insert a background in our working sheet the reference image, named **blueprint**.

For inserting a background image, you need to check **Background Image**, in the *Properties Bar*.

By clicking on **Add Image** and then on **Open Image** a *browser* will appear, from which you can upload a graphic file.

Once opened, you can choose the file type, the color and the chromatic range, the possibility to render the image (**View As Render**), changing the image opacity (**Opacity**), move the image in front or back to the project (**Back** o **Front**) and, most of all, to rescale the image along *x* and *y* (**Scale**), such as to adapt it to the project size. You also can rotate the image (**Rotate**),

261

mirror it according to the *x* and *y* (**Flip**) and shift it with respect to the Cartesian frame origin (**X and Y**).

fig. 305 the *Background Image* panel in the *Properties Bar*

Moreover it is possible and very useful to determine the view type for visualizing the background image, choosing among the options present in the *Axis* menu on the top.

For example, you can insert several background images, such as the top and front view of a house and set their view, respectively, as *Top* and *Front*.

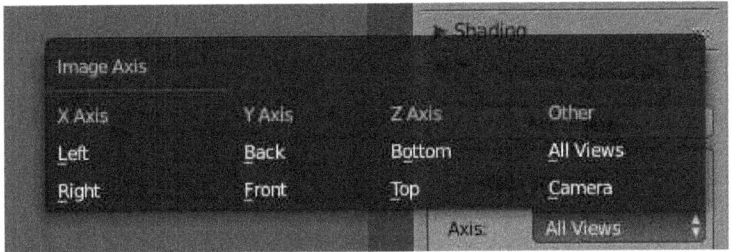

fig. 306 the *Image Axis* menu where you can choose where to visualize the background image

Moreover it is possible to switch off all the backgrounds by unchecking *Background Images* or to separately switch off the various backgrounds deactivating the icon with the eye.

 EXERCISE n. 6: INSERT IN BACKGROUND THE MAP OF A HOUSE AND TRACE IT

In this exercise we will show how to draw a room starting from its map.

For inserting the reference image in background, you first need to check *Background Images*, set the view as *Top* and upload the reference file.

Using the *Top* view (key 7 PAD), insert a plane with SHIF + A. We know that by default the plane size is 2 x 2 meters. You will use it in turn as reference size to rescale the background image.

First of all it is necessary to force the plane in Wireframe view, even if the full project is set on *Texture*. This is necessary to make

263

the plane transparent and thus having always visible the *background* image, until the end of the modeling phase.

Upon selecting the plane, in *tab Object* (icon with shape of a yellow cube) of the *Properties* editor, you must set *Wire* in the option *Maximum Draw Type* of the *Display* panel.

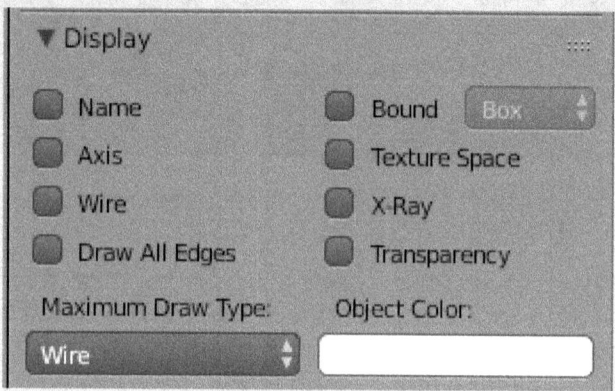

fig. 307 forced *Wire* modality of a mesh

In this way the plane will be visualized in *Wire* modality.

Select now the plane and place it such as one vertex coincides with one map vertex. Rescale the plane, such as its horizontal side have the same length of a known reference side. Reset now the scale with CTRL + A (in *Object Mode*).

Now you must rescale and shift the background image such has the known reference side coincides with the scaled reference plane side.

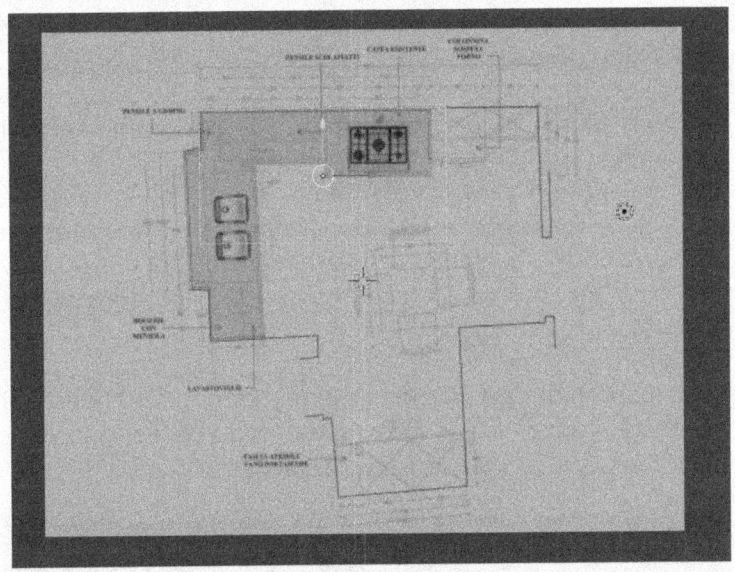

fig. 308 plane recalling according to a known measure

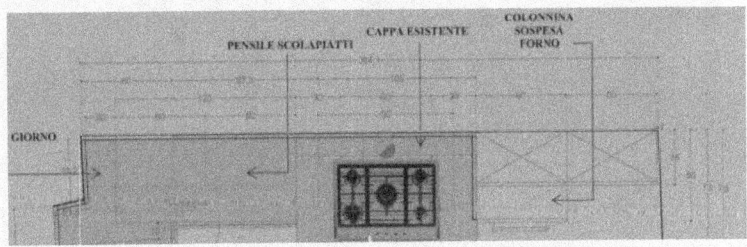

fig. 309 image rescaling and placement with respect to the plane

You can now operate following two different methods.

Following the first method, enter in *Edit Mode* and delete the two vertices not coinciding with the reference wall. Extrude than one of the two remaining vertices, following freely the perimeter of the reference map. At the end you will only need to join the last segment with the second vertex pressing F. Finally, by selecting

265

all the *mesh* vertices, you will need to press F again to fill with a face the full perimeter.

Following the second method, again in *Edit Mode*, shift the lower plane vertices and make them to coincide with the opposite wall, achieving a sort of maximum envelope. Then subdivide in *loops* the surface in correspondence of the offsets and direction changes, adding geometry with the extrusion (E) and eventually arranging the out of square and deleting the vertices not needed.

Remember that for shifting a vertex along an edge (not necessarily along the *x, y* and *z* axes), you only need to press twice the G key (G + G) and choose the direction.

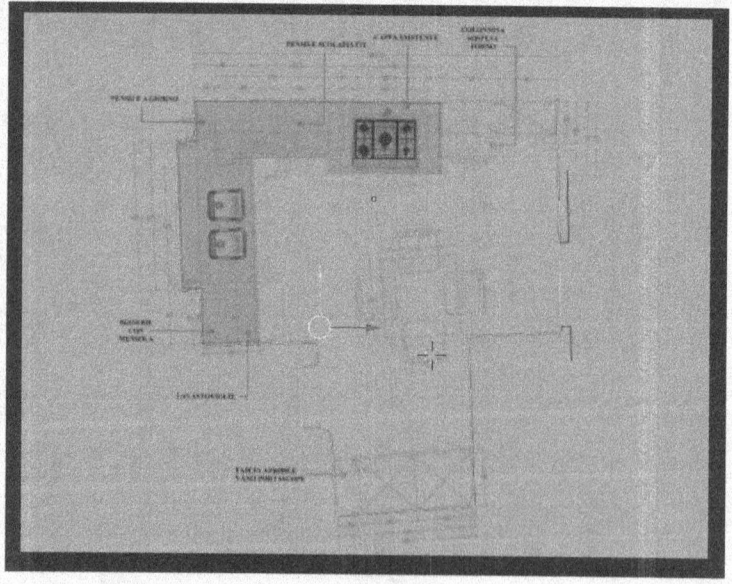

fig. 310 trace a map by the extrusion of a vertex

Depending on the map shape, choose the better and most effective method.

The first method will perform better in case of the map chosen in this example, quite complex and not so regular.

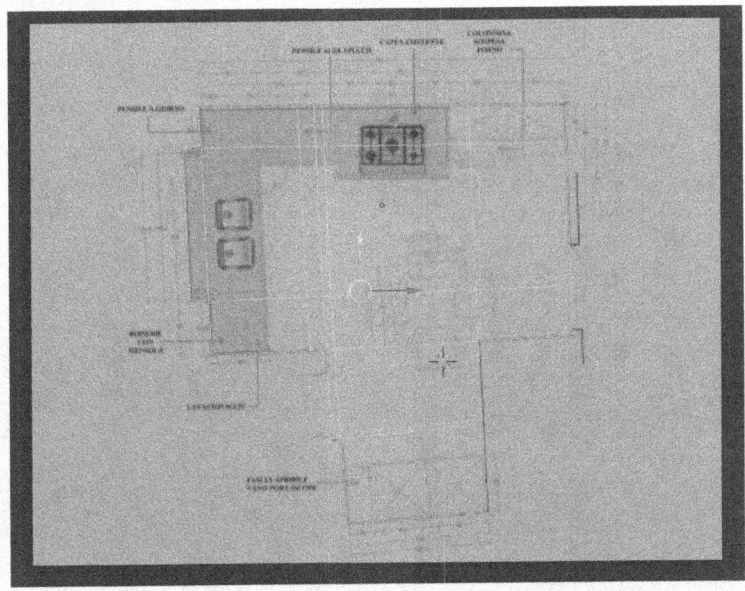

fig. 311 trace a map using the loops

Select now all the mesh vertices in *Edit Mode* and extrude them upward for 3 meters, typing E (+ Z) + 3.

Invert inward the normals such that the inner faces are set for the mapping and the view.

Create now the needed vertical *loops* and place them in correspondence of the openings (doors and windows).

Then create 3 horizontal *loops*, one placed at 2,1 meters from the ground for the door and 2 placed, respectively, at 0,95 and 2,4 meters from the ground for the windows.

Extrude inward (creating the thickness for the masonry) the faces created by the *loops* representing the wall arches. Finally delete the extruded faces.

Restore now in the *tab Object* the visualization *Solid* of the *mesh* and switch off the *background*.

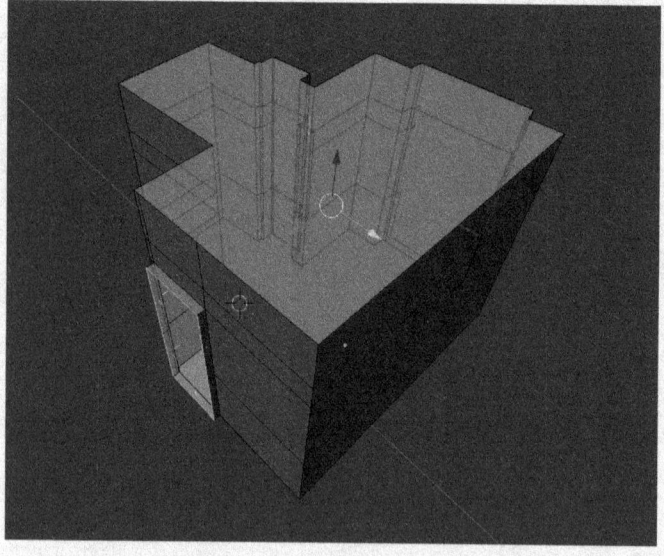

fig. 312 the environment done

4.5.1. A useful *Addon: Image as Plane*

A second method allowing you to trace an image, but not only this, is to insert a plane already mapped and scaled according to an image.

To exploit this opportunity, you need to activate the **Image As Plane** Addon. This *Addon* will allow you to insert a plane once chosen the image from the *browser*.

To insert an already mapped plane, you only need to type SHIFT + A.

In the drop-down menu *Image As Plane* you can find the submenu *Mesh*.

Once inserted, it will be positioned with the center of the gravity corresponding to the *3D Cursor*.

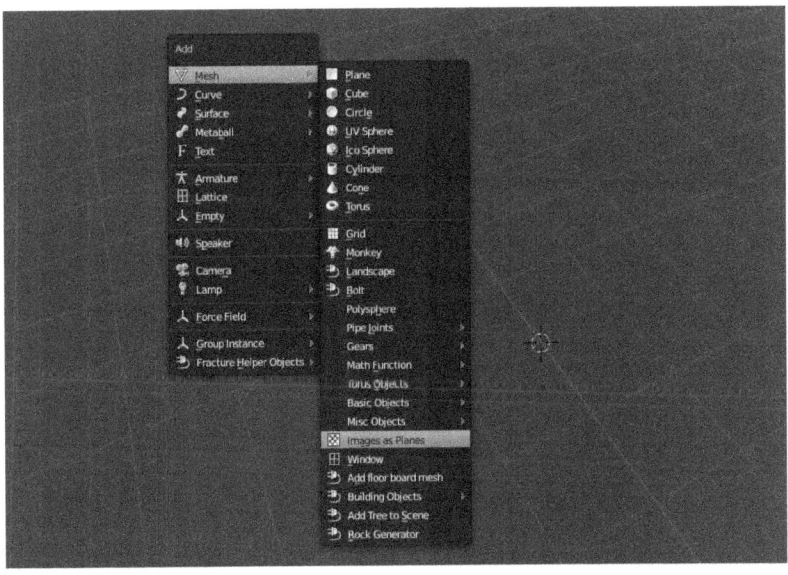

fig. 313 plane insertion with the mapped image

You will notice that a plane has been inserted but no image is visible.

This is because an image applied to a *mesh* is a *texture* and cannot be visualized in the 3D view in *Wireframe* or *Solid* modality. You then need to set the *Texture* visualization style.

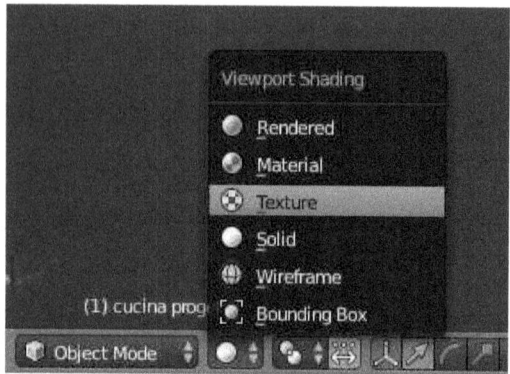

fig. 314 setting of the *Texture* visualization style

The image will be finally visible even in perspective view. It can be rendered and will cast a shadow, if you want it, like any standard *mesh* on which a material has been applied.

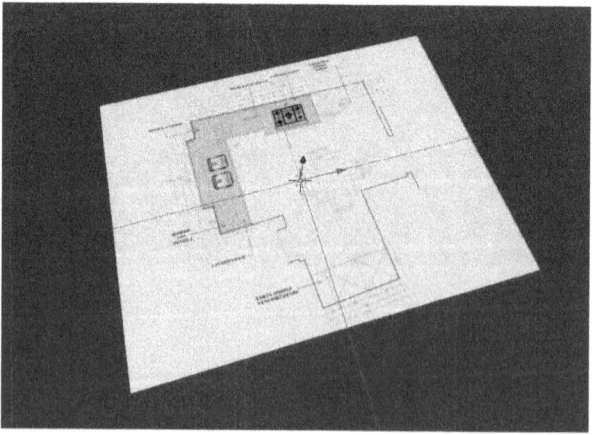

fig. 315 *Image As Plane*

Try to upload the house map of the previous exercise, using *Image As Plane*.

The Blender versatility is a great advantage. In the next three exercises we will show how to model a glass according to three different methods, yielding analogous results.

In all the three examples you will notice that the glass resolution is not very high. You can easily see the faces comprising the object and notice that it is not rounded and smooth as in the reality. Don't worry about: by now what you have learned allows you to achieve only this level of detail. In the next chapter, we will explain in detail the modifiers and, in particular, the *Subdivision Surface*, improving the geometry definition (increasing vertices, edges and faces) and will make the object smoother at the same time.

fig. 316 the glass image in *background* (*Front* view) already scaled with the reference plane

271

For all the three methods i twill be necessary to insert as *background* (in front view, 1 NUM) the reference image and rescale it, using the previously explained method, until to achieve realistic dimensions (for example a height of almost 28 cm).

EXERCISE n. 7: MODELING A GLASS BY FACE EXTRUSION

The first method is based on the extrusion and gradual scaling of a glass section (a circle in this case), following the glass profile.

Create a circle with 12 segments and fill the face with F in *Edit Mode* or directly setting *Fill Type* on *Ngon* in the *Tools Shelf* panel.

Rotate it of 90° around the *x* axis (R, X, 90) and place it in correspondence of the glass base, scaling it such to coincide with the reference circumference.

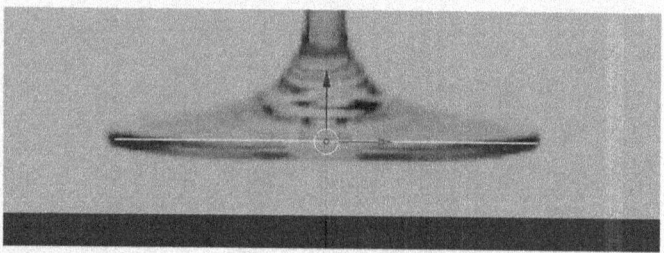

fig. 317 placement of the base circle

Enter in *Edit Mode* and extrude the circle of the base thickness, then extrude again, shifting the extruded face till the stem and scale it.

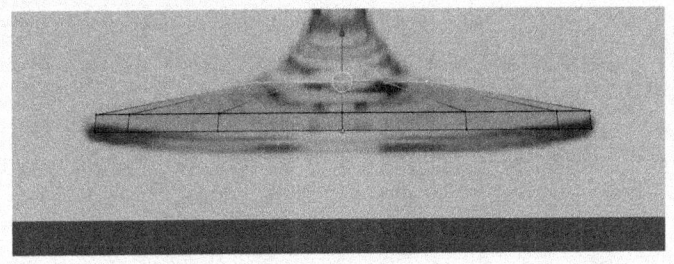

fig. 318 face extrusion along the profile

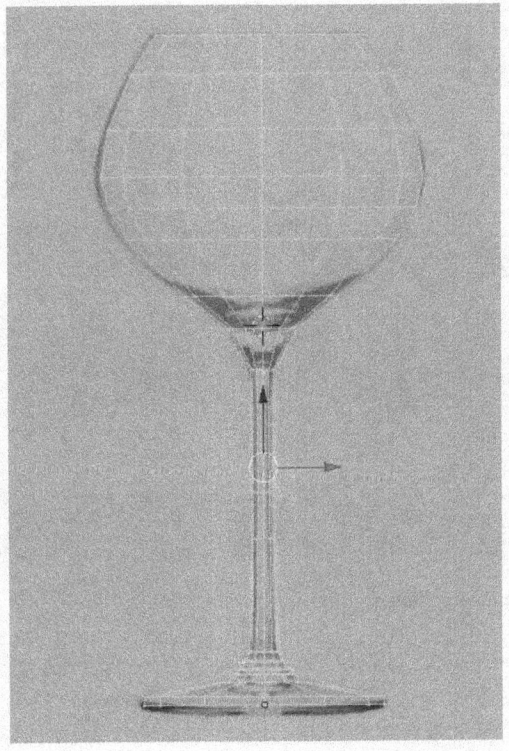

fig. 319 extrusion till the top

Keep on in the same way till the top. Remember that you will not need to make further extrusions. The key points will be sufficient for the future application of the *Subdivision Surface* modifier.

Once you have reached the top, you will need to further extrude inward for creating the glass thickness and convexity.

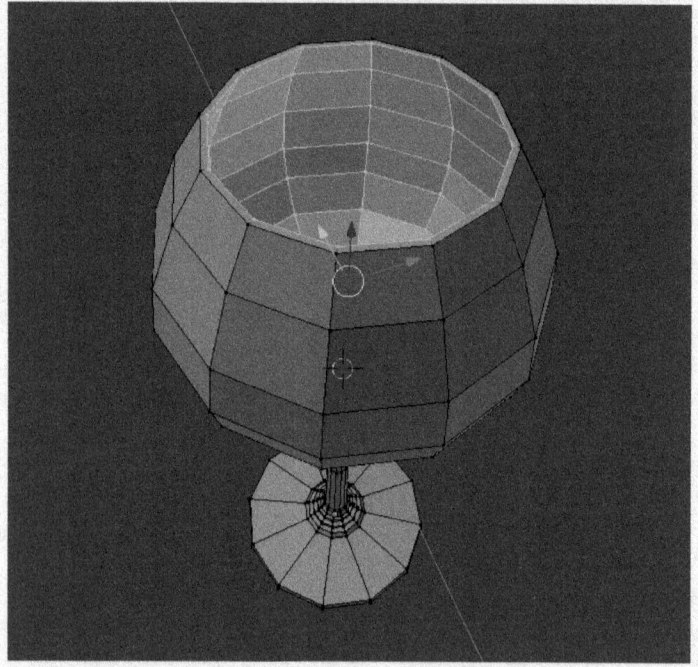

fig. 320 the glass completed

Try to keep you attention on an important aspect. As you remember, it is important that the mesh geometry is based as much as possible on a quadrangular subdivision.

The base and cup bottom are twelve-sided and this will create graphical artifacts when shadings, reflections and materials are being applied.

We than need to transform the non quadrangular figures in four-sided.
Select for example the base circle.

Operate with a sequence of *Inset* (I) inward until the only non-quadrangular left figure be quite small. This will allow you to get also further geometry useful, for example, to raise up the central inner part of the bottom.

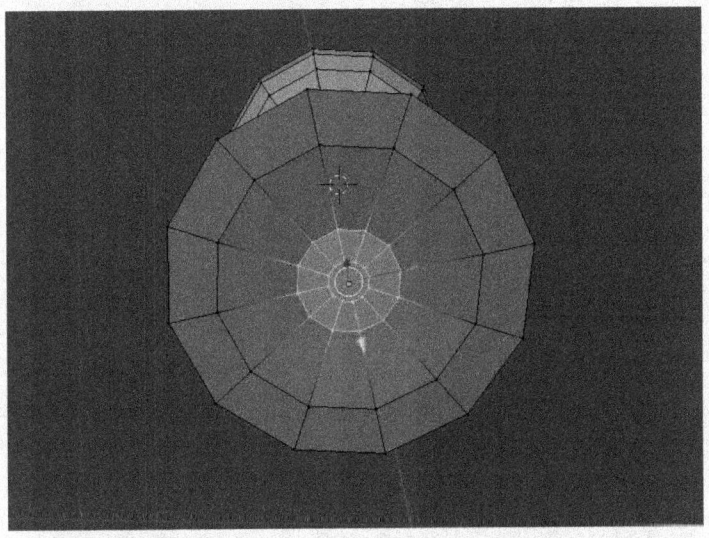

fig. 321 *Inset*

To be precise, you can further subdivide the small twelve-sided figure with the *Knife* tool, paying attention to cut along the correct vertices thus getting 6 quadrangles.

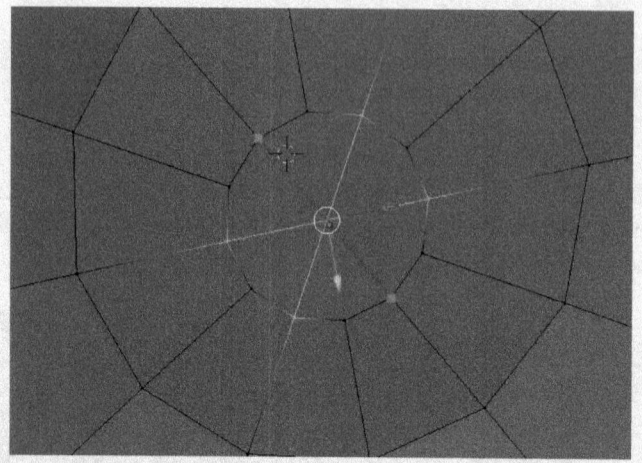

fig. 322 *Knife*

Use finally *Knife* also for the cup bottom.

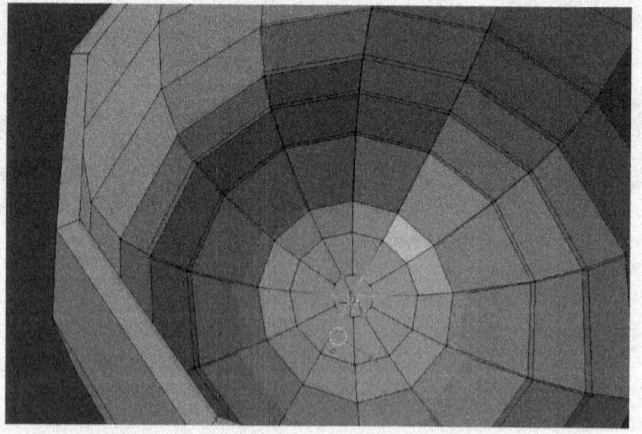

fig. 323 *Knife* on the cup bottom

EXERCISE n. 8: MODELLING A GLASS BY EXTRUDING THE VERTICES AND USING THE SPIN COMMAND

In this exercise you will model the same glass, but using a completely different method.

You will trace half contour of the *background* image and you will use the *Spin* command for rotating the profile of 360° around *z*.

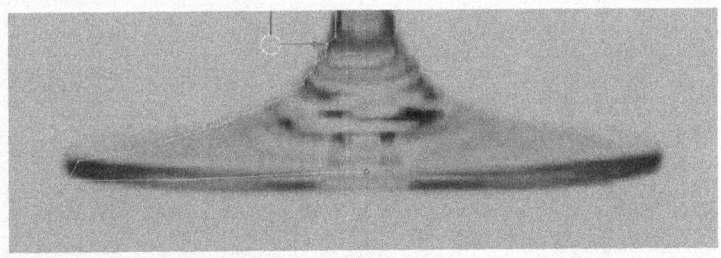

fig. 324 vertex extrusion along the glass profile

Insert a plane on the background image and rotate it of 90° around the *x* axis, enter in *Edit Mode* and delete 3 of the 4 vertices of the plane. Finally, place the left vertex in correspondence of the center of the glass base, operating with a sequence of extrusions.

At the end you should get a contour like this.

Select all the vertices and apply the *Spin* command, setting the parameters in the specific panel of the *Tools Shelf* like shown below.

The achieved outcome is a revolution solid obtained with a complete rotation (360°) around the z axis in 12 steps.

fig. 325 completed glass profile

At the end of the process you will have to delete the overlapped vertices generated due to the figure closure. You only need to select all the vertices with A and press *Remove Double* in the *Tools Shelf.*

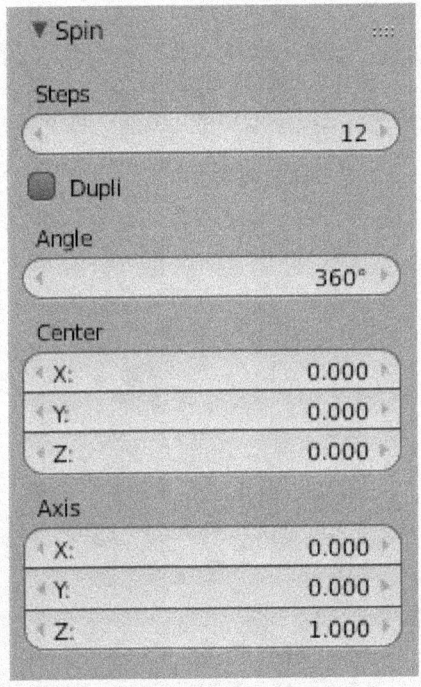

fig. 326 parameter setting for the *Spin* command.

fig. 327 the outcome of the overlapped vertex removal

fig. 328 the completed glass

EXERCISE n. 9: GLASS MODELING BY EXTRUSION OF THE POINTS OF A CURVE, TRANSORMATION IN MESH AND USE OF THE SPIN COMMAND

A third method, much similar to the previous one, is to create a profile starting from a curve instead of a *mesh*, and extrude the vertices, by suitably regulating the handles to archive the correct slope and curvature.

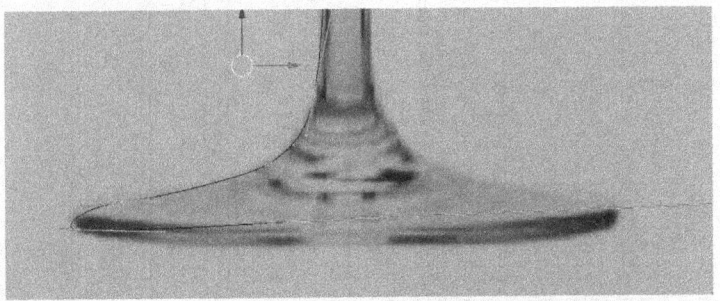

fig. 329 curve vertex extrusion along the glass profile

fig. 330 complete extrusion with the curve

281

The curve will be transformed into a sequence of points.

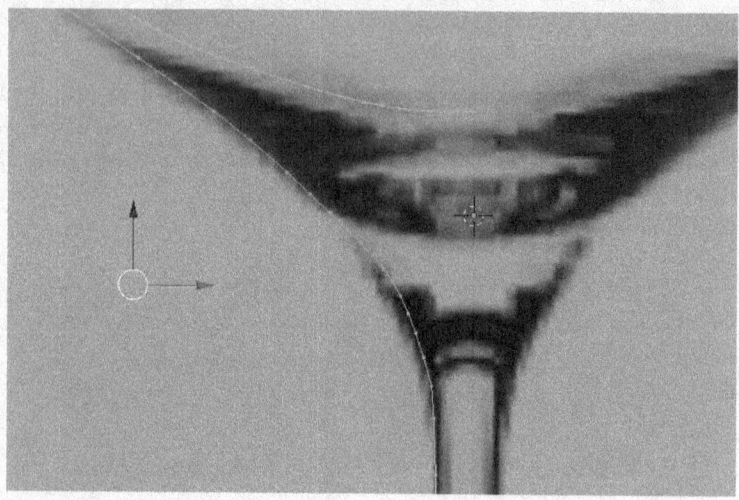

fig. 331 curve transformed into a *mesh*

Now, after selecting all the points in *Edit Mode*, you will use the *Spin* command like in the previous exercise, getting the revolution solid.

Don't forget, also in the present case, to delete the overlapped vertices.

Moreover, after the conclusion of certain operations like the extrusion and the rotation, some faces can invert their positive direction. You can see them because they appear darker and you will need to recalculate their normals with the *Recalculate* command.

fig. 332 the glass obtained with the revolution of a curve transformed into a *mesh*

In the next chapter we will analyze a further method for obtaining a revolution solid, using the *Screw* modifier.

4.5.2. The *Specials* (W) menu

A special drop-down menu which can be recalled in 3D view in *Edit Mode* with W, summarizes many of the functions already seen, and some others regarding object modifying.

This menu applies to *meshes*, curves, surfaces and texts, with some differences. Let us analyze the various cases.

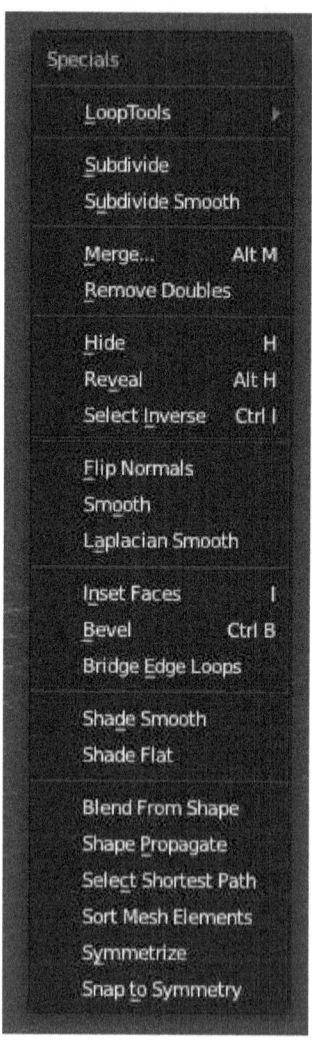

fig. 333 the *Specials* menu for meshes

In case of *meshes*, in *Edit Mode*, a menu can be opened pressing W in correspondence of any point of the 3D view. This menu allows you to execute the following functions and commands:

- **Loop Tools** encloses the same commands previously described;

- **Subdivide** subdivides the selected elements;

- **Subdivide Smooth** subdivides the selected elements, smoothing their shape;

- **Merge** (ALT + M) joins two or more elements, according to what has been already analyzed;

- **Remove Doubles** removes the overlapped vertices;

- **Hide** (H) hides the selected elements, which can be seen again with ALT + H (**Reveal**);

- **Select Inverse** (CTRL + I) inverts the selection regarding the selected elements;

- **Flip Normals** inverts the normals of the selected elements;

- **Smooth** smoothens the shape of the selected elements;

- **Laplacian Smooth** executes the smoothing proportionally involving also the adjacent elements;

- **Inset faces** (I) makes an *inset* of the selected face/faces;

- **Bevel** (CTRL + B) makes a *bevel* on all the selected vertices and edges. The number of iterations can be defined in the

Bevel panel in the *Tools Bar*, once the command has been launched;

- **Bridge Edge Loops** makes a connection between two selected edges;

- **Shade Smooth** shows the selected faces with smooth shading (*Smooth* command);

- **Shade Flat** is the opposite of the previous command, making flat the face shadings.

Then you can find the following other commands:

- **Blend from Shape** and **Shape Propagate** are useful tools for the shape *keying* and will be analyzed in the foregoing;

- **Select Shortest Path** finds the shortest path between two selected vertices;

- **Sort Mesh Elements** modifies the order of the selected elements (vertices, edges or faces) according to the selected method in the submenu;

- **Symmetrize** automatically generates a symmetry axis according to the axis defined in the *Symmetrize* panel in the *Tools Shelf*;

- **Snap To Symmetry** inverts the vertex position with respect to the corresponding mirrored position: *x* on –*x*; *y* on –*y* *z* on –*z*;

SPECIALS MENU RELEVANT TO CURVES AND SURFACES

The specials menu (W), in *Edit Mode* of a curve or surface, allows you to select the following functions:

- **Subdivide** subdivides the object into a number of parts defined in the homonym panel in the *Tools Shelf*;

- **Switch Direction** inverts the normal direction;

- **Set Goal Weight** sets a weight for the selected elements to be used by the *Soft Body* function;

- **Set Curve Radius** sets a numeric value for the curvature radius between selected elements;

- **Smooth** smoothens the curvature of the selected elements;

- **Smooth Curve Weight** smoothens the interpolation between selected elements;

- **Smooth Curve Radius** smoothens the curvature according to the radius;

- **Smooth Curve Tilt** smoothens the twist of a point acted upon by *Tilt*.

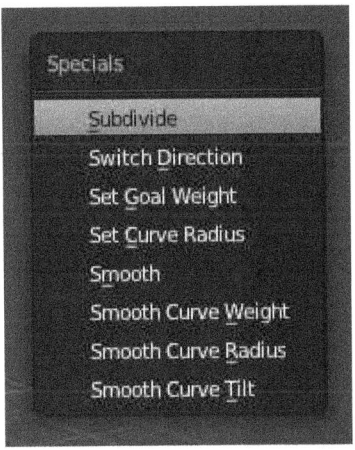

fig. 334 the *Specials* menu for curves and surfaces

The *Specials* menu applied (in *Object Mode*) to texts activates the following menu and functions:

- **Extrude Size** extrudes the text creating a 3D text. It is possible to set an extrusion numerical value after the command has been activated;

- **Width Size** defines the width of the text single characters. The thickness amount can be defined by inserting a numerical value after the command activation;

- **Restrict Render Unselected** and **Clear All Restrict Render** are two parameters for the rendering, which will be explained in the foregoing.

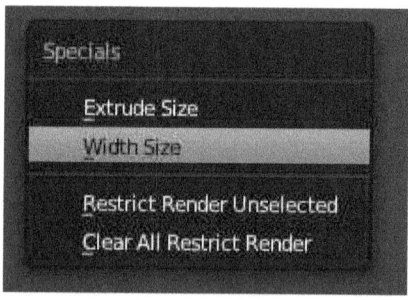

fig. 335 the *Specials* menu for text

4.6. The menus of the 3D view header in *Edit Mode*

The menus in the 3D view header change a lot the items in *Edit Mode* environment and adapt to the type of selected object (*mesh*, curve, text...).

You will already know many of the tools present in these menu, like usually happens in Blender, because they have been already examined.

The Blender interface is organized such that tools and functions are grouped into different thematic environments, and so they can be recalled from different panels, menus and *shortcuts*.

Let us analyze also in this case all the functions, subdivided by object typology.

MESH

A) View

Contains the same tools already analyzed in *Object mode*.

B) Select

In this menu you can find the commands and options relevant to the selection of the mesh elements.

- ***Select Boundary Loop*** selects the external boundaries of the selected faces;

289

- *Select Loop Inner-Region* select the faces inside a selected *loop;*

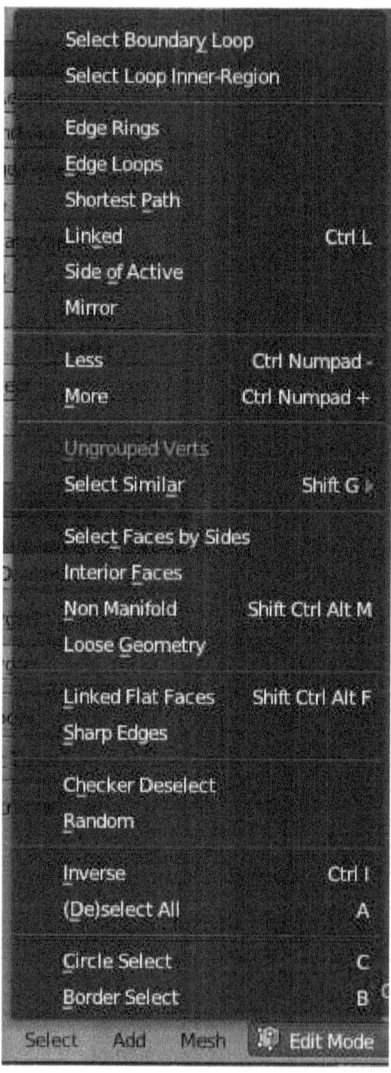

fig. 336 the Select menu

- **Edge Rings** selects one or more specific circular loops (if possible) where one or more selected elements are enclosed:

fig. 337 *Select Boundary Loop*

- **Edge Loops** selects a *loop* between two or more selected elements;

- **Shortest Path** (see **Special**, **W** menu previously described)

- **Linked** (CTRL + L) selects all the vertices directly connected to the selected element/elements of the *mesh*;

- **Side Of Active** selects all the elements of a *mesh* along a specific axis;

- **Mirror** adds a mirrored copy depending on a symmetry axis defined by the selected elements;

- **Less** (CTRL, -NUM) removes vertices, edges or faces, one at each pressure, connected to those already selected;

291

- **More** (CTRL, +NUM) adds vertices, edges or faces, one at each pressure, connected to those already selected;

- **Ungrouped Verts** selects vertices not grouped or (dis)connected to others;

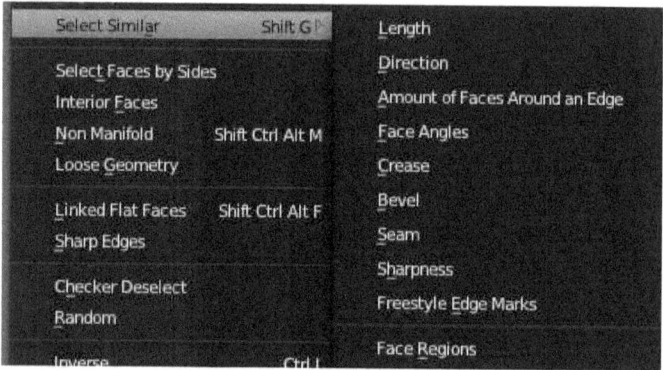

fig. 338 the *Select Similar* menu

- **Select Similar** (SHIFT + G) opens a submenu containing very useful tools for finding elements and mesh parts similar to that/those selected according to well defined criteria, i.e.:

  • Those having the same length (*Length*);

  • Those having the same direction (*Directions*);

  • Those having the same face amount around an edge (*Amount of Faces Around an Edge*);

  • Those having faces with the same angles;

  • Those having the same *Crease* value which, as we will show in the foregoing, reduces the effect of the *Subdivision Surface* on the edges and surfaces;

  • Those having the same bevel (*Bevel*);

- Those unwrapped for the mapping (*Seam*);

- Those with the same sharpness (*Sharpness*);

- Those obtained through a hand-free modeling;

- The same faces (*Face Regions*);

- **Select Faces by Sides** selects the vertex or face number according to the parameters prescribed in the *Select faces by Sides* panel in the *Tools Shelf* and, more specifically:

  - The vertex number (*Number of Vertices*);

  - The selection methodology (drop-down menu *Type*), choosing from equal to..., different from..., less than... or greater than...;

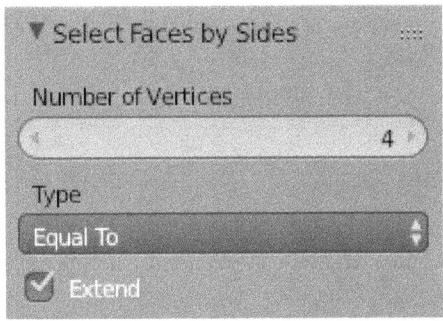

fig. 339 the *Select faces by Sides* panel

- **Interior Faces** selects the faces whose edges are connected at least to two faces;

- **Non Manifold** (SHIFT + CTRL + ALT + M) selects the elements not compliant to a geometry optimal for the 3D print;

- **Loose Geometry** selects the geometry elements not connected to the base geometry;

- **Linked Flat faces** (SHIFT + CTRL + ALT + F) selects the faces interconnected according to the angle specified in the *Linked Flat faces* panel of the *Tools Shelf*;

- **Sharp Edges** selects all the enough acute edges, according to the angle defined in the *Sharp Edges* panel of the *Tools Shelf*;

- **Checker Deselect** deselects all the n-elements of a section (defined in the counter *Nth Selection* of the *Checker Deselect* panel placed in the *Tools Shelf*) starting from the active element (vertex, edge or face). It is a tool useful for automatically selecting misaligned elements;

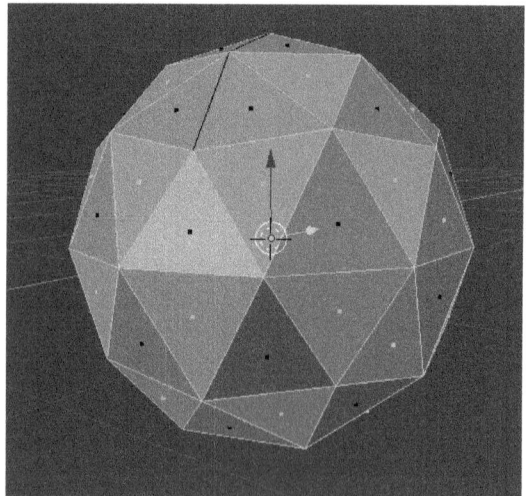

fig. 340 *Checker deselect* set to 2 *Nth* of a *Icosphere*

- **Random** selects or deselects elements (vertices, faces or edges, depending of what has been fixed in the section of the 3D view header) randomly, according to a percentage established in the *Random* panel of the *Tools Shelf*;

294

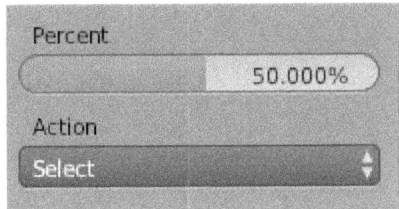

fig. 341 the *Random* panel

- *Inverse* (CTRL + I) inverts the selection;

- *(De)Select All* (A) selects or deselects all the elements;

- *Circle Select* (C) makes the selection with a circular brush;

- *Border Select* (B) makes a rectangular selection.

C) Add

In this menu you can insert *meshes* inside the selected *mesh* in *Edit Mode* environment.

D) Mesh

The specific tools for modifying a mesh are enclose din the *Mesh* menu.

- *Show/Hide* shows (H) or hide (ALT + H) selected parts of the *mesh*;

- *Proportional Editing Falloff*, *Proportional Editing* and the flag *AutoMerge Editing* recall the same commands already analyzed and which can be recalled from the *header* icons;

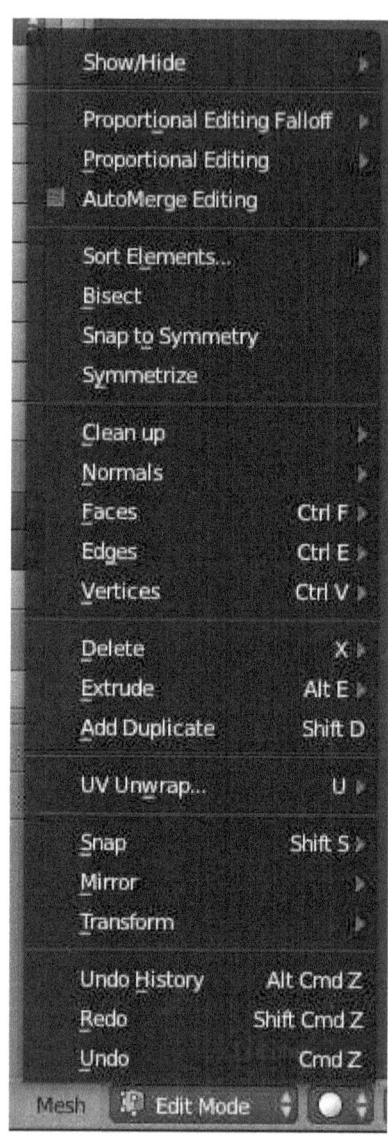

fig. 342 the *Mesh* menu

- **Sort Elements** opens a submenu where you can choose whether you can order the view based on the view along the z or x axis, the cursor distance, the material, the selected elements, randomly or in opposite way with respect to the selection;

- **Bisect** makes a mesh manual cut creating new vertices, edges and faces;

- **Snap To Symmetry** inverts the vertex position with respect to the corresponding mirrored position: x on –x; y on –y z on –z;

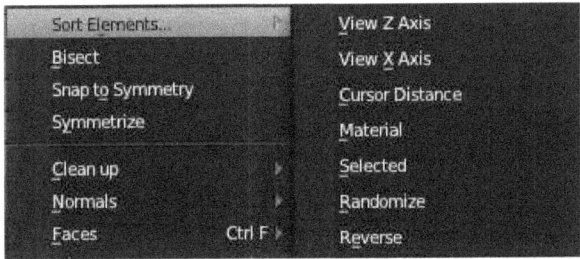

fig. 343 the *Sort Elements* submenu

- **Symmetrize** automatically generates a symmetry axis according to the axis defined in the *Symmetrize* panel of the *Tools Shelf*;

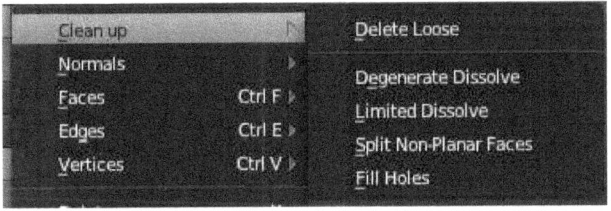

fig. 344 the *Clean Up* submenu

- **Clean Up** collects some commands in a submenu, allowing you to automatically clean the meshes depending on fixed parameters;

- **Normals** open a submenu where you can re-compute the mesh normals inward (CTRL + N), outward (SHIF + CTRL + N), or automatically flip them (*Flip Normals*);

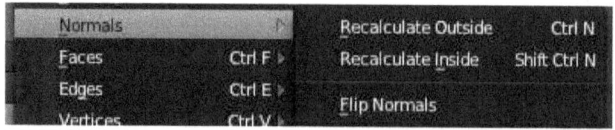

fig. 345 the *Normals* submenu

- **Faces** (CTRL + F) is a menu collecting all the tools for modifying the mesh faces.

  • **Flip Normals** inverts the normals of the selected faces;

  • **Make Edge/Face** (F) joins two vertices with an edge or fills a closed selection of vertices or edges with a face;

  • **Fill** (ALT + F) join as many vertices as possible for creating the face maximum amount in a selection;

  • **Grid Fill** joins selected loops with faces;

  • **Beautify faces** (SHIFT + ALT + F) tries to arrange the shape of some faces, restoring at the best the mesh geometry;

  • **Inset Faces** (I) creates an *inset* of the selected faces, adding new quadrangular faces;

  • **Bevel** (CTRL + B) adds a bevel to selected vertices or edges. It is possible to parametrize the bevel amount adding the numerical value, for example typing CTRL + B, 3;

- **Solidify** extrudes the elected faces giving a thickness to the mesh and creating new geometry, whose value is defined in the *Thickness* counter of the *Solidify* panel of the Tools Shelf;

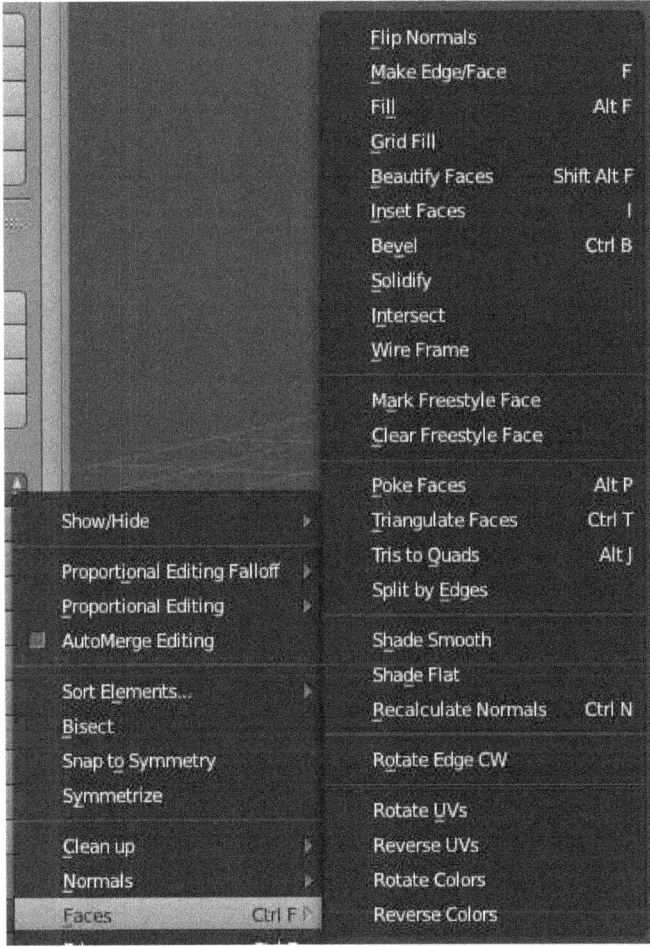

fig. 346 the *Faces* submenu

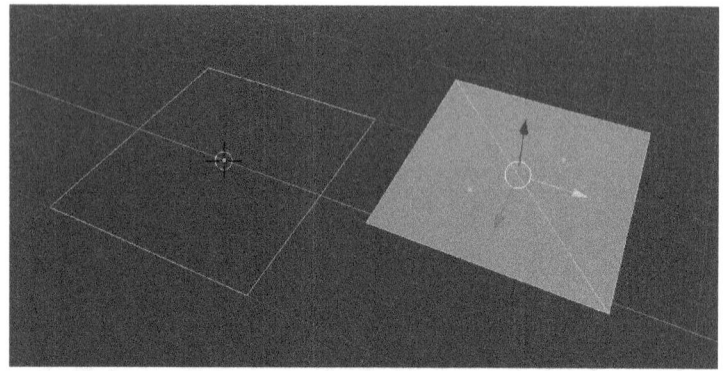

fig. 347 *Fill*

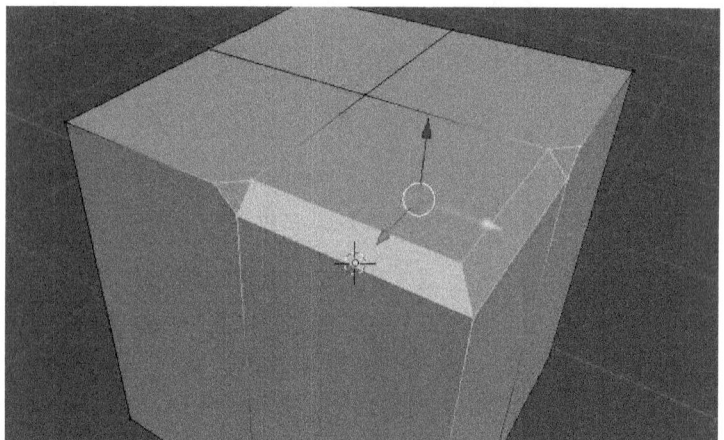

fig. 348 *Bevel* of the selected edges

- ***Intersect*** creates a cut between intersecting faces;

- ***Wire Frame*** deletes the faces of a mesh and thickens the edges by adding new geometry, according to the values in the Wire Frame panel of the *Tools Shelf*;

- ***Mark Freestyle Face*** selects or deselects the hand-free created faces;

- ***Clear Freestyle Face*** deletes the hand-free created faces;

- ***Poke Faces*** (ALT + P) divides a face making, at the same time, an *Inset* of the vertices and a *Merge* at the face center. In the *Poke Faces* panel in the *Tools Shelf* you can define an *Offset* (from -1 to 1) in the merge point of the new vertices;

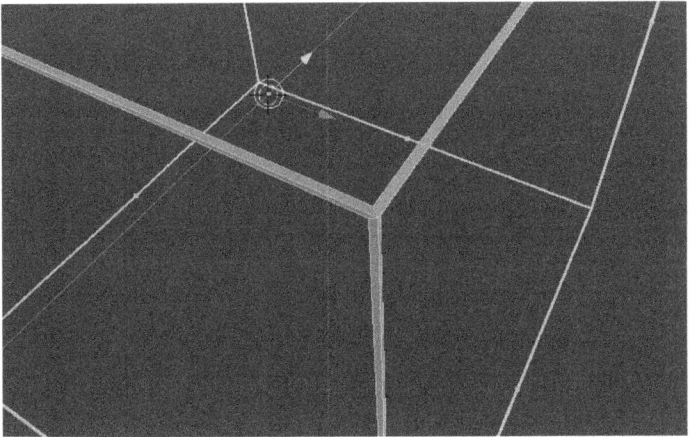

fig. 349 *Wire Frame* on a cube

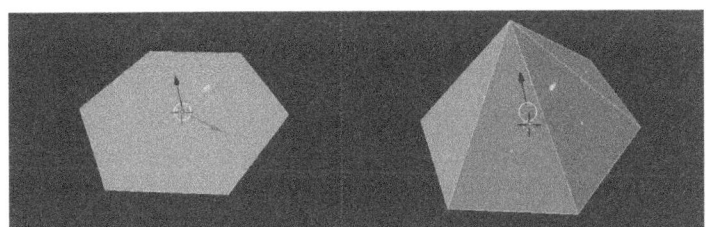

fig. 350 outcome of the *Poke Faces* on a hexagonal polygon which gets transformed into a pyramid due to the *Offset*

301

- **Triangulate Faces** (CTRL + T) tries to transform all the mesh faces into triangles. This function can be useful for the 3D print;
- **Tris of Quads** (ALT + J) executes, among others, the opposite operation with respect to the previously described *Triangulate Faces*: tries to improve the mesh geometry enforcing as much as possible quadrangular faces;
- **Split by Edges** separates the faces from the vertices not connected to them;

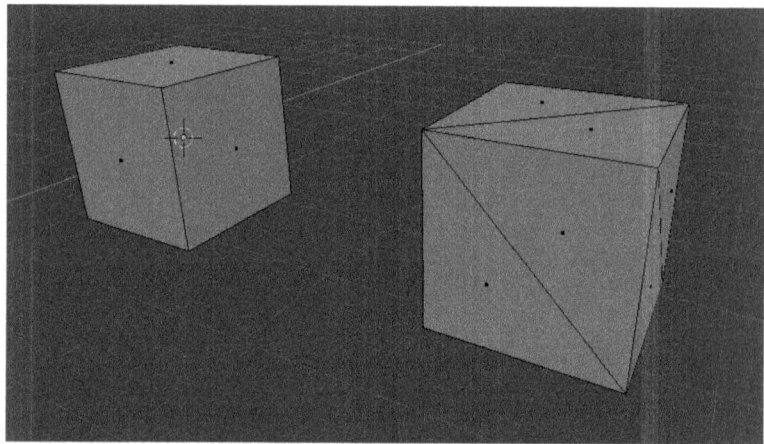

fig. 351 the cube faces divided in triangles with *Triangulate Faces*

- **Shade Smooth** visualizes the smoothened and rounded face effect;
- **Shade Flat** visualizes the face smooth effect;
- **Recalculate Normals** (CTRL + N) executes an automatic re-computation of the elected face normals;
- **Rotate Edge CW** distorts and rotates the selected edges or the adjacent faces;
- **Rotate UVs** rotates the face *UV* coordinates;
- **Rotate Colors** rotates the *Vertex Color* inside the faces;

- **Reverse Colors** inverts the *Vertex Color* direction inside the faces;

- **Edges** (CTRL + E) is a menu collecting all the tools for modifying the mesh edges.

  - **Make Edge/Face** (F) joins two vertices with an edge or fills a closed selection of vertices or edges with a face;

  - **Subdivide** subdivides the selected edges in several parts, adding new vertices, as many as indicated in the *Subdivide* panel of the *Tools Shelf*;

  - **Unsubdivide** reduces the subdivisions of the selected edges;

  - **Edge Crease** (SHIFT + E) assigns to the selected edges a resistance against the rounding action of the *Subdivision Surface* modifier parametrizing this value from 0 (no resistance) up to 1 (maximum resistance). The edges undergoing this resistance will appear colored by violet e thickened according to the assigned value;

  - **Edge Bevel Weight** assigns to the selected edges a resistance against the bevel effect. This tool works analogously to *Edge Crease*: by selecting the desired edges and assigning a value ranging from 0 to 1, these edges will appear colored by light orange, and thickened depending on the assigned value, and will resist to the effect;

  - **Mark Seam** marks in red the selected edges for executing the unwrapping along the mesh edges for the *texture* mapping;

  - **Clear Seam** removes the outcome of the *Mark Seam* previously applied to the selected edges;

- **Mark Sharp** marks the selected edges as not rounded. They will be colored in pale blue;

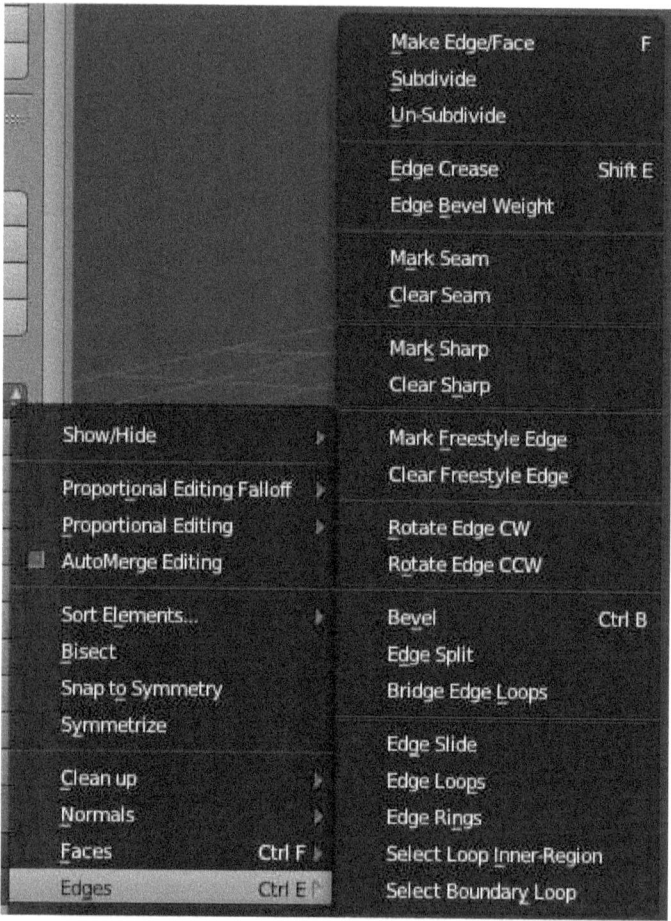

fig. 352 the *Vertices* submenu

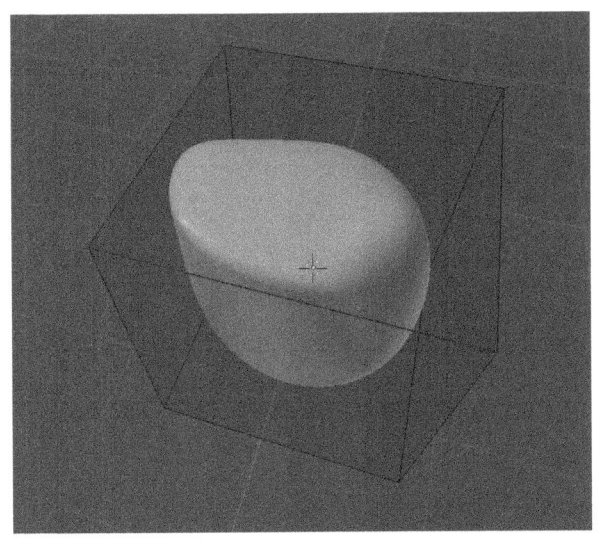

fig. 353 the *Crease* effect set to 0,7

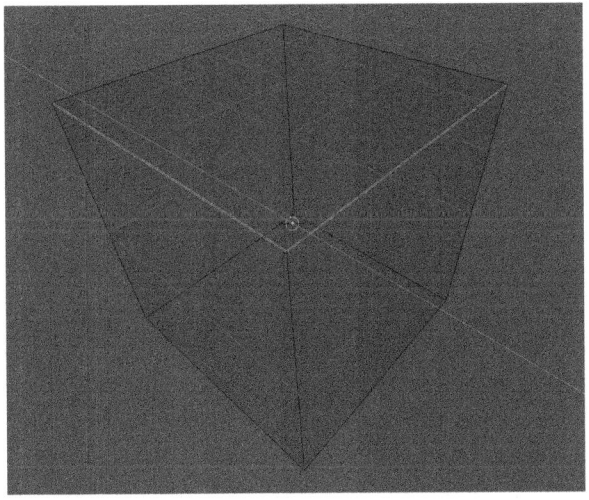

fig. 354 *Bevel Weight* on the edges

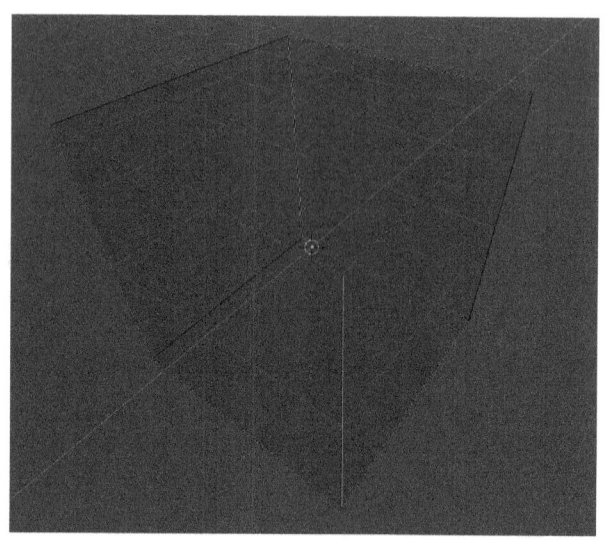

fig. 355 *Mark Seam* on the selected vertices

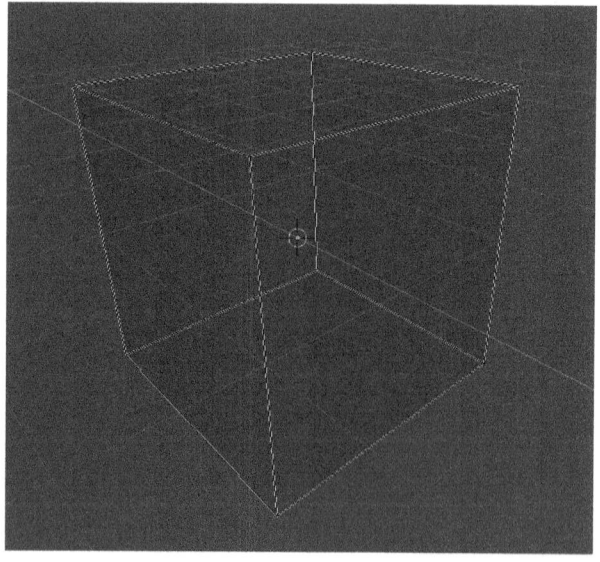

fig. 356 *Mark Sharp*

306

- **Clear Sharp** cancel the previous command from the selected edges;

- **Mark Freestyle Edge** marks all the vertices of a selection belonging to a hand-free modeling;

- **Clear Freestyle Edge** deletes all the vertices of a selection belonging to a hand-free modeling;

- **Rotate Edge CW (CCW)** distorts and rotates the selected edges or the adjacent faces;

- **Bevel** (CTRL + B) adds a bevel to selected vertices or edges. It is possible to parametrize the bevel amount adding a numerical value, for example by typing CTRL + B, 3;

- **Edge Split** creates a copy of the selected edges coinciding with the originals;

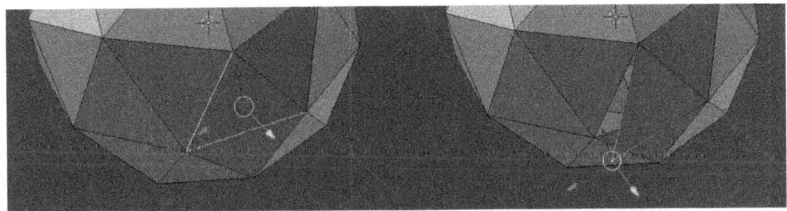

fig. 357 *Edge Split* on some vertices of the Icosphere

- **Bridge Edge Loops** perform a connection between two *loops* (see what already described concerning to *Loop* Tools;

- **Edge Slide** shifts a deselected *loop* along a edge;

- **Edge Loops** selects the whole *loop* related to two or more selected vertices or edges;

307

- **Edge Rings** selects, if existing, closed *loops* where two or more selected vertices or edges are enclosed;

- **Select Loop Inner Region** selects the *loops* inside a selection;

- **Select Boundary Loop** selects the boundary loops *of a selection*.

- **Vertices** (CTRL + V) is a menu collecting all the tools for modifying the mesh vertices.

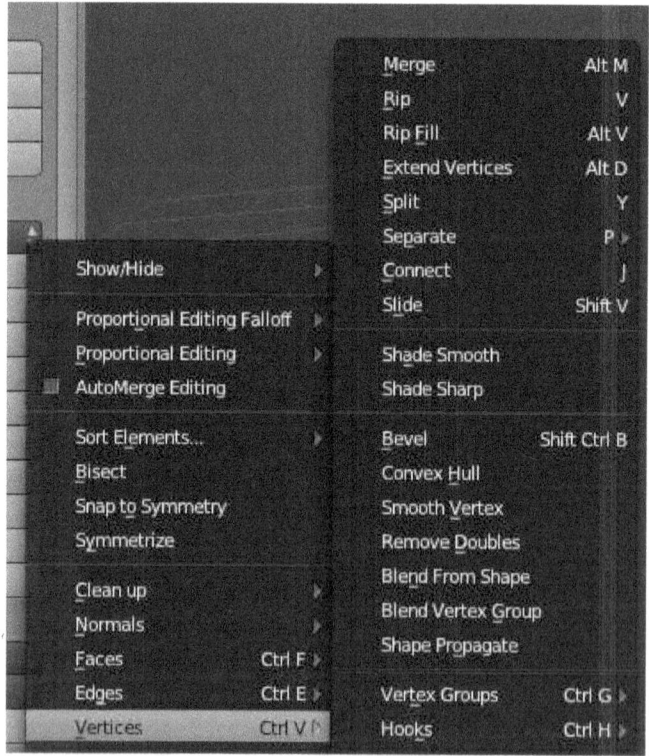

fig. 358 the *Vertices* submenu

- **Merge**, which has been already widely discussed, merge the selected vertices into a single one, according to a certain choice (on the first vertex, on the last one, at the center, collapsing);
- **Rip** (V) separate the selected vertices creating a copy unrelated from the original and from the related loop;

- **Rip Fill** duplicates the selected elements (vertices or edges) keeping a connection with the originals and creating a new *loop*;

- **Extended Vertices** (ALT D) extends the selected vertices creating a new geometry;

- **Split** (Y) creates a copy and physically separates the selected elements from the *mesh*;

fig. 359 outcome of the *Rip* tool

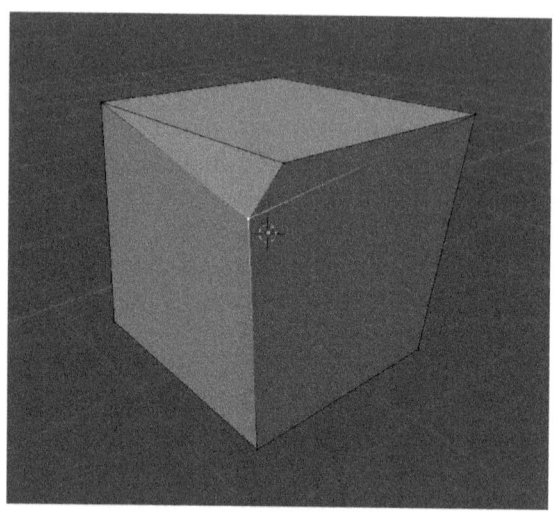

fig. 360 outcome of the *Rip Fill* tool

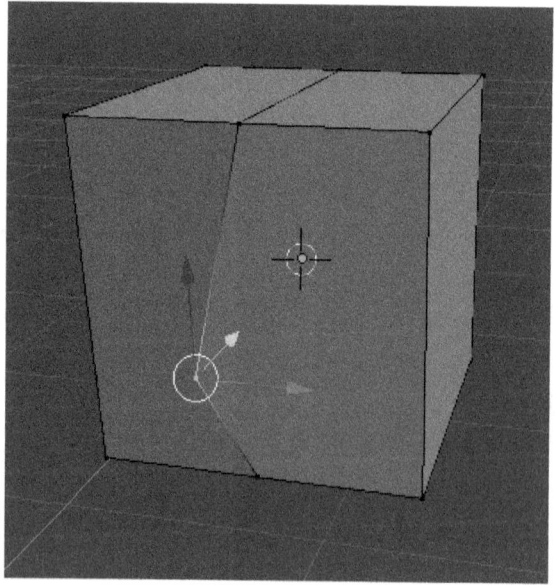

fig. 361 outcome of the *Exteded Vertices* tool

310

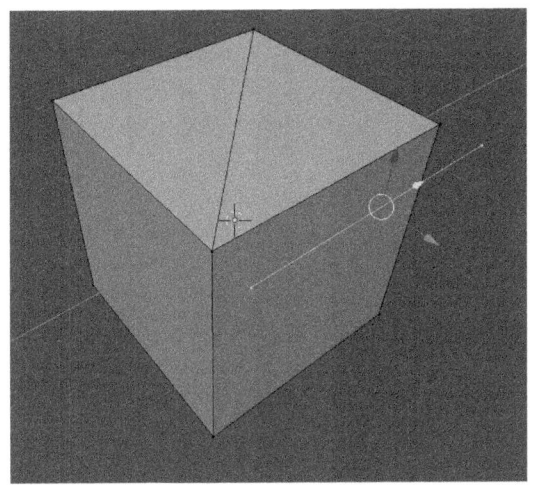

fig. 362 *Separate*

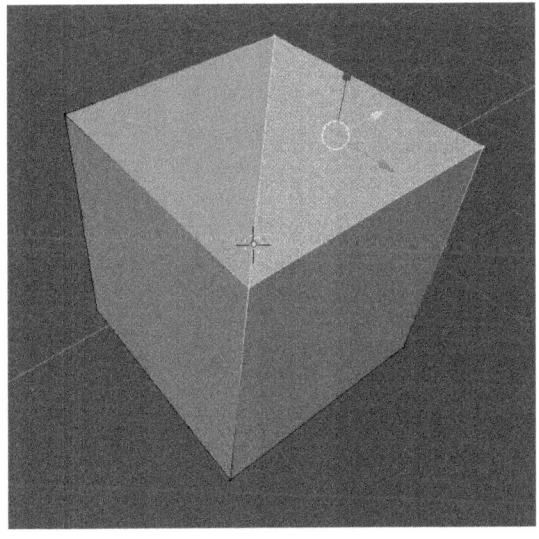

fig. 363 outcome of the *Connect* between two points

311

- **Separate** (P) separates from the mesh the selected elements and creates a new mesh. You can choose to apply the tool by selection, material or by elements disconnected from the mesh (*By Loose Part*);

- **Connect** (J) connects two selected vertices and separates the faces the vertices belong to, with an outcome similar to *Knife*;

- **Slide** (SHIFT + V) shifts a vertex along the adjacent edges. The edge on which the vertex is shifted will be highlighted in yellow when you approach it with the mouse pointer. Confirm with the LMB;

- **Shade Smooth** rounds the *mesh* close to the selected vertices. The *mesh* will be more and more rounded by repeating the command;

- **Shade Sharp** selects the selected vertices marking as sharp the edges connected to them (they will be colored in blue);

- **Bevel** (CTRL + B) adds a bevel to selected vertices or edges. You can parametrize the bevel amount adding a numerical value, for example typing CTRL + B, 3;

- **Convex Hull** tries to modify the selected parts of a concave *mesh* such as to make it convex;

- **Smooth Vertex** places the selected vertices such as to smoothen the *mesh* according to a parameter (from 0 to 1, where 1 yields the maximum smoothing effect) of the *Smoothing* counter, the number of repetitions of the command (*Repeat*) and according to the selected axes (*Axis*) inside the *Smoothing Vertex* panel of the *Tools Shelf;*

- **Remove Double** removes all the overlapped vertices of the selection;

- **Blend From Shape**, **Blend Vertex Group** e **Shape Propagate** are useful tools for the shape *keying* which will be analyzed in the foregoing;

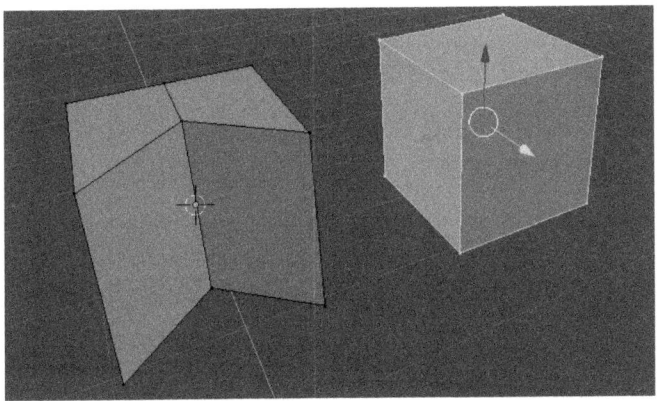

fig. 364 outcome of the *Convex Hull*

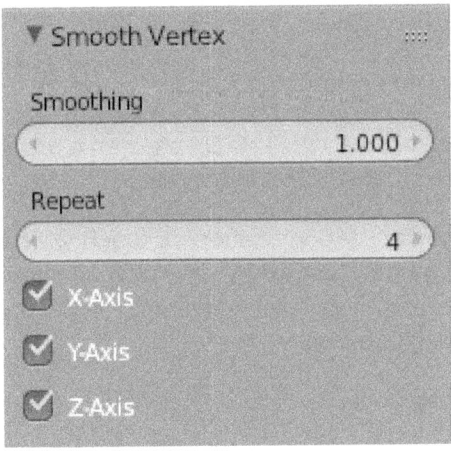

fig. 365 the *Smooth Vertex* panel

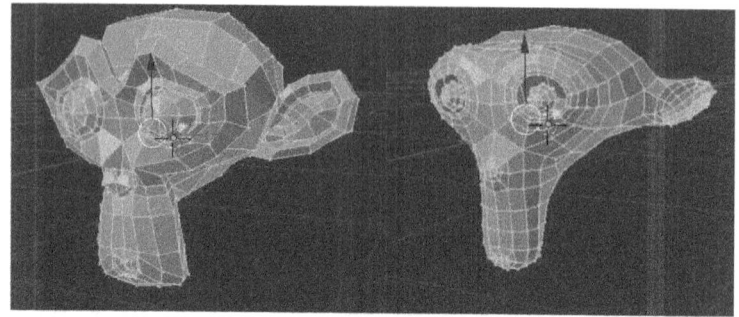

fig. 366 *Suzanne* subjected to the *Smooth vertex* with *Smoothing* to 1 and with 4 repetitions of the command

- **Vertex Group** assigns the selected vertices to a new *Vertex Group* automatically renamed *Group.00x* which can be visualized in the *Vertex Group* panel of the *tab Data* of the *Properties* editor;

- **Hooks** (CTRL + H) adds to a vertex or to a selected vertex group a *Hook* modifier, a hook on which you can assign a specific function. *Hook* will be described in the foregoing;

- **Delete** (X) deletes a selected element;

- **Extrude** (E) encloses the *tools* for the element extrusion;

- **Add Duplicate** (SHIFT + D) creates a duplicate of the selected elements inside a mesh;

- **UV Unwrap** (U) opens a menu, which will be analyzed in detail in the foregoing, enclosing all the methods for unwrapping the mesh elements as a function of the mapping of a *texture*;

- Under **Mesh** menu:

314

- **Snap** (SHIFT + S) snaps the selected elements according to a criterion defined in the submenu. These functions are the same of those previously analyzed in the 3D view header;

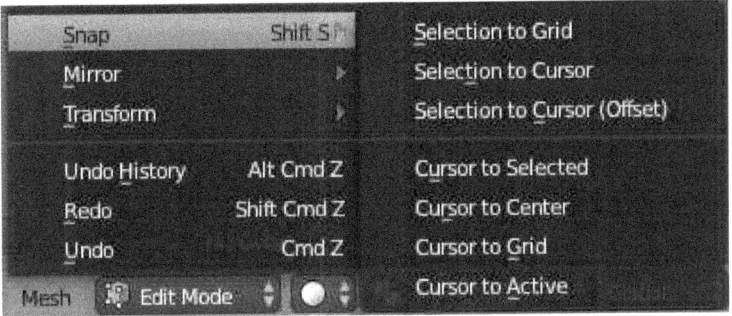

fig. 367 the *Snap* submenu

- **Mirror** (CTRL + M) adds a mirrored image of the selected elements with respect to one of the indicated symmetry axes;

- **Transform** encloses all the transformers (*Grab*, *Rotate* and *Scale*);

- **Undo History** (CTRL + ALT + Z) deletes the history of the operations made;

- **Redo** (SHIF + CTRL + Z) restore the last canceled operation;

- **Undo** (CTRL +Z) cancels the last operation. By repeating many times the command, you can go back in the operation sequence canceling the last operations made.

Analogously to the *mesh*, also with the curves in *Edit Mode*, the menus of the 3D view header present a complete and wide set of commands and tools.

A) *View*

Encloses the same tools already seen in *Object mode*.

B) *Select*

In this menu you can find the commands and operations relevant to the element selection of the selected curve. Some of those are identical to the ones already analyzed in case of a *mesh* and thus they will not be explained here, indicating the corresponding previously sections where you can find their description.

- **Select Less** and **Select More** (see the corresponding commands in *Mesh/Select*);

- **Select Previous**

- **Select Next**

- **(De)Select Last**

- **(De)Select First**

- **Selected Linked** (CTRL + L) (see the corresponding command in *Mesh/Select*);

- **Checker Deselect** (see the corresponding command in *Mesh/Select*);

- **Select Random** (see the corresponding command in *Mesh/Select*);

- **Inverse** (CTRL + I) (see the corresponding command in *Mesh/Select*);

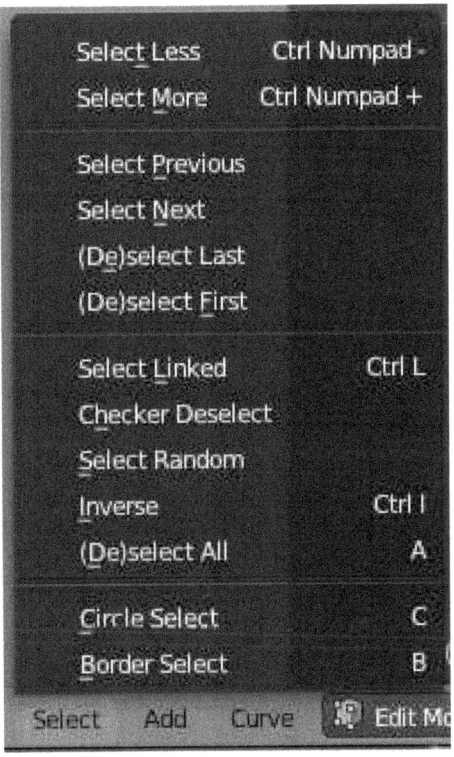

fig. 368 the *Select* menu relevant to curves in *Edit Mode*

- **(De)Select All** (A) (see the corresponding command in *Mesh/Select*);

- **Circle Select** (C) (see the corresponding command in *Mesh/Select*);

- **Border Select** (B) (see the corresponding command in *Mesh/Select*).

C) *Add*

In this menu you can insert other curves inside the selected *Curve* in *Edit Mode*.

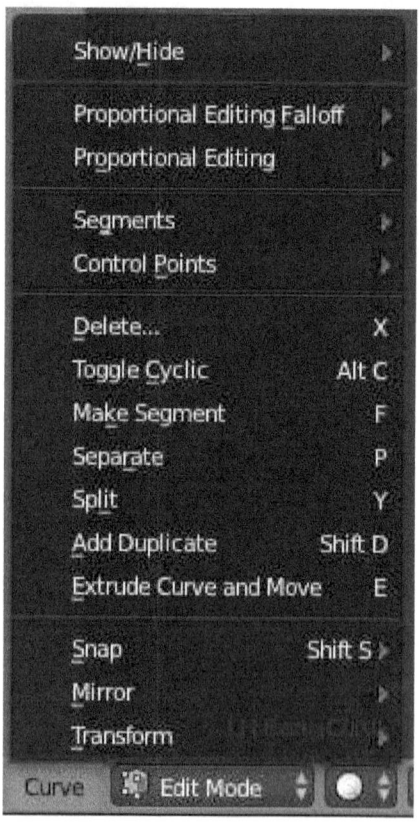

fig. 369 the *Curve* menu relevant to curves in *Edit Mode*

D) *Curve*

Finally in this menu you can find all the tools for modifying a curve, many of them already analyzed. Some of these tools are identical to the corresponding ones applied to the *meshes* and thus, also in this case, they will not be described again.

- **Show/Hide** (H and ALT + H) (see the corresponding command in *Mesh/Select*);

- **Proportional Editing Falloff** and **Proportional Editing** (see the corresponding commands in *Mesh/Select* and in the 3D view header);

- **Segments**

- **Control Points**

- **Delete** (X or CANC) deletes the selected elements;

- **Toggle Cyclic** (ALT + C) closes the curve by joining the two ends;

- **Make Segments** (F) corresponds to *Fill*: merge two points of the curve creating a curve segment;

- **Separate** (P) separates from the curve the selected parts, creating a new curve;

- **Split** (Y)

- **Add Duplicate** (SHIFT + D) creates a copy of the curve selected elements;

- **Extrude Curve and Move** (E) extrudes the curve selected vertices creating new adjacent segments and lengthening the curve;

- **Snap** (SHIF + S) (see the corresponding command in *Mesh/Select*);

- **Mirror** adds a mirrored copy of the curve selected elements according to the specified mirroring axis;

- **Translate** encloses like in *Mesh* all the base transformers for translating, rotating and scaling the elements of a curve.

SURFACE E METABALL

The commands and tools contained in the menus of the 3D view header, referred to the surfaces and the *Metaballs* in *Edit Mode*, are identical to those relevant to the curves.

TEXT

The commands contained in the menus of the 3D view header, referred to the *Text* in *Edit Mode* are few.

A) *View*

Contains the same tools already analyzed in *Object mode*.

B) *Edit*

Let us analyze the commands present in the *Edit* menu.

- **Select All** (A) selects or deselects the whole text;

- **Paste Clipboard** copy in the text the characters of an external selection, even taken from another software from which the selected text has been copied with the standard key combination CTRL + C;

- **Paste File** copy the content of an external text file chosen in the Blender *browser*;

- **Paste** (CTRL + V), **Cut** (CTRL + X) and **Copy** (CTRL + C) respectively: pastes a text previously copied on the *Text* in *Edit Mode* and cuts and copies the selected text.

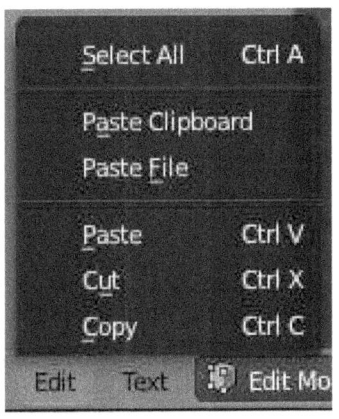

fig. 370 the text *Edit* menu in *Edit Mode*

C) *Text*

Let us finally analyze the commands present in the *Text* menu.

- **Insert Lorem** inserts the text *Lorem Ipsum Dolor...* into the selected text;

- **Toggle Small Caps** (CTRL + P) inserts the characters in small caps modality;

- **Toggle Underline** (CTRL + U) inserts underlined characters;

- **Toggle Italic** (CTRL + I) insert italic characters;

321

- *Toggle Bold* (CTRL + B) inserts bold characters;

- *Special Characters* opens a drop-down menu where you can choose which special character typology insert, chosen from the listed ones.

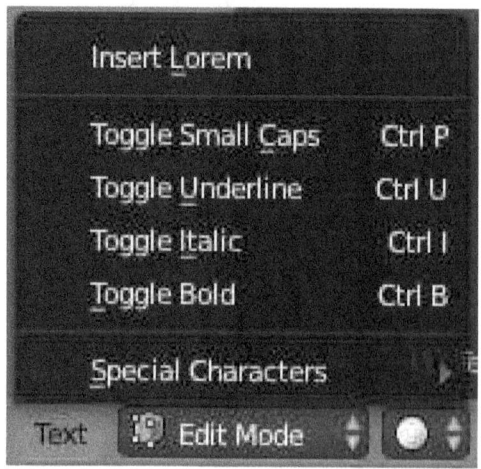

fig. 371 the *Text* menu of the *text* in *Edit Mode*

In the next chapter we will describe in detail the 3D modeling, analyzing one by one, with examples, the modifiers, tools acting in real time on the base geometry of the meshes and curves, and offering a wide range of applications.

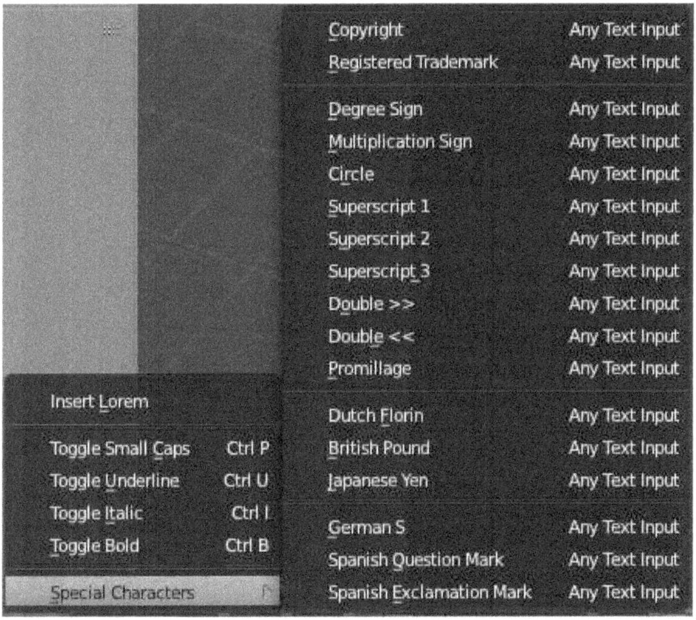

Copyright	Any Text Input
Registered Trademark	Any Text Input
Degree Sign	Any Text Input
Multiplication Sign	Any Text Input
Circle	Any Text Input
Superscript 1	Any Text Input
Superscript 2	Any Text Input
Superscript 3	Any Text Input
Double >>	Any Text Input
Double <<	Any Text Input
Promillage	Any Text Input
Dutch Florin	Any Text Input
British Pound	Any Text Input
Japanese Yen	Any Text Input
German S	Any Text Input
Spanish Question Mark	Any Text Input
Spanish Exclamation Mark	Any Text Input

Insert Lorem

Toggle Small Caps	Ctrl P
Toggle Underline	Ctrl U
Toggle Italic	Ctrl I
Toggle Bold	Ctrl B
Special Characters	

fig. 372 the *Special Characters* submenu

5
ADVANCED MODELING: MODIFIERS

5.1. What are the modifiers?

In this chapter we finally analyze the most advanced modeling. After you learned the basic concepts, you can now start to use new and very important tools, making the modeling much more systematic, complex and adaptable.

The use of some of these tools is quite common and frequent, whereas other tools are less used. As a matter of fact the power of the modifiers in modeling is almost unlimited.
But what are the modifiers?

They are dynamical modeling tools, i.e. they act on an object in real time. They can be enabled or disabled, regulated in any moment or applied to the object permanently.

While the various modifiers will be analyzed, you will notice that many of them present, though in general in a much more complete and advanced fashion, some of the commands and tools previously seen.

We want to stress that the modifiers are not tools alternative to those already analyzed for modifying and transforming an object. They act on objects differently, and can be freely placed in cascade, i.e. in sequence, yielding different results depending on their mutual position in the cascade.

Some modifiers have the same name of the modifying and transformation tools (for example *Mirror, Subdivision Surface, Bevel*). Sometimes they yield a similar result on the object where they have been applied, in other cases they turn out to be more complex and complete.

Summarizing, the transformation and modifying tools act directly on the object, transforming it permanently, whereas the modifiers act on the object with open parameters, which can be regulated anytime, until (but not necessarily) they will not be applied.

This is useful to have a control on the object, which will appear complex, with few points, the original ones.
Two main modifier categories exist: the **Generate** and **Deform** categories.

The former act on the object geometry, increasing or decreasing the vertex, edge and face numbers. The latter don't add or remove geometry, but deform it depending on certain parameters.

5.1.1. Assigning a modifier

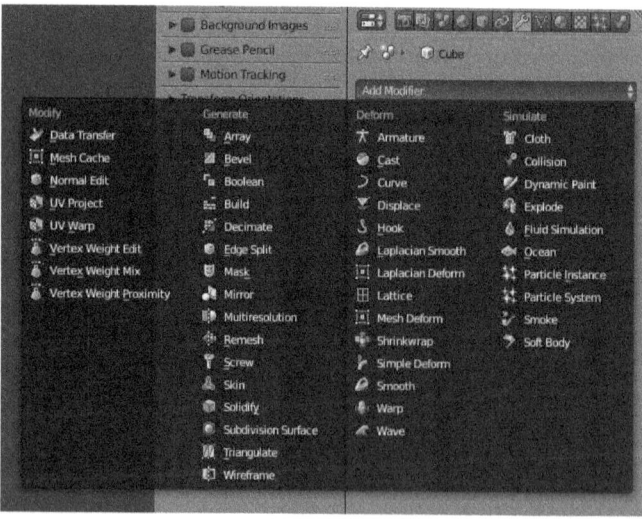

fig. 373 *Add Modifier* drop-down menu

For assigning a modifier to an object you only need, once the object has been selected, to click on the *tab* with the wrench (*Modifiers*) placed in the *Properties* editor. A panel will appear with the *Add Modifier* menu.

By clicking on the menu you will open a drop-down menu enclosing all the modifiers which can be assigned to an object, divided in 4 categories. For now we will only analyze the *Generate* and *Deform* categories.

Each assigned modifier will create in the *Properties* editor a dedicated panel where, valid in general, in the horizontal bar on the top you can find:

- The arrow for maximizing or minimizing the panel;
- The modifier symbol;
- The modifier name;
- The button with the camera managing, if activated, the application of the modifier to the object in rendering environment;
- The button with the eye managing, if activated, the application of the modifier to the object in 3D view modeling environment;
- The button with the cube with 4 highlighted vertices allowing you, if activated, to visualize the modifier outcome when the object is in *Edit Mode*;
- The button with three vertices joint in a triangle which, if activated, allows you to select also the generated elements belonging to the original geometry (vertices, edges and faces);
- The two buttons with the up and down arrows shift the modifier positions in the modifier cascade;
- The button X deletes the modifier and cancels its effect.

fig. 374 the buttons in a modifier head panel

Moreover, each modifier has two further buttons next to the head:

- *Apply* assigning the modifier to the object permanently, and transforming its geometry and shape;
- *Copy* copying all the modifier parameters to paste and repeat them in a modifier of the same kind in the cascade.

In the drop-down menu appearing after the modifier choice you can assign also other modifiers of different nature collected in two groups: **Modify** and **Simulate**. The former assign as a modifier, some functions related to image projection on a mesh, to cache, Vertex Group management etc. The latter automatically visualize as modifier all those operations on the physics and on the special effects, volumetric effects and simulations, which can be applied to an object from the suitable *Physics* and *Particle System* tabs.

This typology will be analyzed more in detail in the foregoing.

5.2. The Generate modifiers

As already said, the *Generate* modifiers actively operate on the geometry of the object they are assigned to.

The first modifier in the menu is **Array**.

This generates a series of linked duplicates of the selected object, similarly to the *Linked* Duplicate command (ALT + D), but in a more much complex way. In fact it is possible to define the number of linked duplicates and the way they will be placed in the 3D space with respect to the original.

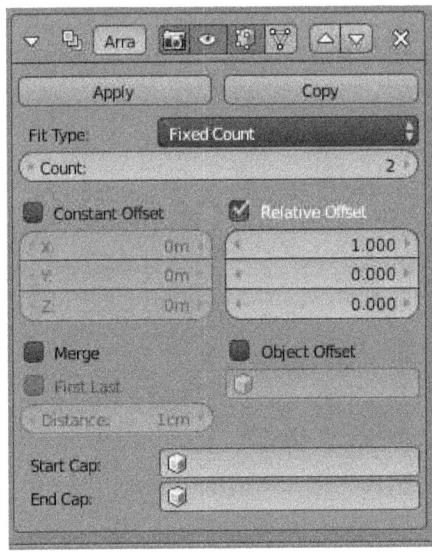

fig. 375 the *Array* panel

331

The **Fit Type** menu allows you to choose the linked duplicate adaptation method.

- *Fit Count* adapts the linked duplicates according to the logic of the number indicated in the repetitions (**Count**);
- *Fit Length* adapts the linked duplicates according the length specified in the **Length** counter appearing in the place of Count;
- *Fit Curve* adapts the liked duplicate disposition according to a curve specified in the **Curve** menu, choosing the curve among those available in the 3D scene.

Moreover, *Array* allows you to arrange the linked duplicates according to three different methodologies (whose outcomes can be eventually overlapped):

- By activating **Constant Offset**, a constant offset is fixed, along to the x, y and z axes, i.e. a fixed distance between the linked duplicates. For example by fixing the value of x at 3 meters for a cube with edges equal to 2 meters?????, the linked duplicates will be spaced by 1 meter, i.e. 3 meters from corresponding vertices;

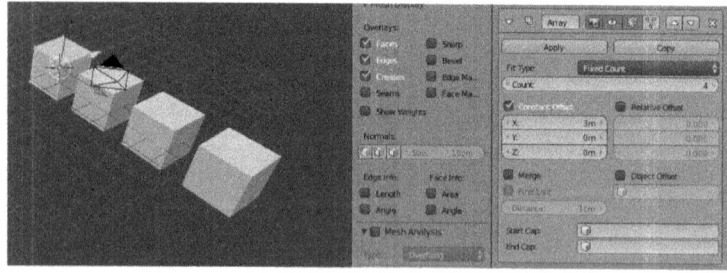

fig. 376 *Constant Offset*

- **Relative Offset** places the linked duplicates along the three axes at a distance (integer or decimal) equal to n times the object length along the three axes. For example, assigning to the cube a relative offset equal to 1 (one time itself) for all the three directions, the linked duplicates will be placed by shifting the cube of the edge length along *x*, *y* and *z* direction.

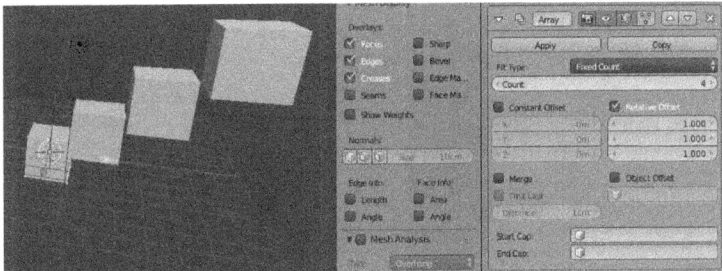

fig. 377 *Relative Offset*

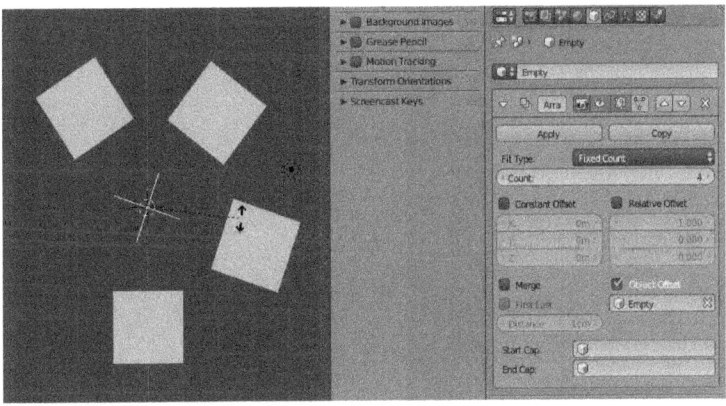

fig. 378 *Object Offset*: by rotating the *Empty* the squares rotate around it

- **Object Offset** determines the linked duplicate placement depending in the behavior of an external object, usually an *Empty*, in the 3D space. The linked duplicates will adapt to the placing, the rotation and also the scaling of the object they refer to as target, and also to the possible deformations the object can undergo to.

> **NOTE: It is essential that the rotation, position and scaling are reset with CTRL +A for the correct operation of the Array modifier on the object on which is applied.**

The flag **Merge** allows you to consider merged the coinciding vertices after the application of the *Array* modifier, avoiding to have duplicate vertices.

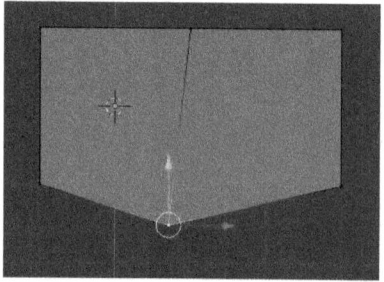

fig. 379 vertices merged with *Merge* after the application of the *Array*

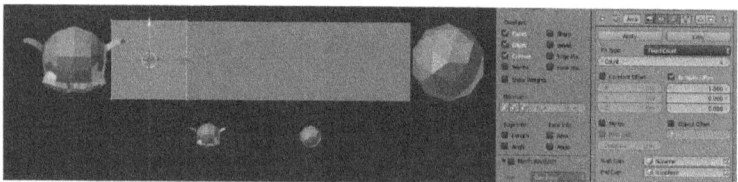

fig. 380 head links

First Last joins the vertices of the first and last linked duplicates.
Start Cap and ***End Cap*** assumes as head links of a linked duplicate sequence, two objects external to the one on which the *Array* modifier is applied. In the image, *Monkey* (*Suzanne*) and an icosphere are used, respectively, as head links of the sequence of 4 linked duplicates of a cube.

EXERCISE n. 10: REALIZATION OF A STAIR

One of the simplest applications of the *Array* is the realization of a stair, starting from a single step.
First model the base step. It will be, in a simplified way, a parallelepiped of dimensions:

$$x = 1 \text{ m}; \ y = 30 \text{ cm}; \ z = 15 \text{ cm}.$$

Reset the scale with CTRL + A and apply the *Array* modifier.

Enter in *Edit Mode* and insert a horizontal *Loop* at 2 cm from the top edge.

Select the top horizontal surface relevant to the step long edge and extrude it outward of 2 cm, such as to create the drip-catcher.

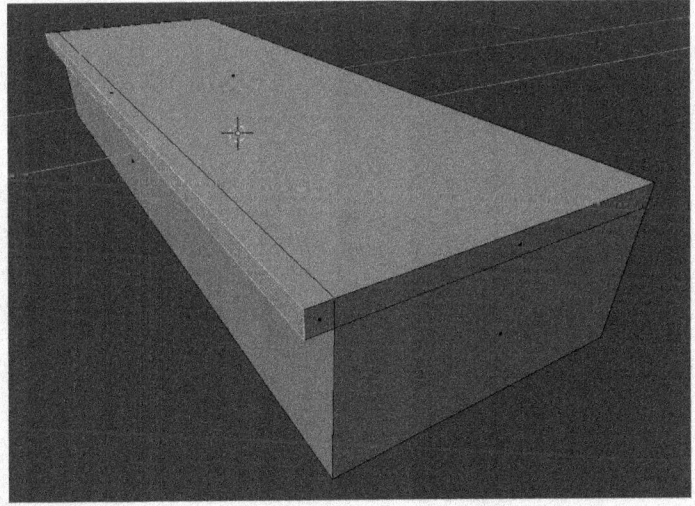

fig. 381 extrusion of the drip-catcher

Select now the 4 lateral faces and extrude them outward of 2 cm with *Extrude Individual*.

In this way you have created also the lateral drip-catchers.

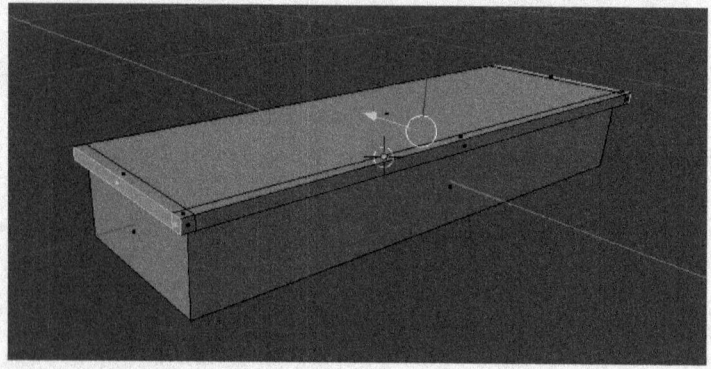

fig. 382 extrusion of the lateral drip-catchers

Apply the *Array* to the mesh and set 10 repetitions (*Count*). For managing the linked duplicate shift, set a mix between the *Relative Offset* for z (1 time itself in z direction) and *Constant Offset* for the y of 30 cm fixed.

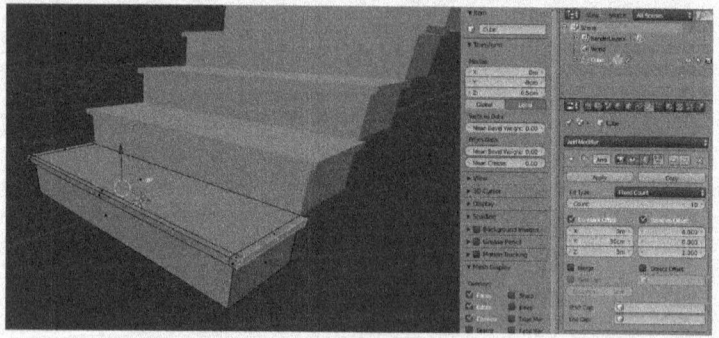

fig. 383 application of the *Array* to the step

Now, you only need to give a thickness to the beam.

Enter in *Edit Mode* and select the two back faces, then extrude them of 30 cm.

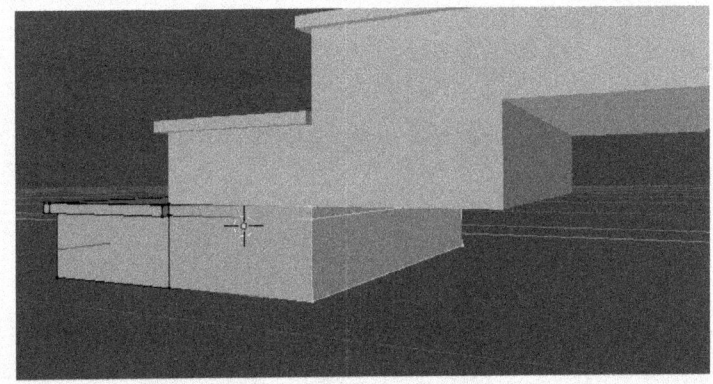

fig. 384 extrusion of the step back faces

Select now the three back vertices on the left of the step extruded faces, starting from the lowest one.

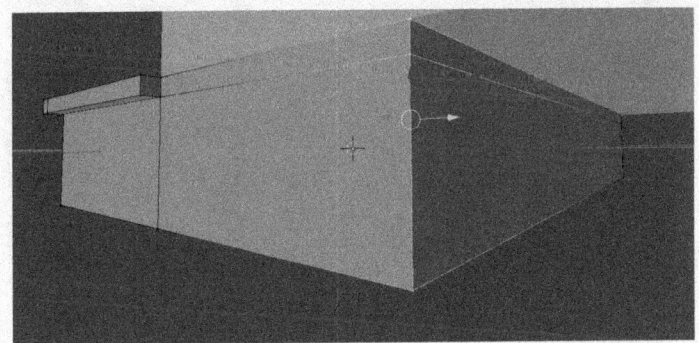

fig. 385 vertex selection

Choose in the *Tools Shelf At Last* from the *Merge* menu to merge
the three points in the last selected position (the active one).

Finally repeat the same operation for the three vertices on the
step right side.

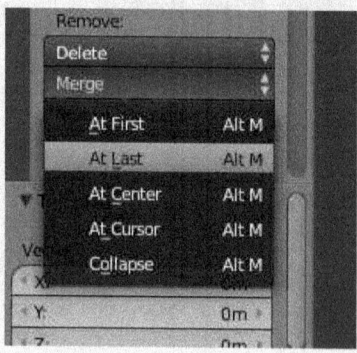

fig. 386 *Merge At Last*

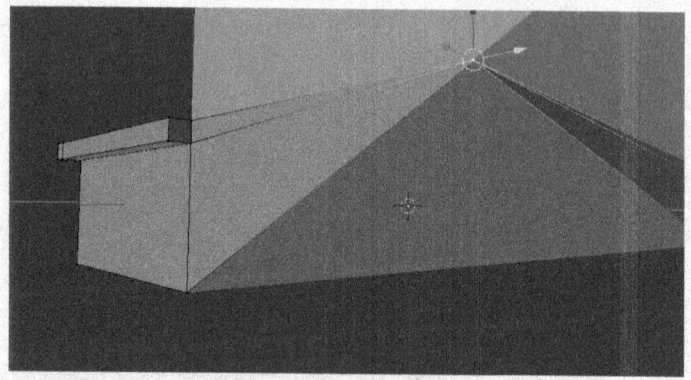

fig. 387 the outcome of the merging of the three vertices on the left side

Triangular faces will be created. However, since they belong to a
flat surface, they will not affect the shading and will not prevent
a correct visualization in *rendering* phase.

Alternatively, you can delete with X + *Dissolve Edge* the edge shared by the two triangular faces, subdivide with W - *Subdivide* the lower diagonal beam edge and, with *Knife*, join the opposite vertices, generating two quadrangles.

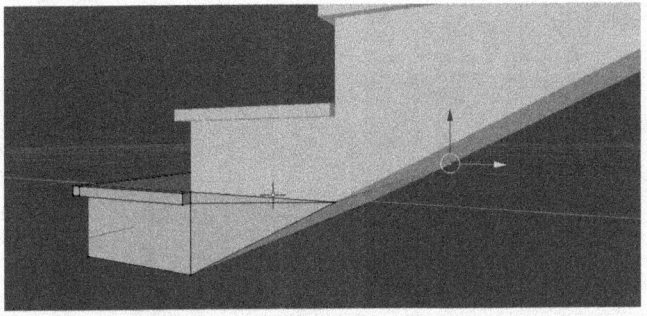

fig. 388 the outcome of the merging of the three vertices on the right side

The stair is finished.

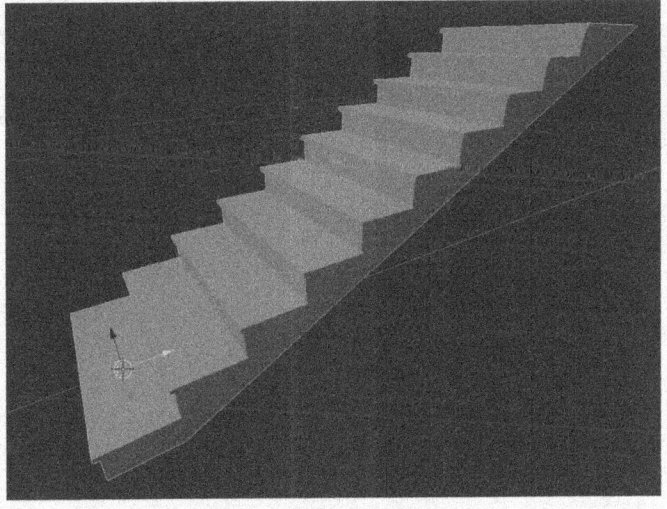

fig. 389 The completed stair

The second, very used modifier is **Bevel**.

This modifier, once applied to a mesh, produces an edge bevel or rounding.

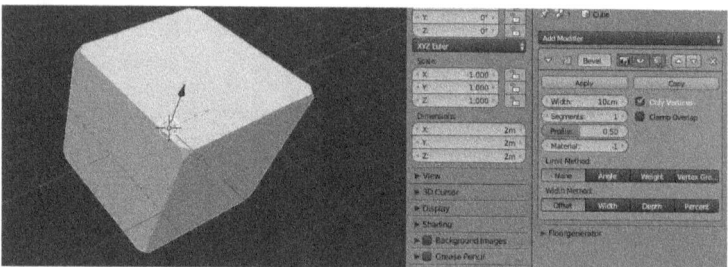

fig. 390 the *Bevel* modifier assigned to a cube

This modifier produces an outcome much similar to the homonym tool in the *Tools Shelf*, with the difference that the modifier acts on all the *mesh* edges and vertices.

Once assigned to a mesh, automatically, *Bevel* rounds by a value of 10 cm all the edges of the mesh itself.

It is possible to set some parameters.

- **Width** defines the bevel dimension.
- **Segments** defines the number of segments producing a rounding (larger values) rather a simply bevel, with cut at 45° (value 1).
- **Profile** determines the shape of the beveled profile. A value ranging from 0.15 (profile inward beveled) to 1 (sharp profile, not beveled) can be set.

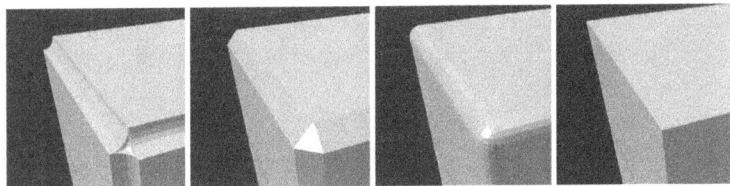

fig. 391 *Bevel* assigned to a cube with 6 division segments and the *Profile* set (from left to right) respectively to 0.15, 0.25, 0.50, 1

- **Material** determines the material comprising the faces created by the *Bevel*, by means of an index (*Index*). This index can be assigned to a material, as we will show in the foregoing. The value - 1 (a fictitious value, since the *Index* is numerated starting from 0) automatically assigns the mesh main material to the beveled faces.

- The flag on **Only Vertices** generates the bevel only on the vertices excluding the edges.

fig. 392 the outcome of the option *Only Vertices* assigning the bevel only to the vertices

341

- *Clamp Overlap* prevents the *Bevel* with a *Width* value large with respect to the mesh dimensions, from creating edges or faces overlaps.

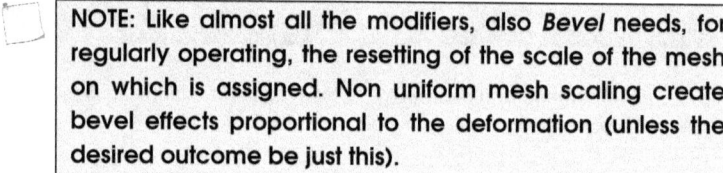

> **NOTE: Like almost all the modifiers, also *Bevel* needs, for regularly operating, the resetting of the scale of the mesh on which is assigned. Non uniform mesh scaling create bevel effects proportional to the deformation (unless the desired outcome be just this).**

- *Limit Method* determines the edges and vertices on which the *Bevel* modifier must be applied, according to 4 modalities:

  • *None* makes the bevel uniformly on all the edges and vertices;
  • *Angle* makes the *Bevel* only on the edges between faces forming an enough acute angle;
  • *Weight* uses the *Bevel Weights* parameters placed into the *Transform* panel of the *Properties Bar* for determining the bevel strength on the various edges where a value of *Bevel Weight* has been set;
  • *Vertex Group* makes the *Bevel* only on the edges and vertices grouped by a specific *Vertex Group* to be indicated in the suitable menu.

- *Width Method* determines *Bevel* behavior type according to 4 possibilities:

  • *Offset* enforces that the *Bevel* must be the result of an offset from the original vertices and edges;
  • *Width* enforces that the Bevel value be the real length of the new created face/faces;
  • *Depth* enforces that the Bevel value be the distance from the edge;
  • *Percent* set the bevel value as a percentage of the adjacent edge length.

The **Boolean** modifier must be carefully used, and only if really necessary.

Remember that an important characteristic for a correct modeling and a control of the geometry is that the latter is composed as much as possible by quadrangles.

Boolean mathematically computes the union, the subtraction or the intersection between two meshes. This fact, though a nice result can be achieved, makes possible the unavoidable formation of triangular or n-sided (*ngon*) faces.

Boolean, once assigned to a *mesh*, allows you to make boolean operations on it.

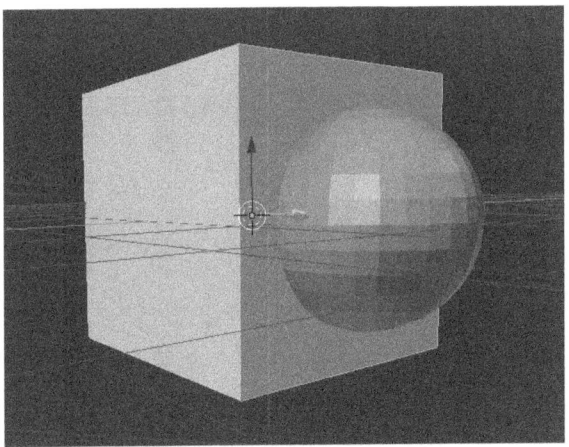

fig. 393 two intersecting meshes on which a boolean operation can be performed

In order to perform a *boolean* operation on a selected *mesh*, the presence of another mesh in the 3D view is necessary, which is the operation object.

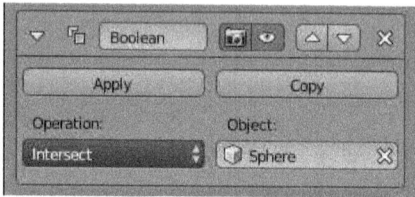

fig. 394 the *Boolean* panel

Once the assigned operation as been applied with *Apply*, the original mesh will be transformed in the operation outcome. It will be then possible to remove the second mesh, which is the operation object.

Operation allows you to choose the boolean operation type, chosen from:

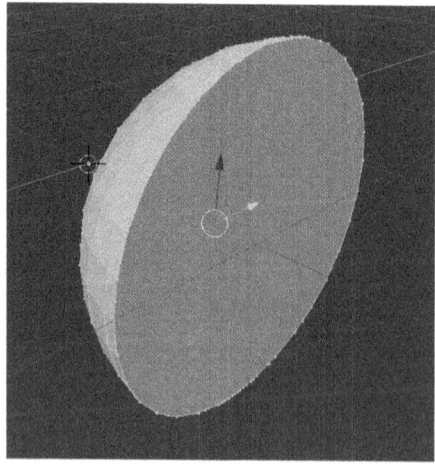

fig. 395 the outcome of the *Intersect* operation

- *Intersect*, performing the intersection between the selected mesh and the intersection object mesh (***Object***).
- U*nion* generates a solid composed by the union between the selected mesh and the object one.

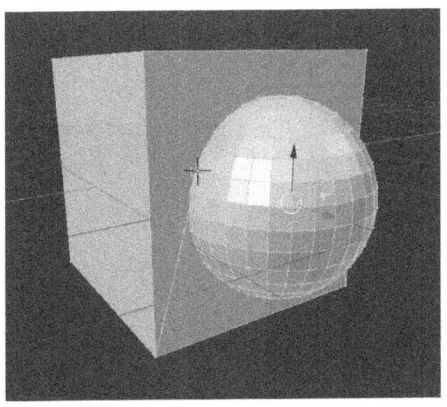

fig. 396 the outcome of the *Union* operation

- *Difference* performs a subtraction between the selected mesh and the object one.

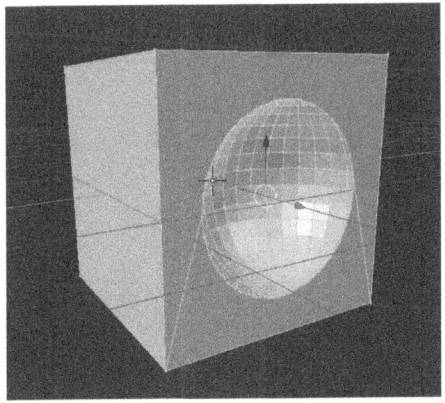

fig. 397 the outcome of the *Difference* operation

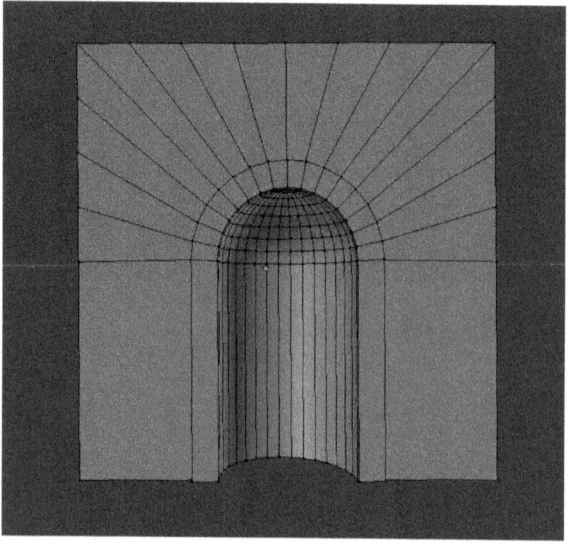

fig. 398 the geometry of this niche, object of a boolean operation, has been corrected by hands, recreating loops and quadrangular faces

BUILD

Build is a funny modifier of *Generate* type allowing you, thanks to the use of an animation, to assemble or disassemble a *mesh* suitably subdivided previously (for example with the shortcut W and the *Subdivide* option).

fig. 399 the panel relevant to the *Build* modifier

Start and **Length** refer to the frames of the *Timeline*, i.e., respectively the starting frame and the frame number for the animation duration. In order to visualize the outcome of the *Build* modifier i twill be necessary, in fact, to launch the animation with ALT + A.

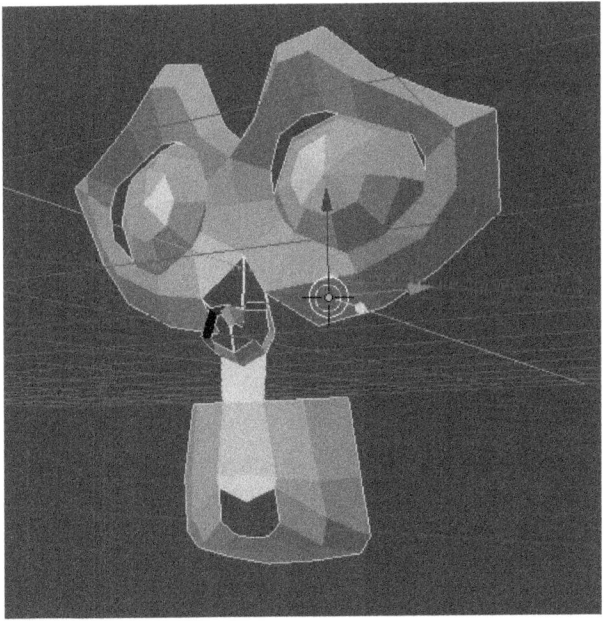

fig. 400 *Suzanne* during construction, face after face

The **Reversed** flag inverts the command, i.e. de-assembles the mesh, face after face, until it disappears during the indicated frame duration.

The **Randomize** flag operates the mesh assembling or de-assembling according to a random logic, whereas in the **Seed** counter the random configuration associated to *Randomize* can be numerated.

DECIMATE

Decimate tries to simplify the mesh geometry, suitable subdivided and being enough detailed.

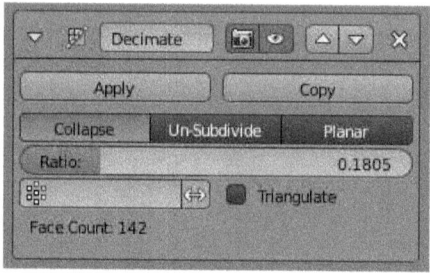

fig. 401 the panel relevant to the *Decimate* modifier with the *Collapse* method

The modifier acts on the *mesh* according to some parameters and the method chosen from:

- *Collapse* simplifies the mesh, collapsing some vertices;
- *Un-subdivide* generates an algorithm inverse to the face subdivision. As a matter of facts it does not subdivide;
- *Planar* simplifies the *mesh* try to flatten the faces thus making the solid sharper.

fig. 402 the outcome on Suzanne of the *Decimate* modifier

All the three methods activate different submenu and specific settings. Let us analyze them in detail.

1) *Collapse*

The **Ratio** cursor, available only for the *Collapse* method, determines the amount of mesh simplification. The value is inversely proportional to the modifier action (0 = maximum simplification, 1 = no simplification).

The flag **Triangulate**, available only for the *Collapse* method, makes the algorithm to generate triangular faces during the geometry simplification process.

The menu with the icon of the **Vertex Group** assigns the simplification, valid only for the *Collapse* method, to the selected *Vertex Group*.

fig. 403 the *Vertex Group* menu

The present number of faces is indicated below (**Face Count**).

2) *Un-Subdivide*

The **Iterations** cursor (values from 0 to 100) is available with the *Un-Subdivide* method and determines the number of iterations for going back in the subdivision process.

fig. 404 the panel relevant to the *Decimate* modifier with the *Un-Subdivide* method

3) *Planar*

Angle Limit dissolves only the edges below the specified angle (from 0° to 180°).

The flag **All Boundaries** dissolves all the vertices placed at the boundaries of adjacent coplanar faces.

Delimit determines the geometry merging limit and gives three possibilities:

- *Normal*, according to the face normals;
- *Material*, according to the assigned material;

-   *Seam*, keeping the unwrapping margins (*unwrap*).

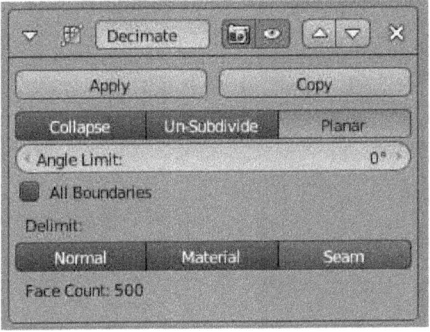

fig. 405 the panel relevant to the *Decimate* modifier with the *Planar* method

This useful modifier prevents the *Smooth* command to operate on flat surfaces yielding shading artifacts.

fig. 406 the *Smooth* command (cube on the left) generates shading artifacts on flat surfaces. By applying the *Edge Split* the shadings are respected

Usually this modifier is assigned when the *Smooth* or the *Bevel* is present, when you want to preserve the linearity of the flat surfaces, achieving at the same time a rounded effect of the piecewise constant entities.

For example the bevel of a lacquered wood panel will be rounded, whereas the flat surface will not produce the same kind of shading.

First a 4 division *Bevel* has been applied, then a *Smooth* and finally an *Edge Split*, to modify the shading on the flat surfaces.

fig. 407 the correct shading of the bevels and the flat surfaces

Let us examine the parameters of the *Edge Split* modifier.

Edge Angle determines the angle between two faces below which the modifier will operate.

Sharp Edges sharply divides the shading between the edges marked as *Mark Sharp* in the *Edges* menu (CTRL + E).

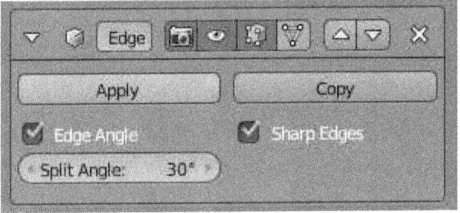

fig. 408 the panel relevant to the *Edge Split* modifier

fig. 409 the *Mark Sharp* option

MASK

Mask makes visible, in a *mesh* on which this modifier is assigned, only the vertices collected in a **Vertex Group** specified in the modifier menu or associated to an armature (**Armature**), useful for the *rigging* and placement of a *character*.

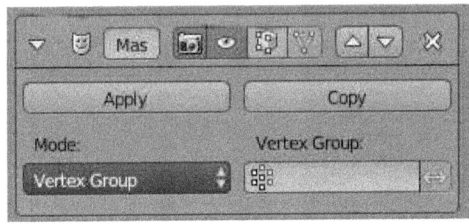

fig. 410 the panel relevant to the *Mask* modifier

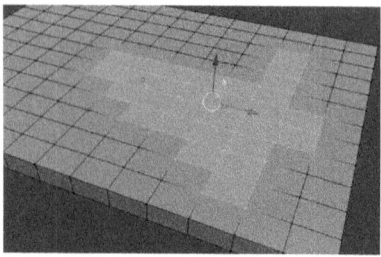 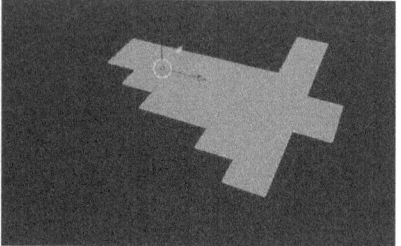

fig. 411 a vertex group (image on the left) is associated to a *Vertex Group* and is made visible (hiding the rest of the *mesh)* with the *Mask* modifier

MIRROR

Mirror is a very useful modifier used for creating a mirrored copy of a selected object, according to one or more assigned symmetry axes, an external object like an *Empty,* or other specific parameters.

fig. 412 the panel relevant to the *Mirror* modifier

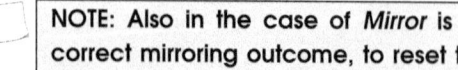

NOTE: Also in the case of *Mirror* is very important, for a correct mirroring outcome, to reset the scale, the position and the rotation of the selected object.

The mirroring occurs according to one or the three axes x, y e z (**Axis**) at the same time, with respect to the object origin. This means that if we are trying to mirror an object with regular shape with respect to its center of gravity, the outcome will be almost identical to the original object.

For example, insert a *Monkey*, shift and rotate it, then, with the key combination SHIFT + CTRL + ALT + C shift the origin making it to coincide with the *3D Cursor* (*Origin To 3D Cursor*).

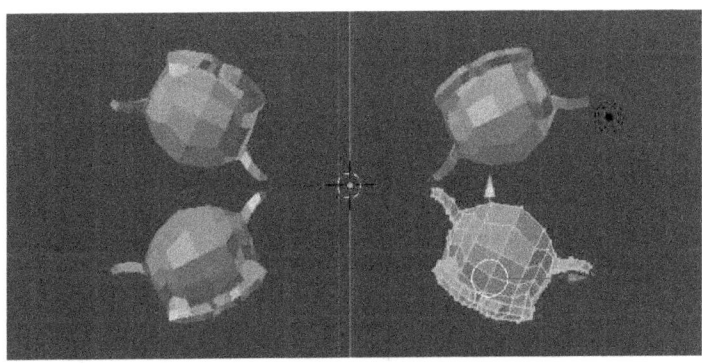

fig. 413 a double *Mirror* (x and y) on *Monkey*

fig. 414 mirroring along x and y with respect to an *Empty* translated and rotated in turn

355

Check *x* and *y* in the *Mirror* panel and see how the monkey will be mirrored with respect to the *x* and *y* axis at the same time.

The mirroring can occur also with respect to another object (usually an *Empty*), by inserting the object name in the **Mirror Object** menu.

Clipping, if checked, prevents, in the event of interpenetration of the object with its mirrored copy, the interpenetrated vertices from going below the symmetry axis, whereas **Merge** merges the coinciding vertices, avoiding the presence of overlapped vertices after the modifier action.

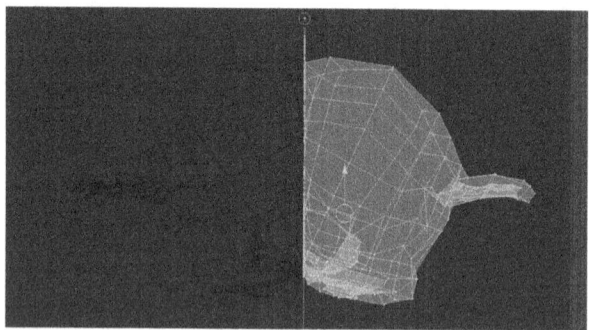

fig. 415 mirroring with *Clipping*

Merge Limit determines the maximum distance within which the vertices will be merged, if the *Merge* flag is activated.

The check on **Vertex Group** mirrors the vertices belonging to a group, if present, whereas the checks on **U** and **V** mirror also the texture mapped on the mesh along its relative coordinates *u, v*, with respect to the image center.

Mirror is a very useful and versatile tool. By exploding the mirroring according to three directions, you can work on the base element, automatically modifying also the mirrored elements. A typical example is the construction of a column capital: you need to work any on half (or event a quarter) of this element to get the full figure.

EXERCISE n. 11: REALIZATION OF A COLUMN STEM USING THE MIRROR, EDGE SPLIT AND ARRAY MODIFIERS

In this exercise we will show how simple and fast can be to build the stem of a classic column.

Insert a 24 segment sphere and, in *Edit Mode*, in top view (7 NUM), first delete half of the lower vertices, then repeat the same operation in front view (1 NUM), deleting half of the upper vertices. Only a quarter of sphere will be left.

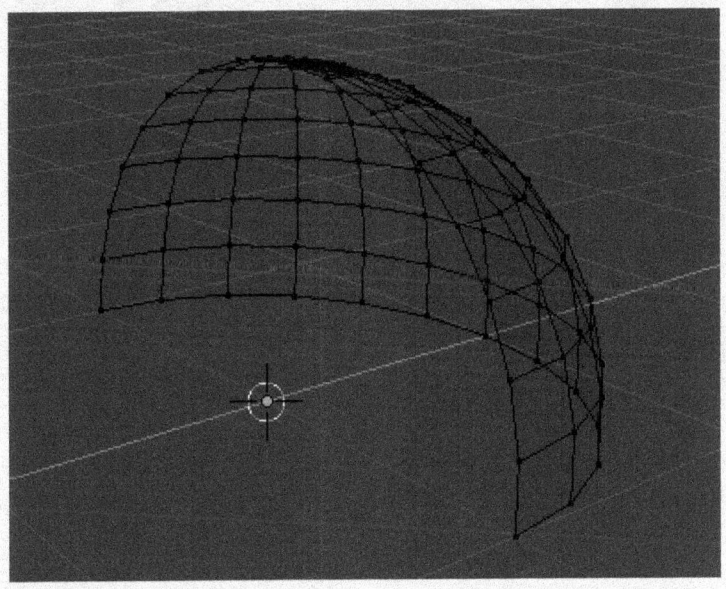

fig. 416 a quarter of sphere

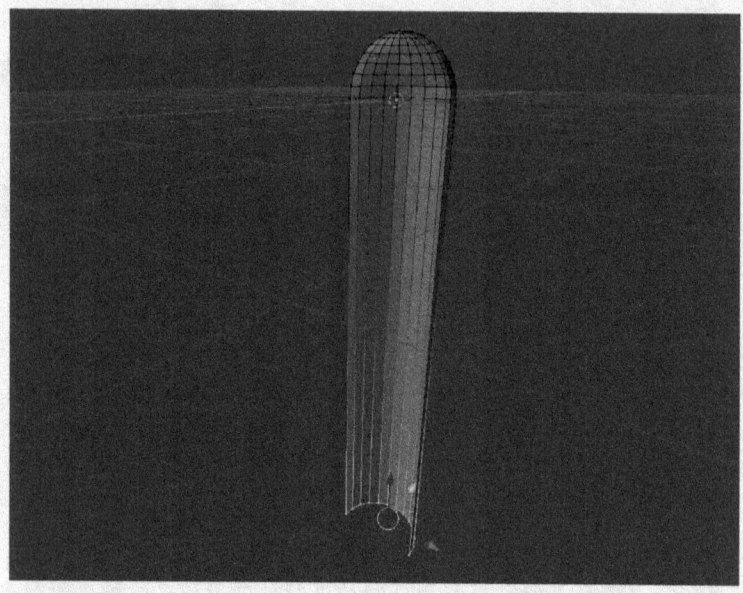

fig. 417 extrusion of the base *loop*

Now select the *loop* of the base vertices and extrude downward. Invert the face normals with *Flip Direction*.

Select now, in front view (1 NUM), the left half part of the element and apply a *Mirror* modifier with respect to the *x* axis, activating the *Merge* and *Clipping* options.

Select now the external boundary and extrude it to the right (E, X) of a small amount, then rescale these vertices by 0 with respect to the *x* axis for vertically aligning them.

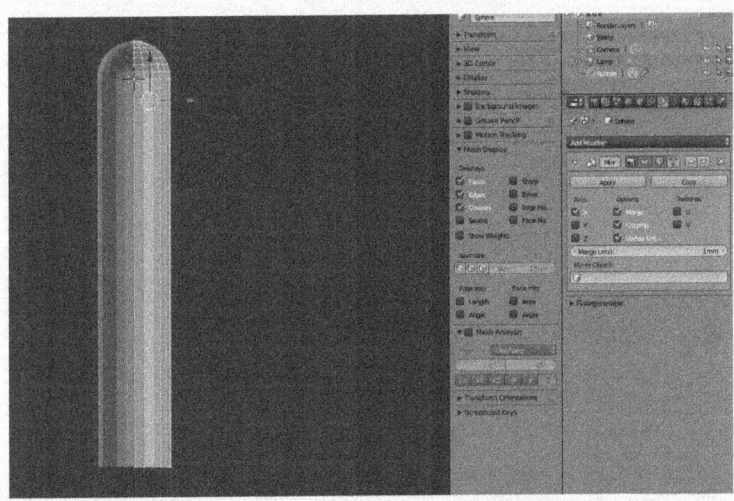

fig. 418 *Mirror* on half of the groove

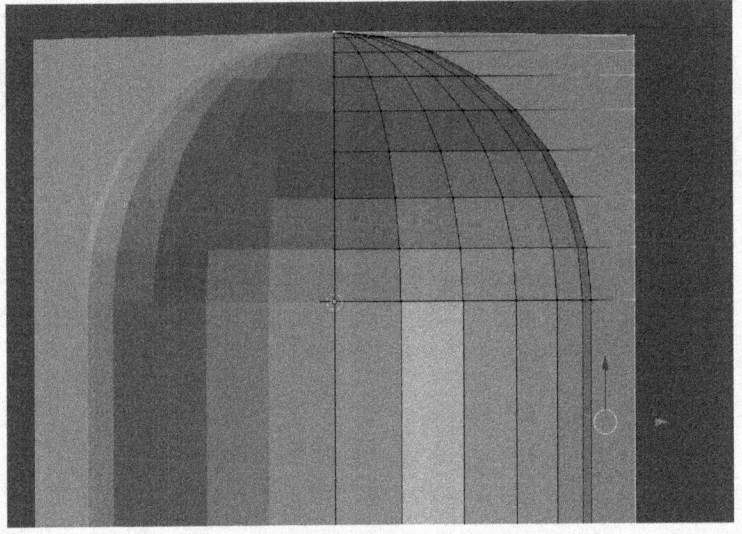

fig. 419 boundary extrusion and scaling on *x* of 0

Note the triangular face on the top. To remove it, subdivide in two (W, *Subdivide*) the top segment and align with the magnet the new vertex, first on *x* and then on *z*.

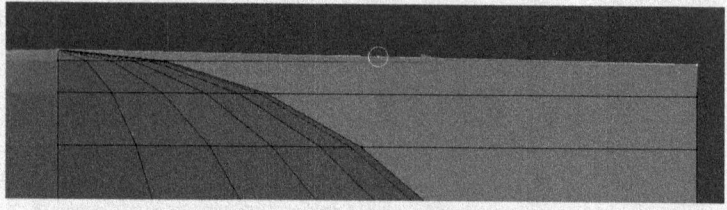

fig. 420 top segment subdivision

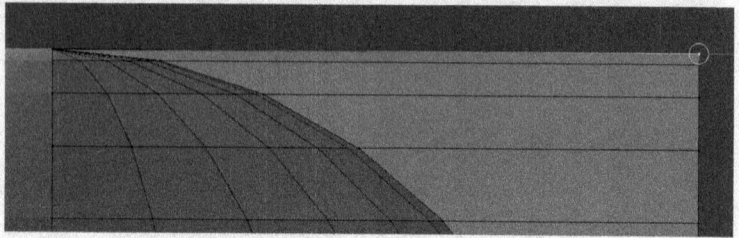

fig. 421 alignment on *x* and *z* of the new vertex

Select now the top edge and extrude it upward.
Return in *Object Mode* and create a 24 segment circle, rotating it of 7.5 degrees and scaling it such that each segment measures as the width along *x* of the built groove.

Then select the circle segment on the bottom in *Edit Mode* and type SHIFT + S, choosing the *Cursor to Selected* option.

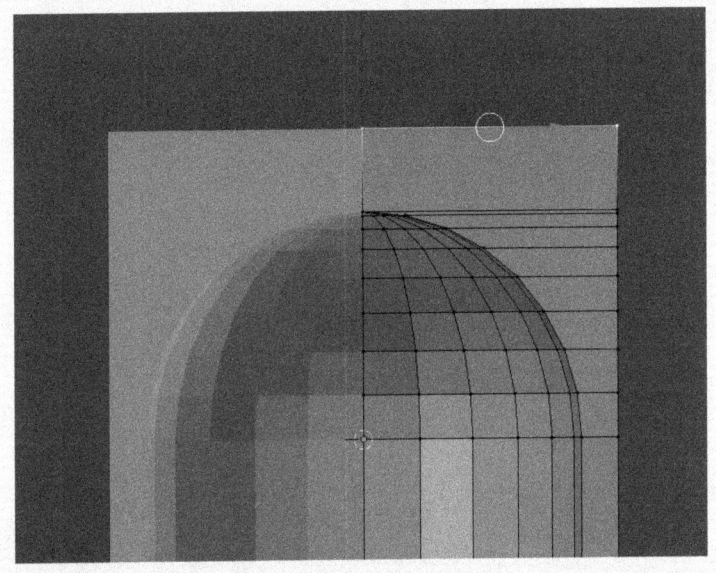

fig. 422 extrusion of the top part

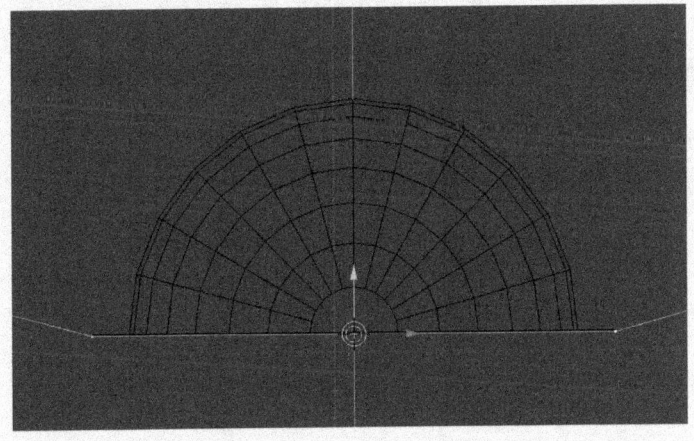

fig. 423 placement of the *3D Cursor* at the center of the circle segment

Reset the scale.

With the two vertices selected, read in the *Properties Bar* the *x* position. This will be the segment length, which should coincide with the groove *x* dimension.

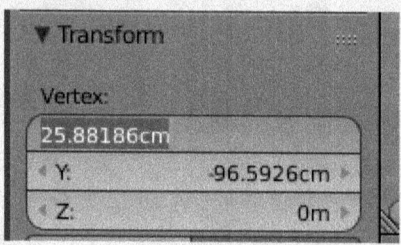

fig. 424 segment dimension

Copy the value in the box with CTRL + C, then return in *Object Mode*, select the groove object, already suitably proportioned and copy with CTRL + V the previous measure in the *x* dimensional box in the *Properties Bar*.

Finally, with SHIFT + S, choose the option *Selection To Cursor* for making the groove origin coincident with the *3D Cursor*.

Place then the *3D Cursor* at the center (SHIF + S and *Cursor To Selected*), insert an *Empty* object and assign to the groove the *Array* modifier.

Reset also the groove object location, then set the *Object Offset* parameter of the *Array* to *Empty*.

Activate the *Merge* and assign 24 repetitions (*Count*).
Finally rotate of 15 degrees the *Empty* object and look to the result.

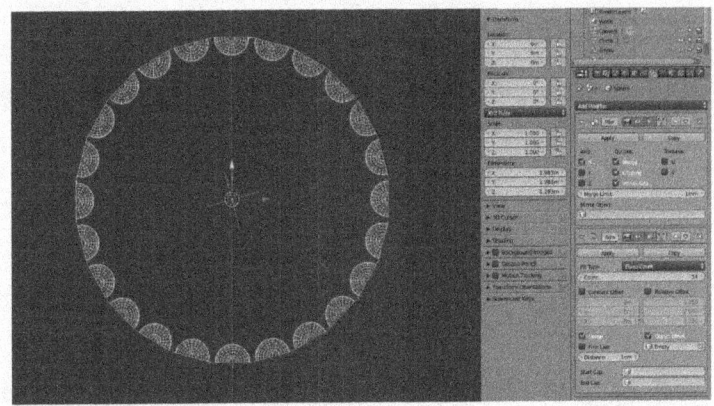

fig. 425 *Array*

Add the *Smooth* and the *Edge Split* modifier to the column.

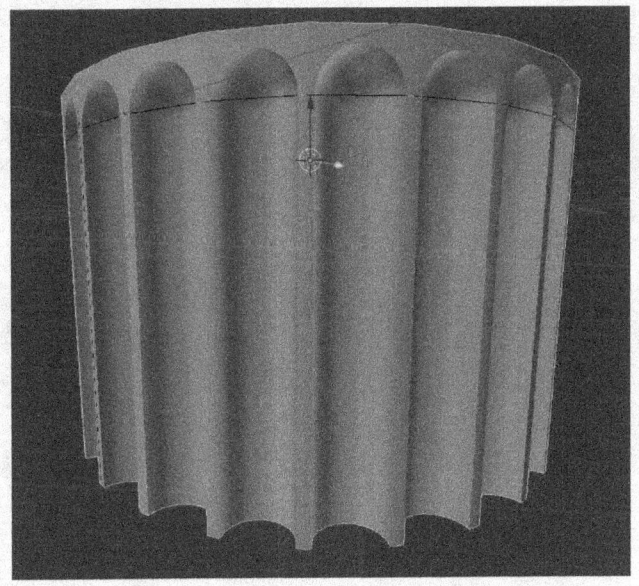

fig. 426 the column with the *Smooth* and the *Edge Split* applied

Multiresolution is a modifier very similar to the **Subdivision Surface**, which we will analyze in more detail in the foregoing.

This modifier subdivides the mesh geometry uniformly along the three directions and tries at the same time to smoothen it.

The closer will be two or more loops, less rounded and less sharp the mesh will result.

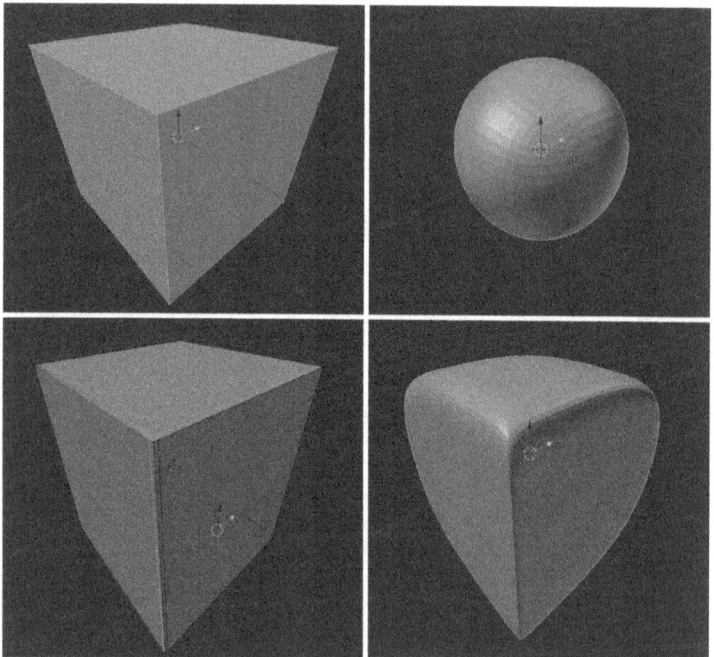

fig. 427 from left to right and from top to bottom: cube in *Edit Mode*, cube in *Object Mode* with 4 divisions *Multiresolution*; cube in *Edit Mode* with two added *loops* near an edge, cube with *loops* in *Object Mode*. Note the cusp reducing the roundness in correspondence of the edge and the loops

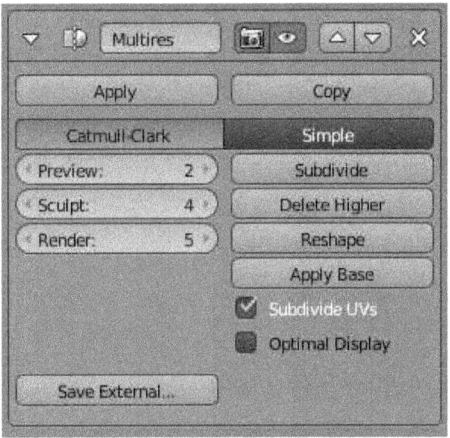

fig. 428 the *Multiresolution* panel

The panel interface of this modifier is less simple, but definitely more complete than the one of the *Subdivision Surface*.

On the top you can find the double switch determining the algorithm between *Catmull-Clark* and *Simple*. The latter preserves the mesh original shape, without rounding it.

Just below, on the left, there are three counters indicating the number of mesh subdivisions respectively in pre visualization phase, i.e. in the 3D view (*Preview*), in *Sculpt Mode* ambient and in final rendering (*Render*). Differently from the *Subdivision Surface*, in fact, the *Sculpt* ambient is added and even different subdivision values can be given to the three ambients. Usually a lower number of subdivisions is chosen for the pre visualization, not to weigh down the system, especially in case of very complex scenes.

On the right the **Subdivide** button, pressed many times, add subdivisions to the *mesh*. For example, if we want to subdivide 4 times, the button must be pressed 4 times. Once assigned, the subdivision number can be varied in the three *Preview*, *Sculpt* and *Render* ambients.

Delete Higher reduces to the lower level the subdivision number set in *Preview*, *Sculpt* and *Render*.

Reshape assigns to the mesh vertices the same vertex coordinates of another analogous mesh. In order to use this command, you first need to select a different mesh object with similar vertices, then holding pressed SHIFT, select the object where you want to copy the vertex coordinates and click *Reshape*.

Apply Base modifies the original not subdivided *mesh* giving it the shape of the subdivided mesh.

Activating **Subdivide UVs**, also the UV mappings will be subdivided, i.e. the coordinates for all the new faces created by the modifier will be virtually added.

If the check **Optimal Display**, in *Wireframe* visualization, is activated, the wires of the new subdivided edges will not be colored in light orange during the mesh selection in *Object mode*. As a matter of facts, only the edges corresponding with those of the original geometry will be colored.

Save External saves the *displacement*, i.e. the new vertex quotes, in an external *.btx* file.

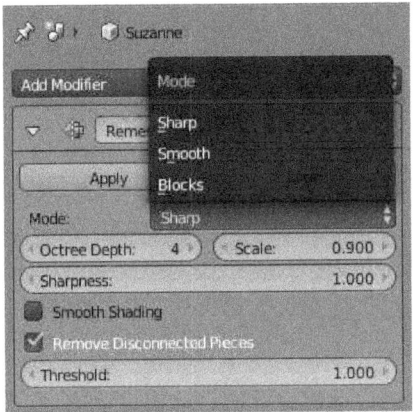

fig. 429 the *Remesh* panel

Remesh tries to create a new and different topology to the *mesh* on which the modifier is assigned.

It is a modifier useful for fixing corrupted meshes, or meshes subdivided with *ngon* or triangular surfaces, or text converted into *mesh* from which the triangles must be removed, or for creating particular shapes starting from an original mesh.

The **Mode** menu allows you to choose the operation methodology from the options:

- *Smooth*, subdividing the mesh with faces such as to obtain a surface the most rounded as possible;
- *Sharp*, which, similarly to *Smooth*, rounds a surface, but preserving the main angularities of the original mesh;
- *Bricks*, which, with the geometry subdivision, makes the mesh the less rounded as possible, producing a brick effect.

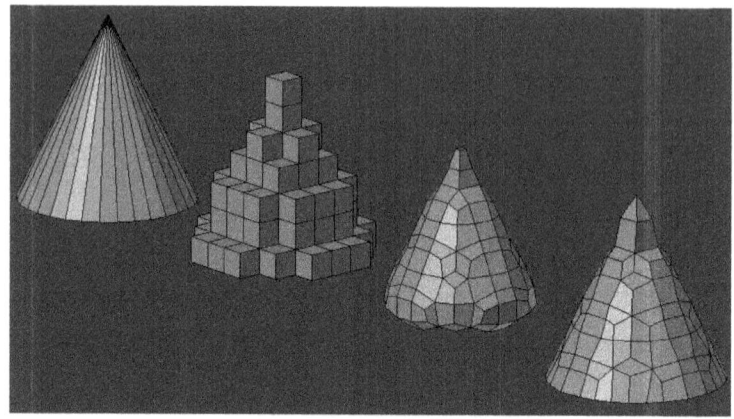

fig. 430 from left to right: the original cone, with the *Bricks* option, with the *Smooth* and with *Sharp*

Insert for example a cone and apply to it the *Remesh* modifier, testing the three options.

Note the difference between *Smooth* and *Sharp*, where *Sharp* preserves the angularity with the cone base.

Octree Depth regulates the effect resolution, for which at low values, faces of larger dimensions will be obtained and thus lower resolution, whereas in correspondence of higher values, smaller faces and hence greater detail.

Scale sets a fine resolution regulation such as to achieve greater detail for lower values.

Sharpness is a parameter available only with the *Sharp* option and determines the edge sharpness for higher inserted values.

Smooth Shading forces the shading in smooth mode instead of flat (*flat*) analogously to the *Smooth* command in the *Tools Shelf*.

Remove Disconnected Pieces automatically removes *mesh* elements disconnected from the main ones.

Threshold determines the dimensional threshold value for the disconnected element to be removed.

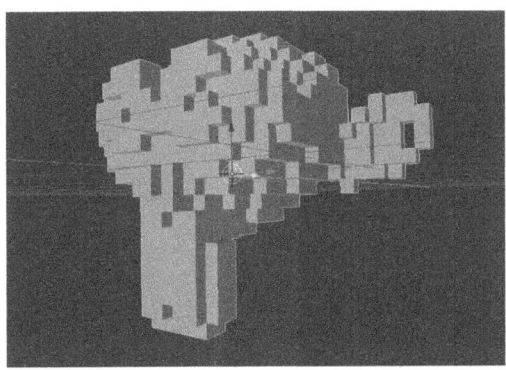

fig. 431 *Suzanne* visualized after the application of *Remesh* with *Bricks* modality

fig. 432 a text in 3D transformed into *mesh* (top) and then modified with *Remesh* (bottom) the *ngon* or triangular faces have been converted into quadrangles

Screw operates similarly to the corresponding tools of the *Tools Bar*, *Spin* and *Screw*, joining their functions.

fig. 433 the *Screw* panel

Screw generates a revolution solid starting from a *mesh* or a *curve*, around a specific revolution axis (**Axis**).

AxisO sets an external object as revolution axis (rotation around an object).

Angle determines the revolution degree number (from 0 to 360) around the axis.

Steps sets the number of steps, or better, of slices in the arch set in Angle, determining the detail and resolution of the generated revolution solid. For lower values the solid will appear sharp, whereas for higher values, will appear rounded and smooth.

Render Steps assigns the step number to the final render.
The check on **Smooth Shading**, analogously to that of the *Remesh* modifier, smoothens the *mesh* shading.

370

The **Screw** parameter is fundamental. It generates the screwing effect in the symmetry axis direction. It is very useful when you want to model the screw or bolt thread, a circular flight of stairs and other screw solids.

Object Screw is activated with *AxisO* and set as screw value the distance between the origins of two objects.

Calc Order re-computes and reorders the mesh edges (does not work with the curves).

Flip re-computes and inverts the mesh normals directed inside the revolution solid.

Iterations sets the screw spin number.

Stretch U and **Stretch V** stretch the mapping coordinates in U and V directions, if assigned to the *mesh*.

 EXERCISE n. 12: CREATION OF A SCREW

In this exercise we will briefly model a screw starting from a vertex sequence placed like in the figure.

Remember to reset the scale, position and rotation.

Note (or copy) the mesh height (*z*), add then the *Screw* modifier. Set 360°, *z* as revolution axis, 16 *steps*, the *mesh* height as *Screw* value and at least 6 *Iterations*.

Check then the *Smooth Shading* option for smoothing the shadings of the rounded regions and add the *Edge Split* modifier for preventing the shading of the flat regions.

The outcome (very simple) should be the following one.

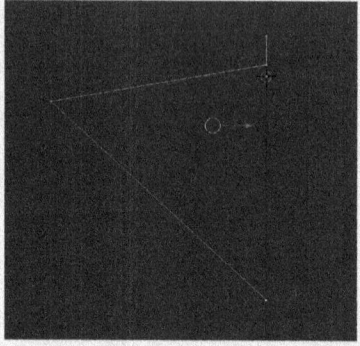

fig. 434 profile of the revolution solid

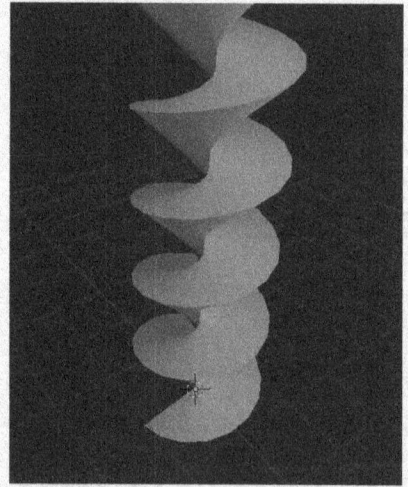

fig. 435 the screwed revolution solid

Try to model with the *Screw* modifier the glass considered in the exercises n. 8 and 9, starting from the mesh and curve profile.

The **Skin** modifier add body, thickness to the mesh edges.
Let us analyze the modifier panel before starting a clarifier exercise.

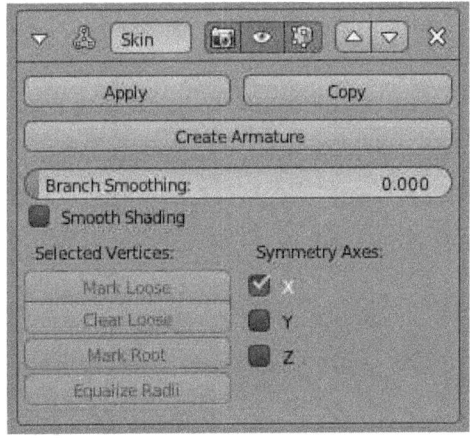

fig. 436 the *Skin* panel

The **Create Armature** button creates the armature and activates the relevant panel for the rigging configuration and control, starting from the *layout Skin* geometric distance.

Branch Smoothing rounds and make more complex the geometry around thickened segments. It is a cursor whose values to be assigned range from 0 (minimum geometry value) to 1 (maximum value).

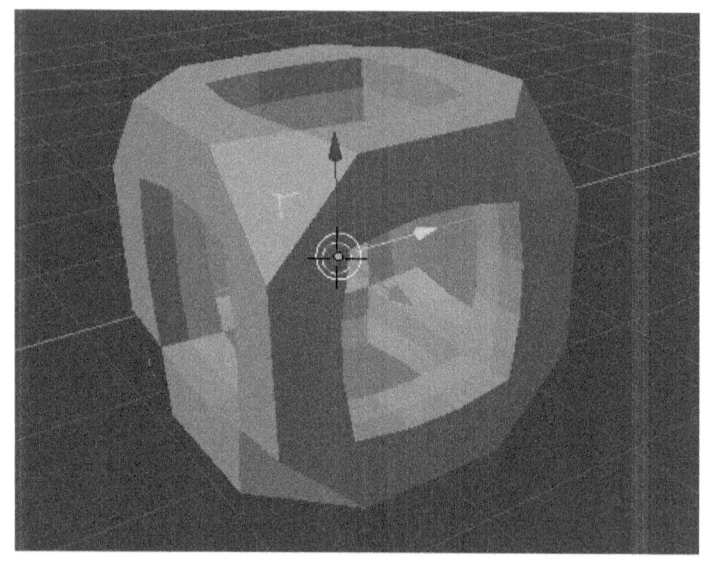

fig. 437 *Skin* applied on a cube by default

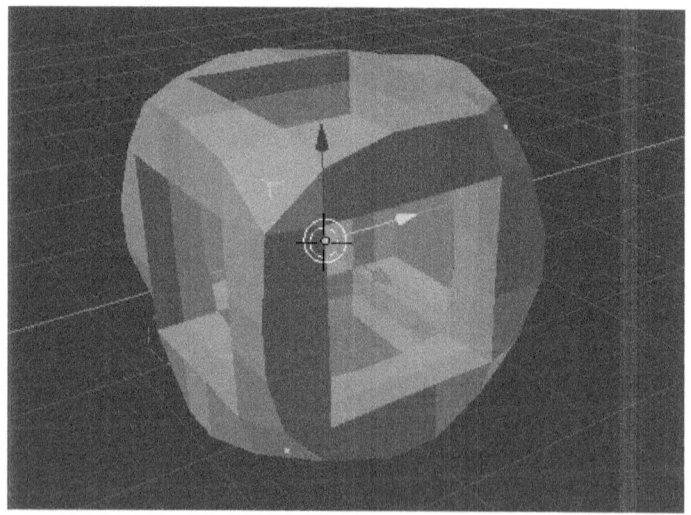

fig. 438 *Branch Smoothing* set to 1

374

By checking **Smooth Shading**, a rounded shading will be visualized.

Selecting in *Edit Mode* some mesh vertices, 4 modifier buttons will be activated.

- **Mark Loose** marks the selected vertices and exclude them from the thickening operation;

- **Clear Loose** cancels the effect of the previous common and restore the vertices as taking part to the thickening operation;

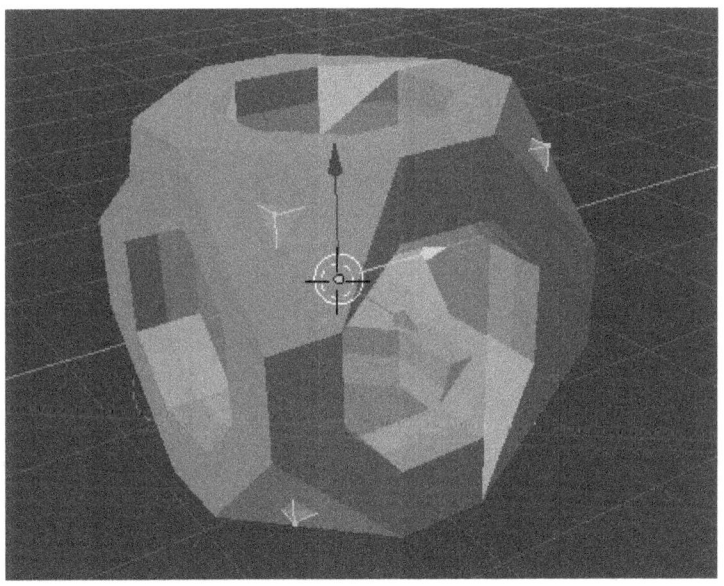

fig. 439 *Mark Loose*

- **Mark Root** marks the selected vertices as *root* of armature bones, such as the vertices be considered as rotation center of the connected bones and limbs. The roots are identified in the 3D view with a red circle dashed around the selected vertices.

375

- *Equalize Radii* enforces thickening radius around the selected vertices be uniform in any direction.

Symmetry Axes, finally, allows you to check the x, y and z axes such as to avoid the creation of quadrangular asymmetric faces with respect to the three axes x, y and z.
In *Edit Mode* is finally possible set the thickening value of the selected vertices.

Typing the combination CTRL + A and moving the mouse the thickening amount of the edges will be previewed in light gray, before confirming with the LMB.

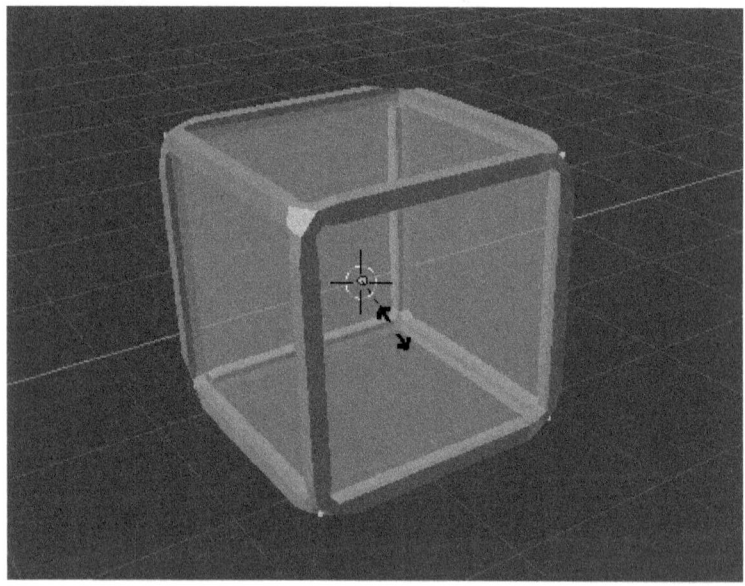

fig. 440 edge thickening regulation with CTRL + A in *Edit Mode*

EXERCISE n. 13: MODELING OF A BRANCH USING SKIN

In this exercise we will show how to model a branch starting from the vertex extrusion and finally thickening the *silhouette* edges with the *Skin* modifier.

Starting from a Plane, where 3 of the 4 vertices will be deleted, operate by extruding the left vertex such as to obtain the *silhouette* of a branch, eventually with secondary branches.
Placing the extruded vertices in the *Front* (1 NUM) and *Right* (3 NUM) views, you will follow an irregular path.

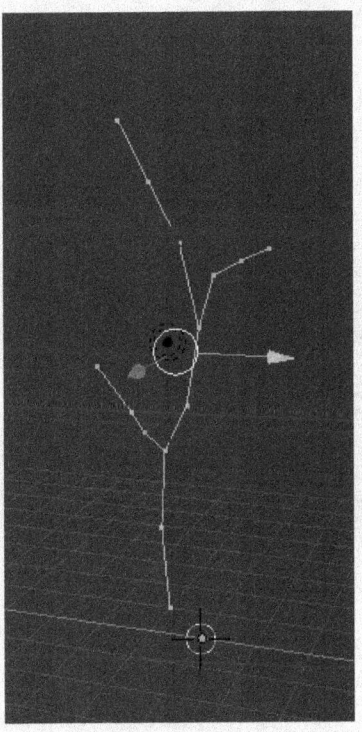

fig. 441 realization of the *silhouette* by point extrusion

Once the extrusion operation has been concluded, add the *Skin* modifier to the *mesh*, enter in *Edit Mode* and freely rescale the thickness with CTRL + A.

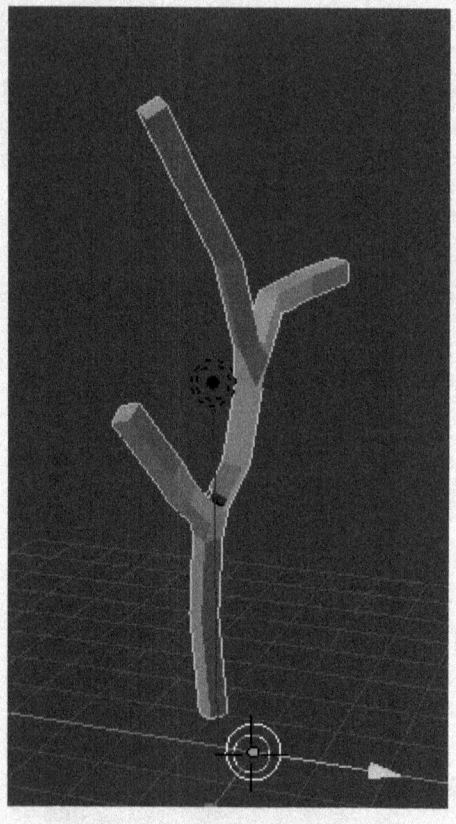

fig. 442 thickness regulation in *Edit Mode* with CTRL + A

Add the *Smoothing Shader.*

Now let's go on a little bit: add to the *mesh* the *Subdivision Surface* modifier to the modifier cascade, placing it after *Skin.* Set 3 as subdivision value in *View* and in Render.

This modifier will increase, analogously to Multiresolution, the mesh geometry, tending to round the surface.

fig. 443 the modifier cascade

The trunk and its branches will be much less sharp, and the ends will be definitely rounded.

Remember that close loops reduce the rounding and locally generate cusps.

For each branch, then, select the two end vertices and add a vertex between them. You have two possibilities:

- Once the two vertices have been selected, press W and choose *Subdivide* among the options. The segment will be subdivided in two parts, with the new vertex added;

- with CTRL + R add a loop between the two end vertices. A vertex (in violet) will be added, a real mono dimensional *loop* between the two.

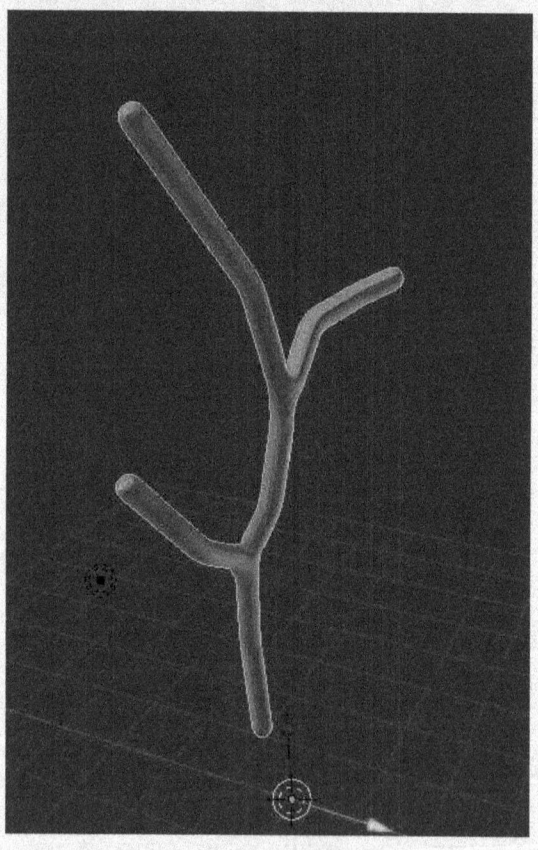

fig. 444 the branch after the addition of the *Subdivision Surface* modifier

Now you only need to shift the new vertex near the branch end vertex pressing G twice.

Remember that this command moves a vertex along the closest edge.

Automatically the roundness of the branch end will be flattened, resembling a broken branch.

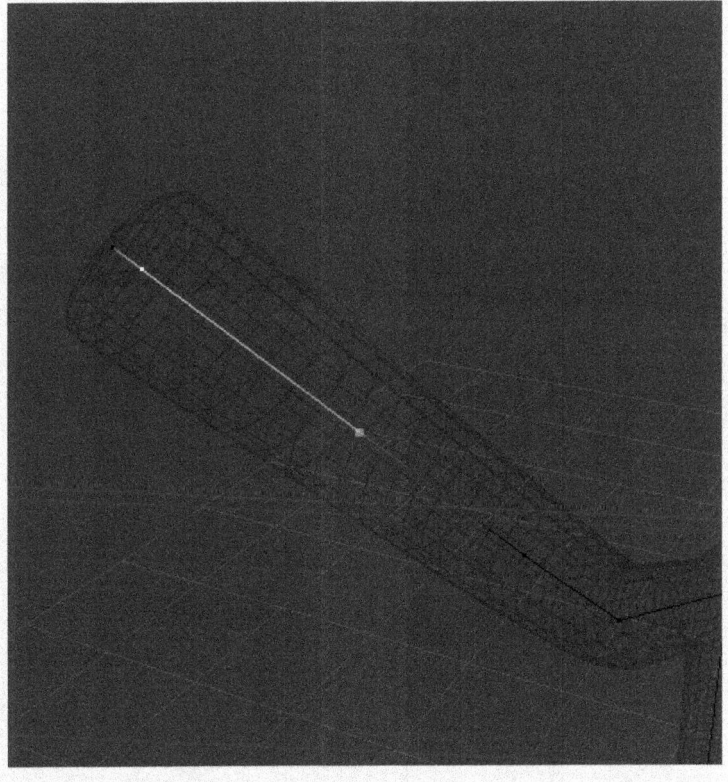

fig. 445 addition of a new vertex and shift of the latter near the end vertex with GG

You now need to repeat the same operation for all the other branches.

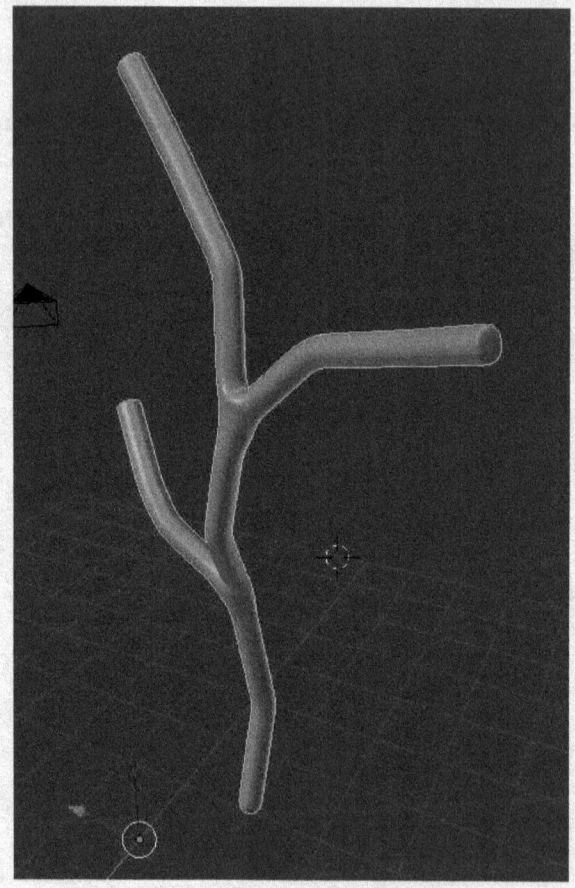

fig. 446 the final outcome

The **Solidify** modifier is much simple in operation, useful and interesting.

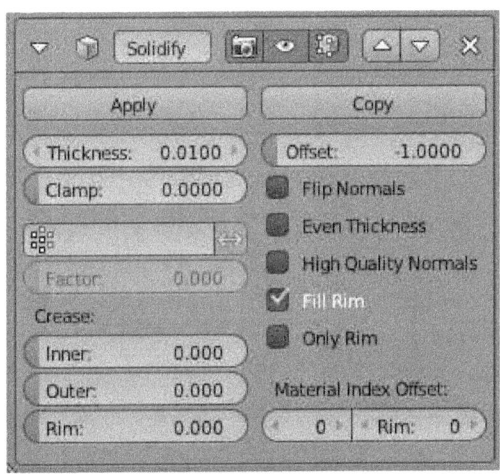

fig. 447 the *Solidify* panel

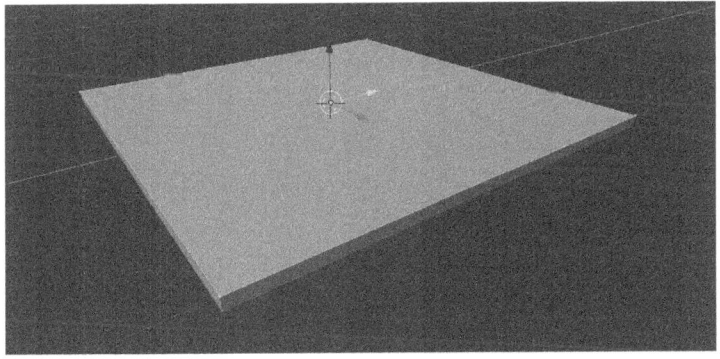

fig. 448 application of the *Solidify* to a plane

As can be understood from its name, the modifier has an effect very similar to the transformation tool *Extrude*. In fact, it gives thickness to the mesh faces on which is applied, along the normal direction.

Thickness allows you to set the extrusion thickness, expressed according to the project units.

Offset specifies the extrusion direction with a parameter from -1 to 1. (-1 totally downward, 1 totally upward, 0 to the center).

fig. 449 *Solidify* with *Offset* set to 0

Clamp prevents auto-intersection of the faces of more complex meshes. It is possible to choose a value from 0 to 2 for the effect regulation.

Vertex Group extrudes only the area delimited by an inserted *Vertex Group*, if present.

Factor is a parameter being activated only if a *Vertex Group* is inserted. It determines how much the vertex relevant weights are considered during the extrusion:

- setting the value to 0, the vertices with 0 weight (0) will not have thickness (no extrusion);

- setting the value 0.5, the vertices with 0 weight will result twice less thick of those with maximum weight.

- Finally, setting the value to 1, the weights will be neglected and the thickness value is separately assigned for each vertex.

The parameters of the **Crease** group are directly related to the *Subdivision Surface*.

- *Inner* enforces that the inner boundary be sharply marked and not rounded;

- *Outer* enforces that the outer boundary be sharply marked and not rounded;

- *Rim* enforces that the front boundary (the section) be sharply marked and not rounded.

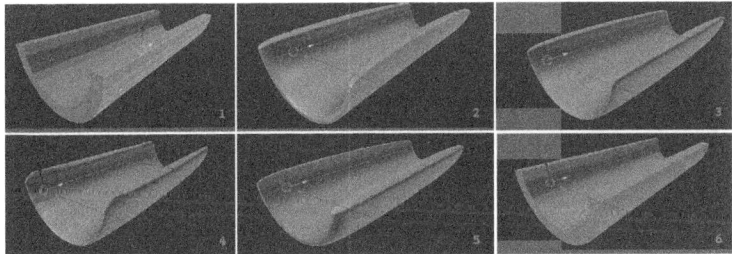

fig. 450 1) Semicircle extruded along y with Solidify; 2) the addition of the *Subdivision Surface* rounds the surface; 3) *Crease Inner* effect; 4) *Crease Outer* effect; 5) *Crease Rim* effect; 6) overall effect *Crease* making the surface flat and the edges sharp

Flip Normals allows you to invert the normals of the solid created by the extrusion, if necessary.

Even Thickness, if checked, keep the thickness regulating the sharp edges. Sometimes it improves the quality but also increases the computing time.

High Quality Normals re-computes the normals to produce a more uniform thickness. Also in this case, the quality improves but also the computing time increases.

Fill Rim is checked creates the faces along the extrusion. If unchecked, parallel faces are generated, not connected to the original ones. As a matter of facts, a simple *Offset* is generated, of the mesh faces on which the modifier is assigned.

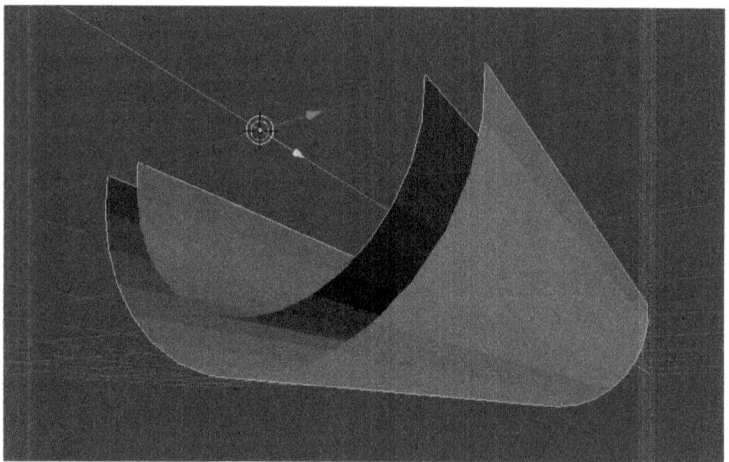

fig. 451 the removal of the fag *Fill Rim* generates a simple *offset* of the mesh faces, not connected to the original ones

Only Rig yields an outcome inverse to the previous one: generates only the thickness belonging to the extrusion, but not the original face offset.

Material Index Offset allows you to choose a different material to be used for the new geometry created by the extrusion. This material is applied on the *offset* and on the rim, depending on the index indicated in the underlying boxes.

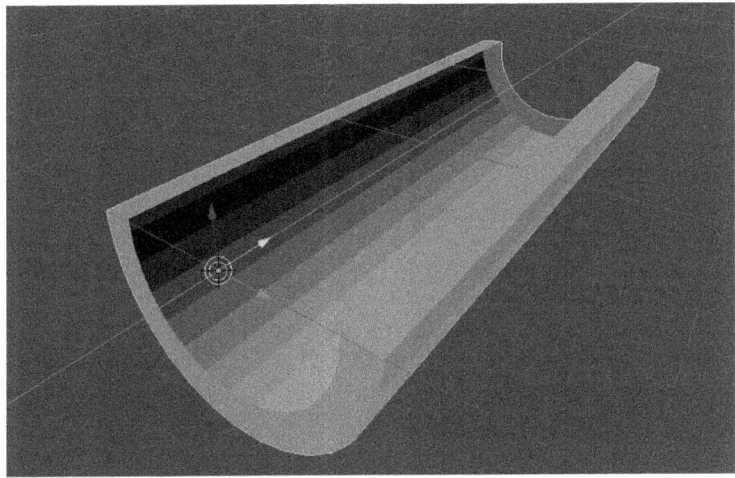

fig. 452 *Only Rig*

The 0 value means that the same material will be used.

A value with positive sign (for example $n = 1$) means that a material with index of refraction lower than the original material one.
A negative value means that materials will be used with index of refraction higher than the original material one.
Similarly, in the *Rim* box, you can assign a different material to the rim faces.

SUBDIVISION SURFACE

It is the most useful and most versatile modifier in Blender.

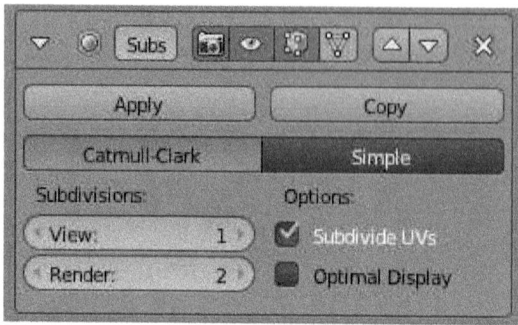

fig. 453 the *Subdivision Surface* panel

Its operation, similar but simpler regarding the settings than that of the *Multiresoliution* modifier, is to subdivide the *mesh* producing more geometry, and at the same time to round it toward the curved surface closest to the original piecewise flat surface.

Like for the *Multiresolution*, it is possible to set the subdivision algorithm, through the two-choices switch: *Catmull-Clark* and *Simple*. The latter keeps the original mesh shape, without rounding it.

Subdivisions allows you to determine the mesh subdivision number and set them differently in the 3D view (*View*) and in the final *rendering* (*Render*). It is recommended not to use too high values in *preview* because they could slow down a lot the system due to the high computation effort of the processor.

Subdivide UVs allows you to subdivide together with the mesh also the *u* and *v* coordinates, making their grid regular, for a more precise texture mapping.

By checking the option **Optimal Display**, if you are working in *Wireframe* modality, the wires of the new subdivided edges will not be visualized, i.e. only the original geometry boundaries will be drawn.

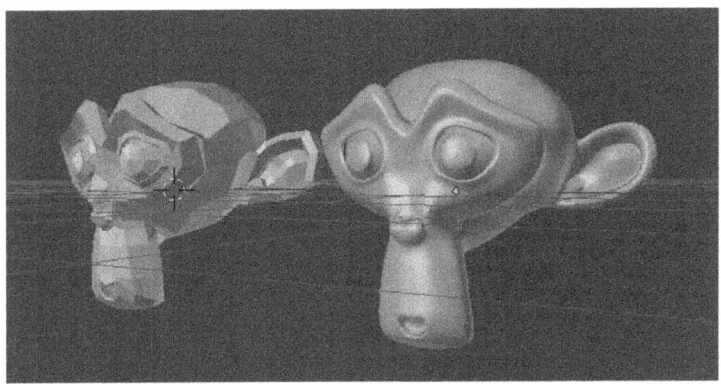

fig. 454 *Monkey* without subdivisions (on the left) and with the assignment of the *Subdivision Surface* (on the right)

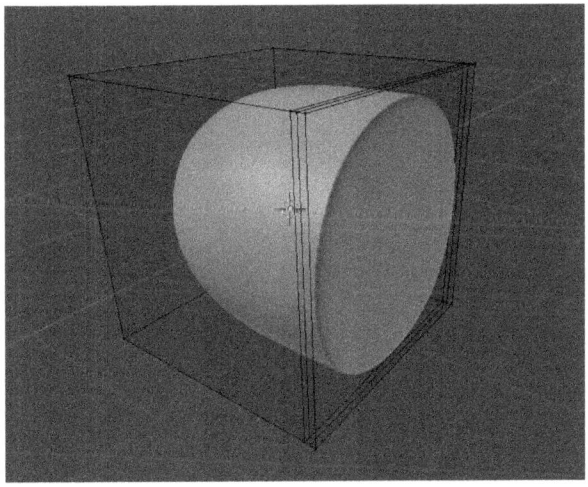

fig. 455 the *loops* reduce the rounding produced by the modifier: in this cube the *Subdivision Surface* modifier with 4 subdivisions has been applied. The modifier has rounded the mesh making it to approximate the sphere, but near the close loops the edges become sharper and the face flatter

The modifier depends on the edge marking *Mean Crease*, favoring a mesh rounding gradually limited to the set value. Analogously the mesh loops are fundamental for the rounding curvature radius.

Very close *Loops* will yield angularities or a very small curvature radius, like those of a *Bevel*.

By combining the modifier with a subdivision value high enough with the *Smooth* command, a perfect and smooth surface shading is achieved.

> **NOTE: It is very important to pay attention to the modifier position in the modifier cascade. The subdivision achieved by placing the modifier at the end of the cascade could not produce the same outcome as the one achievable by placing the modifier in the middle of the cascade.**

EXERCISE n. 14: SUBDIVISION AND ROUNDING OF THE GLASS CONSIDERED IN THE EXERCISES nn. 7, 8 AND 9 BY USING THE SUBDIVISION SURFACE MODIFIER

Retrieve the glass considered in the previous exercises and apply the *Subdivision Surface* modifier.

Set 3 subdivisions in *View* and in *Render*, then add also the *Smooth* command.

The glass surface will be now smooth and soft.

fig. 456 the glass with the *Subdivision Surface* modifier and the *Smooth* command

Once the modifier has been applied, it could be convenient to modify the geometry in *Edit Mode*, by eventually adding some loops for reducing the excessive rounding.

This is what we will do along the cup border, at the base and in correspondence of the moldings of the glass stem.

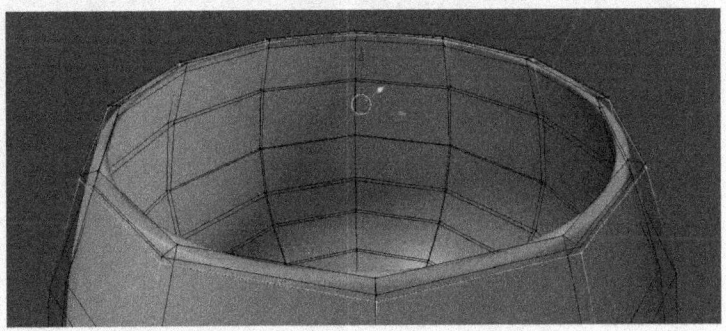

fig. 457 addition of *loops* on the cup border

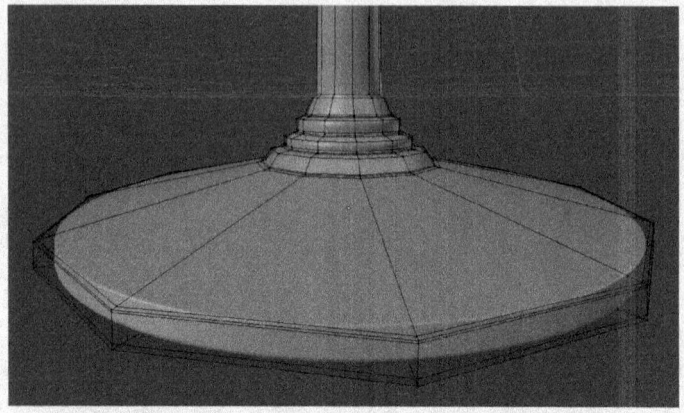

fig. 458 addition of *loops* at the base and at the moldings of the stem base

On the top of the panel, among the previously described icons, there is one (Cage) used for visualizing the mesh segments such as the lay along the curved and rounded surface.

fig. 459 the *Cage* icon

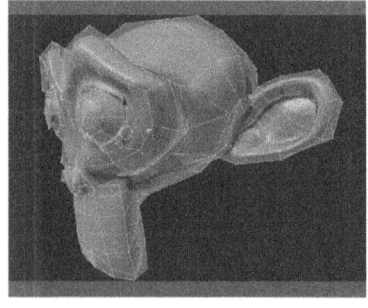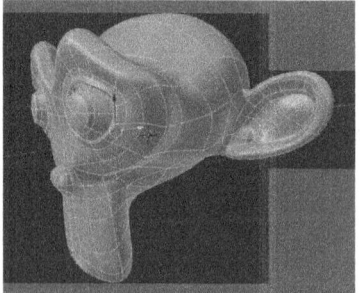

fig. 460 in *Edit Mode* the mesh grid represented without the activation (on the left) and with the activation of the *Cage* icon

fig. 461 the *Triangulate* panel

This modifier recreates the mesh geometry and tries to subdivide it in triangles.

One of the uses of a triangulated mesh is related to the 3D printing. Often the 3D printers manage in a better way a triangulated surface, instead of a surface divided in quadrangles.

Quad Method activates a menu where you can choose the subdivision method of the quadrangular faces into triangles.

fig. 462 the *Quad Method* menu

- *Shortest Diagonal* along the shortest diagonal;

- *Fixed Alternate* such that the diagonal is connected between the second and the fourth quadrangle vertices;

- *Fixed Fixed* such that the diagonal is connected between the first and the third quadrangle vertices;

- *Beauty* such that the triangles be the as regular as possible.

Ngon Method activates a menu where you can determine the way the triangles are derived from the *ngon* faces.

- *Clip* generates triangles such as to divide the *ngons* using a fill scanning algorithm;

- *Beauty* such as the triangles be as regular as possible.

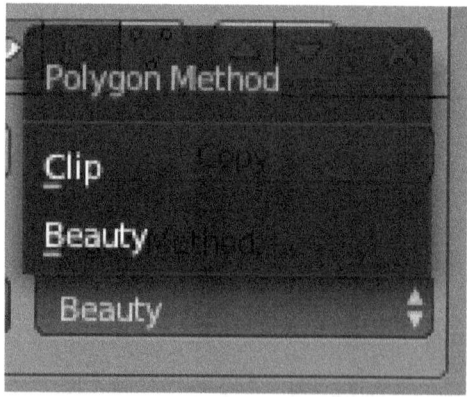

fig. 463 the *Polygon Method* menu

fig. 464 *Monkey* subdivided in triangles

The last modifier available in the *Generate* group is **Wireframe**.

This modifier, like the corresponding modify tool previously described, assigns a minimum thickness to the mesh edges such as to appear to be able to render an object made by iron wires, provided those edges are part of a face.

Edges contained in *Meshes* without faces, in fact, cannot be visualized in *Wireframe*.

fig. 465 the *Wireframe* panel

The **Thickness**, **Vertex Group**, **Factor**, **Offset** and **Even Thickness** parameters have the same meaning than the corresponding ones in the *Solidify* modifier.

Crease Edges, conceived to be used in association to the *Subdivision Surface* modifier, folds the boundaries on the junctions in order to prevent crossings near the curves.

Crease Weight defines the junction folding amount between the edges, choosing from 0 (no fold) to 1 (maximum fold).

Relative Thickness determines the edge thickness by considering the length as boundary – longer edges as thicker.

Boundary creates the wireframe on the *mesh* margins.

Replace Original replaces the original mesh with the wireframe. If unchecked, place the wireframe above the original mesh.

Material Offset assigns the material index (*Index*) of the mesh or of another material to the new geometry.

fig. 466 a *mesh* rendered in *Wireframe*

5.3. The Deform modifiers

The second group of modifier that we will analyze in this chapter is named **Deform**.

The modifiers belonging to this group, differently from the previous ones, do not add geometry to the object on which are applied, but deform it according to certain algorithms, paths and references to external objects.
In most cases the object, to be deformed, must posses an enough detailed geometry. This means that the object must posses a high enough number of vertices, to be shifted according to a certain criterion.

Let's start to introduce the available modifiers, except **Armature** which will be analyzed later.

CAST

The **Cast** modifier tries to modify the shape of an object and transform it in a cubic, spherical or cylindrical shape object, depending on the choice.

A similar function, though more limited, included in the *Edit Mode* transformers is *To Sphere*.

Given a *mesh* with a suitable geometry, you need to choose the deformer type in the menu **Cast Type**, among **Sphere**, **Cylinder** and **Cuboid**.

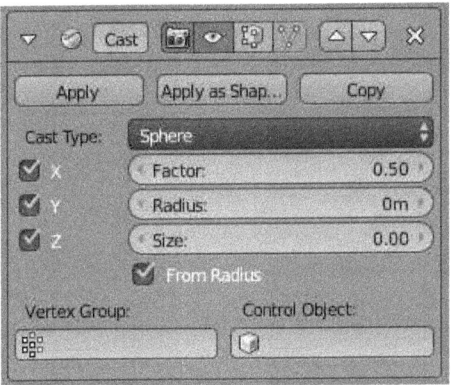

fig. 467 the *Cast* panel

Let us consider for example a cube, subdivide it with W *Subdivide* in 10 parts for each side and apply *Cast, Sphere*.

The **Factor** parameters determines the deformation amount. For negative values the object will tend to implode in correspondence of the central parts, for positive values less than 1 will tend to a sphere, whereas for values greater than 1 each face will tend to individually inflate, yielding efflorescence.

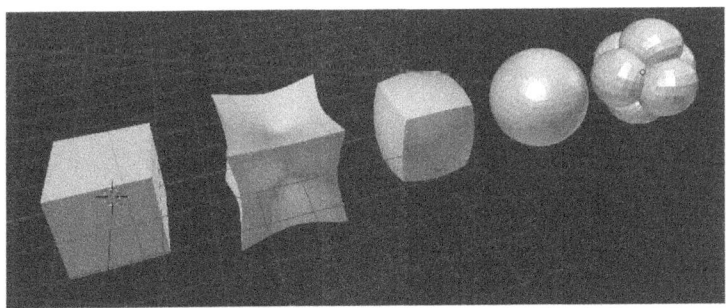

fig. 468 applying *Cast* to a cube and setting the *Cast Type* as a *Sphere*, different deformations can be achieved, depending on the assigned *Factor* parameter. From left to right, *Factor* has been set to: 0; -1; 0.5; 1; 2

Set now *Cylinder* in the *Cast Type*.

399

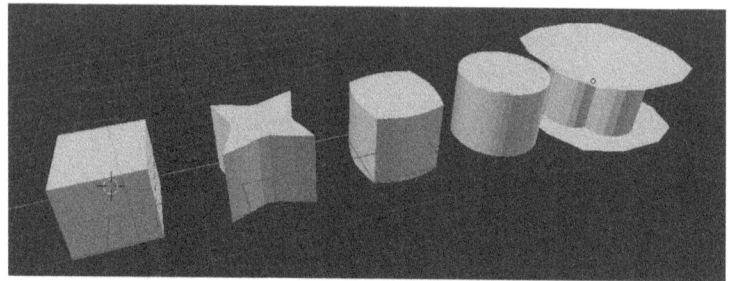

fig. 469 setting the *Cast Type* as Cylinder, depending on the *Factor* parameter, shapes tending to a cylinder will be achieved. From left to right, *Factor* has been set to: 0; -1; 0.5; 1; 2

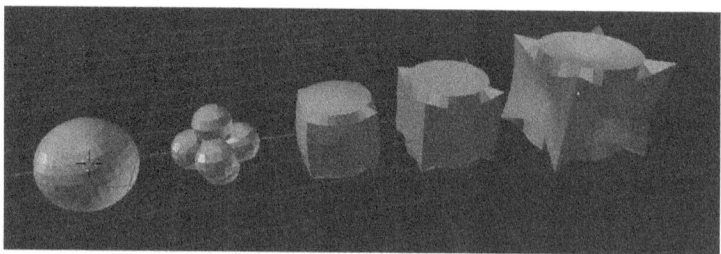

fig. 470 setting the *Cast Type* on the sphere as Cuboid, depending on the *Factor* parameter, shapes tending to a cube will be achieved. From left to right, *Factor* has been set to: 0; -1; 0.5; 1; 2

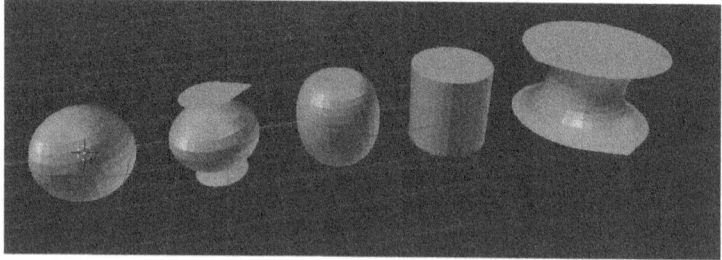

fig. 471 setting the *Cast Type* on the sphere as Cylinder, depending on the *Factor* parameter, shapes tending to a cylinder will be achieved. From left to right, *Factor* has been set to: 0; -1; 0.5; 1; 2

Finally create a sphere and set first *Cuboid* and then Cylinder in the *Cast Type*.

Shapes tending respectively to a cube and a cylinder will be achieved, with differences depending from the *Factor* parameter.

The checks **X**, **Y** and **Z** able and disable the transformation in the axes direction.

Radius defines the influence radius (spherical) of the modifier with respect to the *mesh*.

Size allows you to insert an alternative dimension for the shape to be obtained;

The check **From Radius**, if activated, automatically computes the *Size* value from the influence radius.

Vertex Group limits the deformation effect to only the vertices belonging to a loaded *Vertex Group*, eventually also as a function of the weight assigned to the vertices with the *Vertex Paint*.

Finally, by inserting the name of an external object in the **Control Object** box, the object will influence with its shape the deformation of the object to which the *Cast* modifier is assigned, based on its position and the origin.

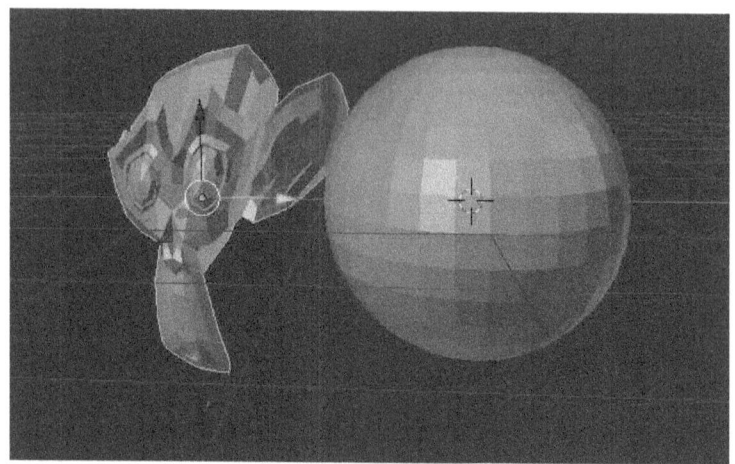

fig. 472 the sphere influences the *Monkey* deformation

CURVE

This modifier is very useful to get twisted shape for a mesh, paths, *mesh* sequences (*Array*).

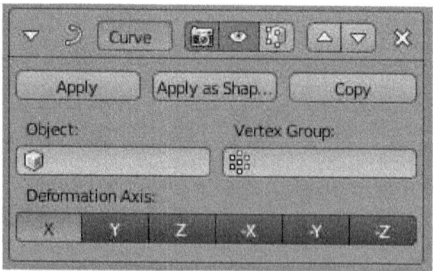

fig. 473 the *Curve* panel

Assigning the modifier to the *mesh* and setting as **Object** a curve in the 3D view, the *mesh* will be deformed according to the curve displacement along the dominant axis X, Y, or Z defined in

402

Deformation Axis. For deforming the *mesh*, you only need to translate it (or translate the curve) along the dominant direction (by default, the X axis).

It is possible to deform only some mesh vertices, defined in an assigned *Vertex Group*.

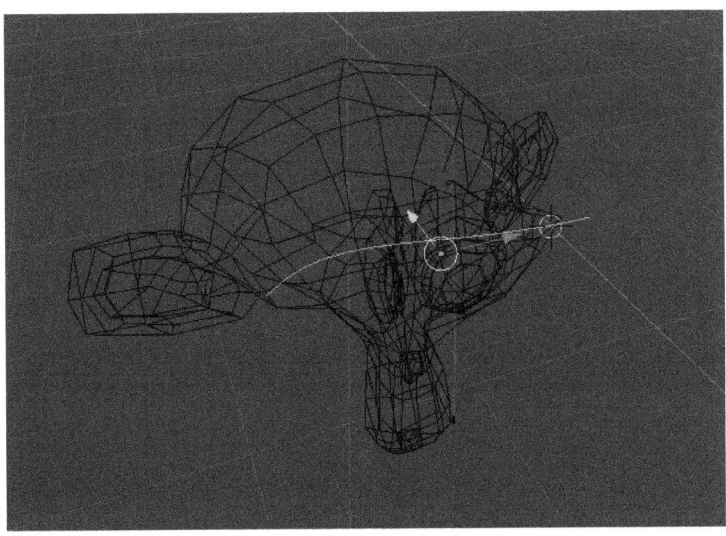

fig. 474 *Monkey* is deformed along the *Bézier* curve

 EXERCISE n. 15: A PEARL NECKLACE

Insert a sphere and a *Bézier* curve defining the necklace path, like it were the *nylon* wire holding together the pearls.
Assign the *Array* modifier to the sphere with a large enough number of repetitions, and then the *Curve* modifier. Set the *Bézier* curve as object of the modifier and shift the sphere sequence along the dominant direction.

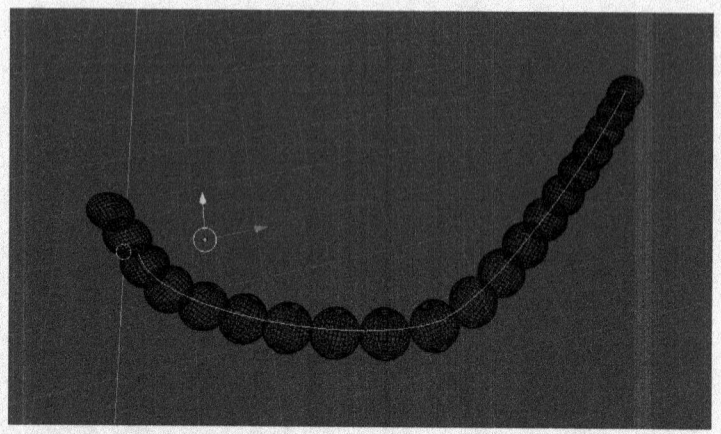

fig. 475 the sphere sequence follows the *Bézier* curve object of the *Curve* modifier

 EXERCISE n. 16: THE ROLLER COASTERS

Similarly try to create the railway of the roller coasters.

First create the typical node, comprising two lateral cylinders (the train railway) and a cylindrical central part.

First insert a cylinder and in *Top* view (7 NUM) move it toward left along the *x* direction.

Reset the *Location* and apply a *Mirror* with respect to the *x* axis (*y* will then be the symmetry axis of the mirroring operation).

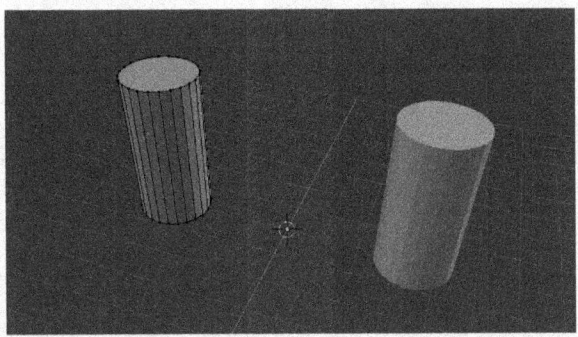

fig. 476 the cylinder mirrored with respect to x

Insert now another cylinder in *Object Mode*, with a larger radius and placed in the center, but shifted along y with respect to the another two cylinders.

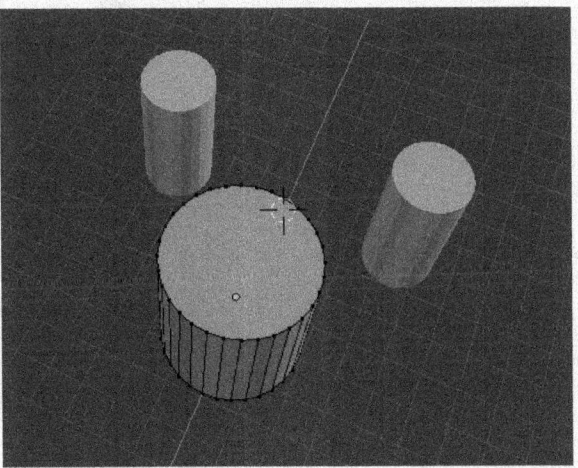

fig. 477 the larger cylinder

Starting from a plane, insert two *loops* and modify in *Edit Mode* the position of some vertices as shown in the figure. Then assign to the plane the *Mirror* modifier with respect to x. This element will the starting element for the connecting structure between the rails and the central beam.

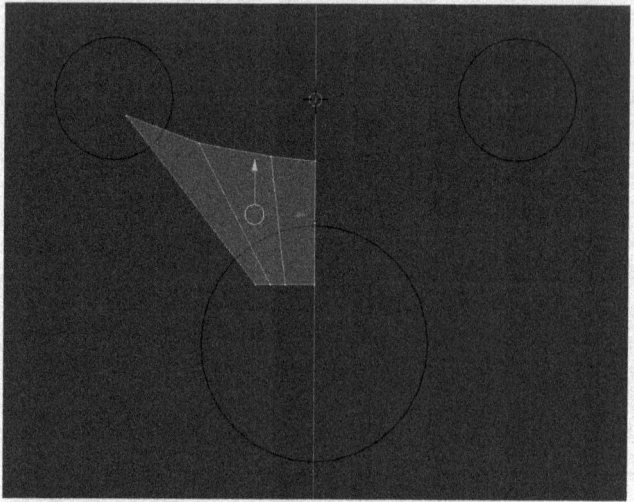

fig. 478 realization of the connecting element

Extrude then the plane of an amount smaller than the cylinder length.

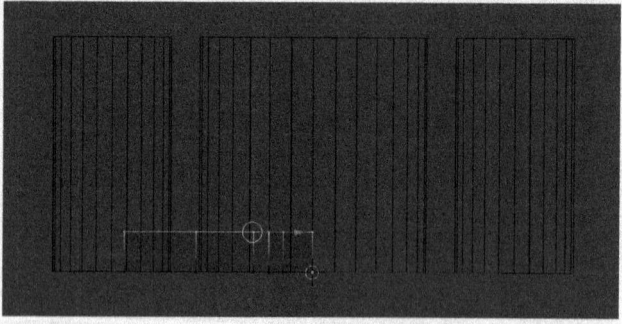

fig. 479 connecting element extrusion

Then apply definitively (Apply) the *Mirror* modifier to all the objects.

Select all the objects and join them in a single *mesh* by typing CTRL + J.

Reset the scale, rotation and position, then rotate the *mesh* of 90° with respect to the *x* axis (R, X, 90).

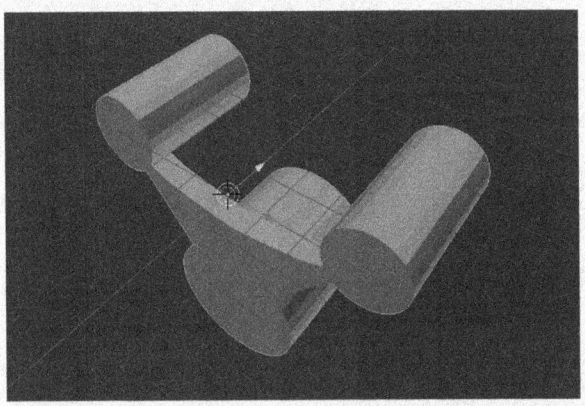

fig. 480 the typical element of the roller coasters

Now we must realize the path followed by the railway. It will be long, twisted, with pirouettes and spins.

Starting from a *Bézier* curve, try to give a glimpse to fantasy, realizing this path such as it is proportionate to the typical element just defined. You can operate with a sequence of extrusions of the curve end vertex.

It is important to pay attention, during the extrusions, to the correct rotation of the vertices and the normals, such has the constitutive elements don't experience unwanted spins and are uniformly placed along the path.

To make the task easier, it is recommended to extrude and shift the curve vertices using the *Top*, *Front* and *Right* views.

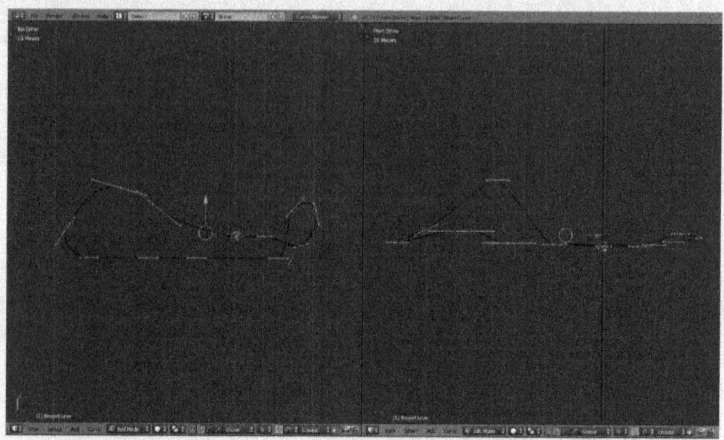

fig. 481 the *Bézier* curve path in orthogonal projection

At the end close the path, by selecting the starting and ending vertices and typing F.

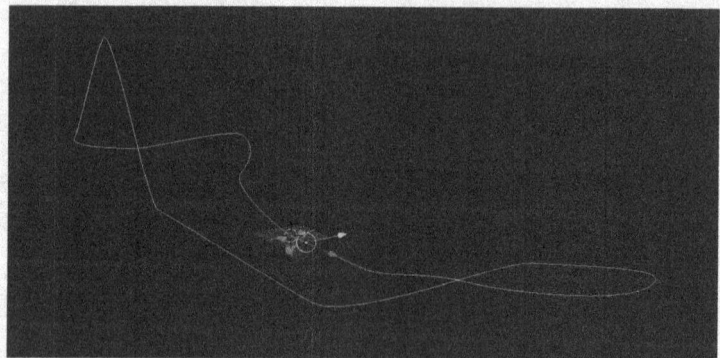

fig. 482 the *Bézier* curve path in the 3D space

Select now the typical element and assign to it the *Array* modifier, setting the *Relative Offset* equal to 1 (equal to itself) and a repetition number (*Count*) suitable to cover the full path length.

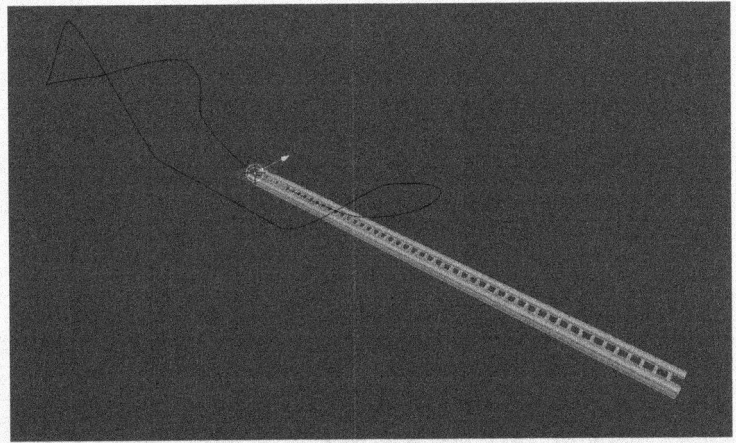

fig. 483 *Array* on the typical element

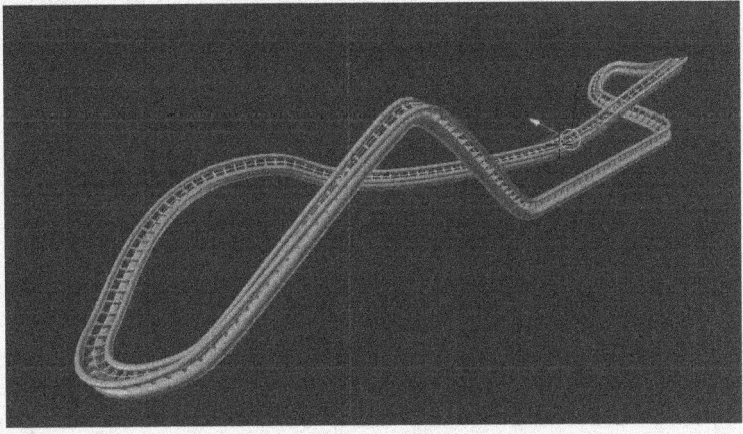

fig. 484 the railway obtained by the deformation of the *Curve* modifier

Finally assign to the typical element also the *Curve* modifier, setting the *Bézier* curve as *Object*. The railway is ready. You can eventually correct the vertex rotation with the *Tilt* tool in the *Transform* panel of the *Tools Shelf*. Add *Smooth* for rounding the surfaces.

DISPLACE

With this modifier we introduce a very important concept: the relief.

The **Displace** term means the possibility of replacing the mesh vertices along their normals or specific directions, achieving a relief.

Many methods exist for obtaining a material relief. We will analyze them in detail in the foregoing. For now, you must know that the relief can be assigned to a mesh as an effect (**bump**) or as a true vertex displacement (**displacement**). In order to be able to apply this latter method, the *mesh* must have a sufficiently detailed geometry.

In order to exactly define the quote of each vertex a texture is used. This can be a monochromatic image or a mathematical model (named procedural texture) which il be discussed later.

Blender interprets the *texture* according to the color tone. The gray scale determines the height of the corresponding vertices in that *texture* position, suitably scaled as a function of the mesh faces, such as the darker areas are lower positioned whereas the clearer areas higher, depending to the enforced strength (**Strength**).

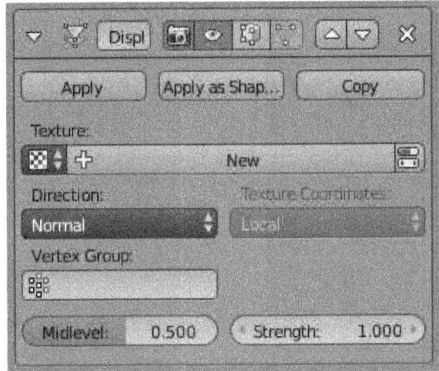

fig. 485 the *Displace* panel

Let us make a practical example for clarifying the concept.
Insert in the 3D view a sphere. Assign to it a *Subdivision Surface* modifier with two subdivisions and apply it permanently such as to obtain a finer grid. Apply permanently the *Subdivision Surface* modifier.

Add now to the sphere the *Displace* modifier.

In the **Texture** box click on *New*.

In the *Properlies* editor enter the *tab Texture*.

fig. 486 *tab Texture* icon in the *Properties* editor

In the panel appearing in the *Properties* editor click on *New* and choose from the *Type* drop-down menu the *Distorted Noise* procedural texture.

411

The latter can be freely modified acting on the *Distortion*, *Nabla* and *Size* parameters (which will be analyzed in the foregoing), adapting it to the *mesh* shape and dimension.

Set:

$$Distortion = 1.50$$
$$Nabla = 0.10$$
$$Size = 0.15.$$

The *texture* will appear much more fine and refined.

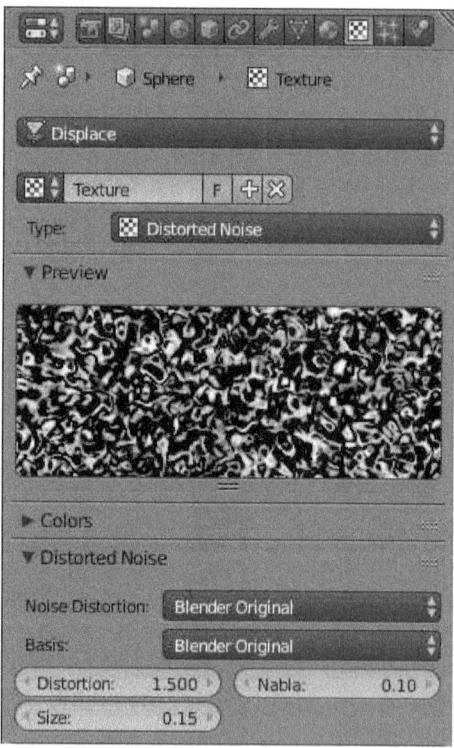

fig. 487 settings of the procedural texture

Return to the *tab Modifiers* and set the *Midlevel* and *Strength* values of the *Displace* modifier respectively equal to 0.20 and 0.10.

Add then a *Subdivision Surface* modifier with 2 subdivisions for further rounding the effect and the *Smooth*.
The *texture* will act as parameter on the quote of each of the mesh vertices, raising them in correspondence of the tones tending to the white and crushing them in correspondence of the darker tones.

> **NOTE: The *texture* associated to the *Displace* do not color the mesh but only determines its relief.**

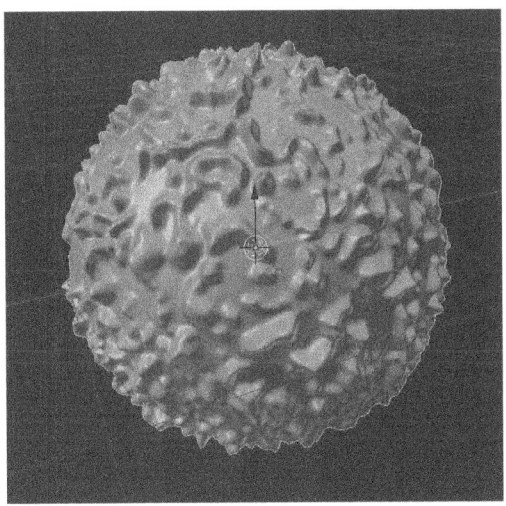

fig. 488 *Displace* effect on the sphere with the *Strength* parameter set to 0.1

Try now to set a negative value to the *Strength*, for example - 0.1. The effect will be inverted and the vertices which had been raised in the previous example, will be now crushed down.

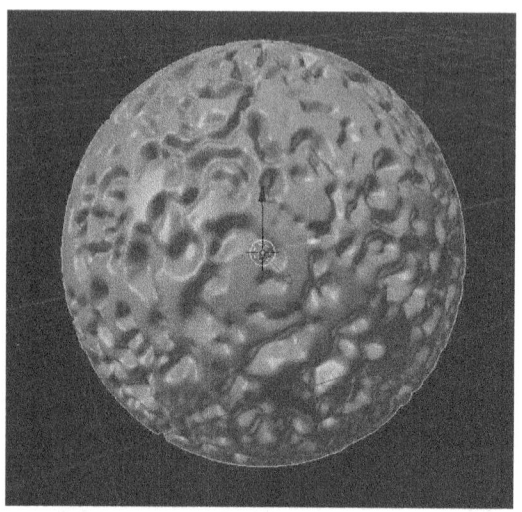

fig. 489 the *Displace* effect on the sphere with the *Strength* parameter set to - 0.1

This modifier is suitable to model organic and natural creatures, like virus and bacteria, or the complex patterns of the asteroid and planet reliefs.

While the **Strength** parameter regulates the action intensity of the assigned texture on the relief effect, **Midlevel** acts as fine regulation of the effect. The *Midlevel* value (between 0 and 1) is subtracted from the numeric value of the *texture* color.
Direction defines the direction for the vertex shift. This direction can be chosen as:

- *X, Y, Z,* along a local axis;
- *Normal,* along the normal in that point;
- *RGB to XYZ,* along the local axes, according to the texture RGB components (red values for the displacement along X, green along Y, blue along Z). This method is referred to as Vector Displacement.

Texture Coordinates defines the mapping system along the coordinates such as to assign the texture values for each vertex. The system can be defined according to one of the following methods:

- *UV*, using the texture coordinate system specified in the underlying menu *UV Map*;
- *Object*, using the coordinate system of another object specified in the underlying menu *Object*;
- *Global*, using the project global coordinate system;
- *Local*, using the object coordinate system.

Vertex Group enforces that the *displacement* be active only on the vertices belonging to the specified group.

HOOK

This modifier is used for deforming a *mesh*, a curve or a *Lattice* object, using another object (usually an *Empty*).

By moving the hook object, the mesh vertices are dragged with it and indirectly undergo the same transformation applied to it, similarly to what happens using the proportional *editing* on a *mesh*.
For example, insert a *mesh* suitably subdivided. Enter in *Edit Mode* and assign to a *Vertex Group* the vertices which must be deformed with the *Hook* modifier, after having selected them.
Then create the *Hook* object (an *Empty*, or a small sphere).

Select the mesh to be deformed and apply to it the *Hook* modifier, setting the hook object (the *Empty* or the small sphere) as *Object* and the vertex group to be deformed as *Vertex Group*.

fig. 490 the *Hook* panel

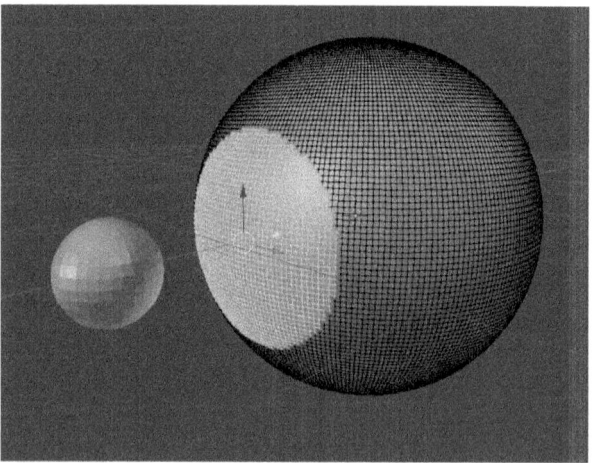

fig. 491 assignment to the *Vertex Group* of the mesh vertices to be deformed

Then assign the hook strength in deforming the vertices with the **Strength** parameter (from 0 to 1), the hook action range with respect to the vertices (**Radius**) and the proportional deformation type in the **Falloff Type** menu.

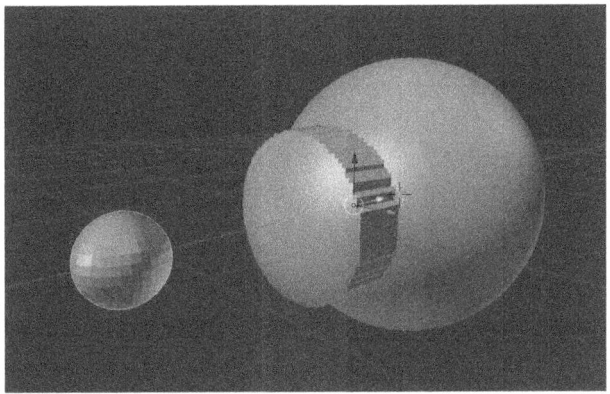

fig. 492 the hook effect on the mesh selected vertices

By moving, rotating or scaling the hook object, the vertices belonging to the mesh *Vertex Group* undergoing deformation will follow the transformation according to the chosen proportional method.

The check on **Uniform Falloff** is useful when you use hooks on objects in scale, in particular when non uniform scales may affect too much the hook action.

In the lower part of the *Hook* panel, you can find 4 buttons referring to the functions of the *Vertex Group* panel:

- **Reset** re-computes and deletes the offset transformed by the hook;
- **Recenter** sets the hook center to the position of the *3D Cursor*;
- **Select** selects the vertices subjected to the hook deformation;
- **Assign** assigns the vertices selected in the *mesh* to the modifier.
- *Hook* can also be directly assigned to a selected vertex group by typing CTRL + H.

This modifier is based on the curvature flux of the Laplace Beltrami mathematical operator. Often used for the meshes reconstructed by means of a 3D *scanner* 3D from objects of the real world, tries to reduce the mesh noise, suitably subdivided, acting on the mesh shape and geometry in a non invasive way.

The **Repeat** counter allows you to repeat the modifier application several times. Each repetition enforces a new mesh curvature flux and, as result, removes the noise at each iteration.

fig. 493 the *Laplacian Smooth* panel

Factor regulates the displacement amount of each vertex along the curvature flux.

Using a low value, especially in correspondence of more repetition (*Repeat*), it is possible to remove the mesh noise without significantly affecting the geometry.

On the other hand, using a high value, a very rounded version of the shape is achieved, paying a loss of the geometry details.

Finally, using a negative value the shape can be improved, preserving the geometry. When the factor is negative, several iteration can increase the noise.

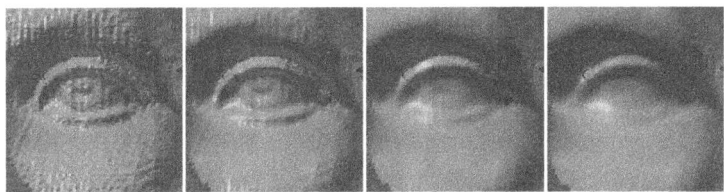

fig. 494 effect of the *Laplacian Smooth* modifier on a *mesh* with the *Factor* value set (from left to right) to 0; 0.5; 2.5; 5

Since there are no methods available for calculating the curvature flux on the mesh boundaries, the latter must be separately checked. The boundaries are managed using a much more simple methods, using **Border** for controlling the influence.

For positive values the vertex position will be smoothened whereas, for negative values, the improving changes will occur in the opposite direction.

The checks on (**Axis**) X, Y and Z will operate the changes along the specified directions.

For very high values of *Factor* and *repeat*, the smoothing process may induce a mesh contraction. By checking **Preserve Volume**, Blender will try to limit the contraction and preserve the mesh original dimensions.

On the other hand, checking **Normalize**, Blender will try to smooth possible vertex peaks which may prevent the soft and uniform surface curved behavior.

419

Finally, inserting a specific vertex group, the *Laplacian Smooth* deformation will affect only the vertices belonging to that group.

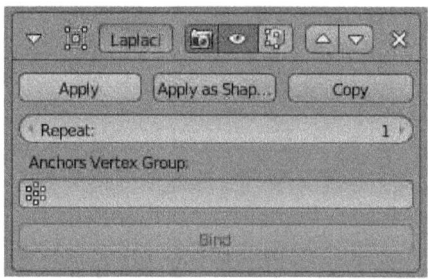

fig. 495 the *Laplacian Deform* panel

Though a simple control panel interface, the **Laplacian Deform** modifier is extremely complex.

This algorithm adapts the displacement of specific vertex groups of a mesh, to which the modifier is assigned, such as to proportionally act also on the neighboring vertices, achieving a smooth geometry of the *mesh* undergoing the vertex displacement.

Analogously to the previous modifier (*Laplacian Smooth*), the **Repeat** counter executes the modifier several times on the *mesh*. In the **Anchor Vertex Group** box the name of the vertex group undergoing the deformation is indicated.

The best way for clarifying the operation of this interesting modifier is to make a practical example.

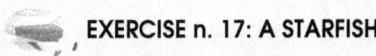 **EXERCISE n. 17: A STARFISH**

First you must build the starfish geometry.

It will have 5 tips, so you can start by inserting a circle whose segment (or vertex) number be three times the tip number, i.e. 15. Before confirming check *ngon* in the *Tools Shelf* panel, or, selecting all the vertices in *Edit Mode*, press F to fill the surface.

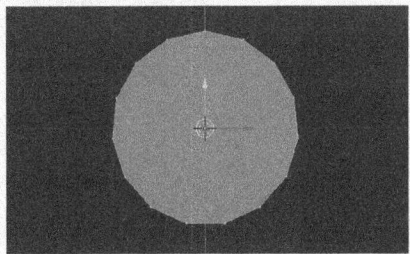

fig. 496 insertion of the circle with 15 segments

Selecting vertex groups, alternating two consecutive and one free, starting from the second on the top-right, scale them like in the figure.

fig. 497 alternate vertex scaling to create the star rays

421

Selecting with A all the vertices, make twice an *Inset* with I.

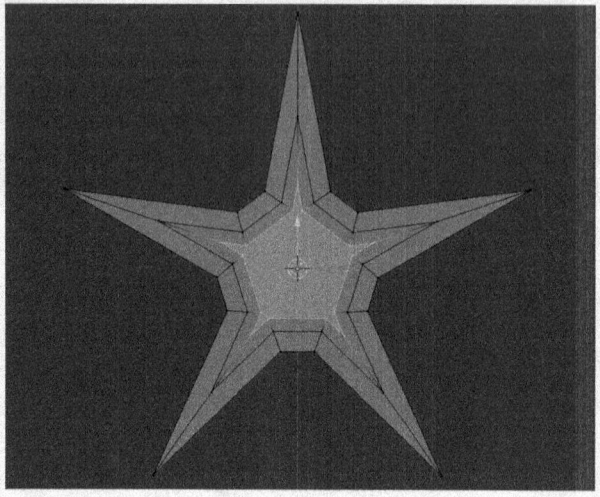

fig. 498 application of a double *Inset*

Then extrude the *mesh* to achieve thickness.

Return in *Object Mode* and assign a *Subdivision Surface* modifier with 4 mesh subdivisions. Apply permanently the modifier.

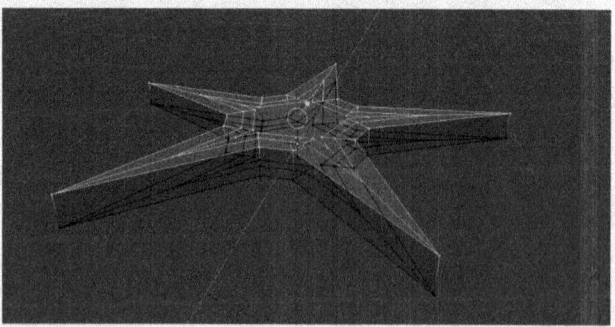

fig. 499 extrusion

fig. 500 application of the *Subdivision Surface* modifier

In *Top* view (7 NUM) and in *Wireframe* modality (Z), with the circular selection command C, select some vertices of one of the star rays

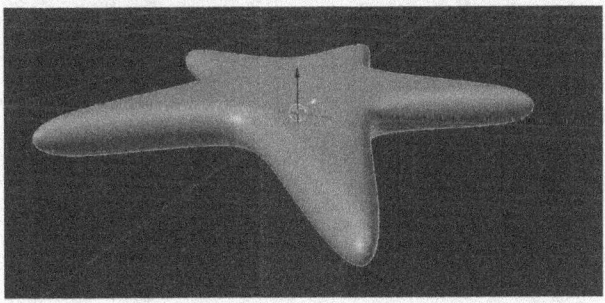

fig. 501 the star in tridimensional view

Assign those vertices to a new *Vertex* Group (in the suitable *tab* of the *Properties* editor) and, by typing CTRL + H and choosing *Hook to New Object* assign to that vertex group a *Hook*.

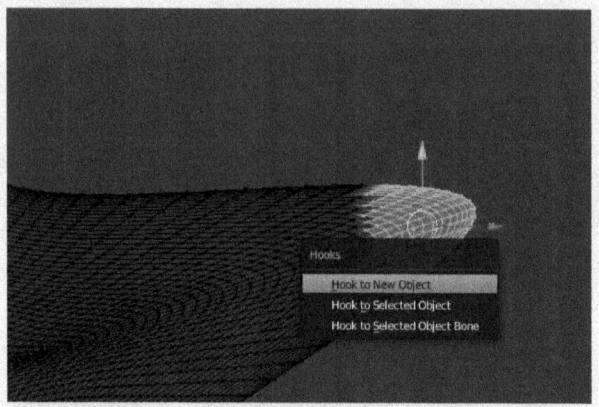

fig. 502 assignment of the selected vertices to a *Vertex Group* and a *Hook*.

Operate in the same way also for the remaining 4 rays and the star central area.

In the *tab Modifiers* 6 *Hook* modifiers in cascade will be appeared, assigned to the relevant *Vertex Groups*.

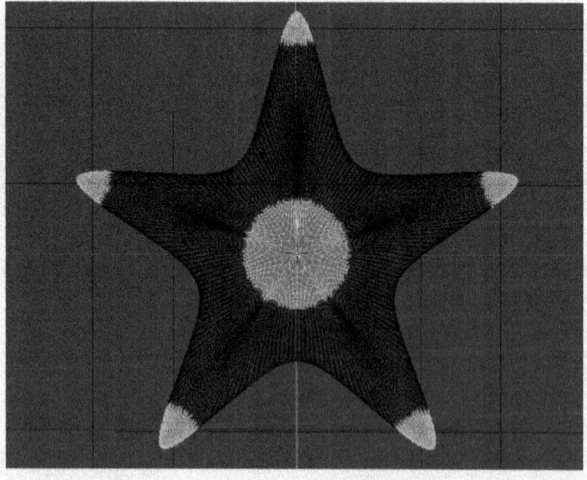

fig. 503 assignment of all the *vertex Groups* and the relevant *Hooks*

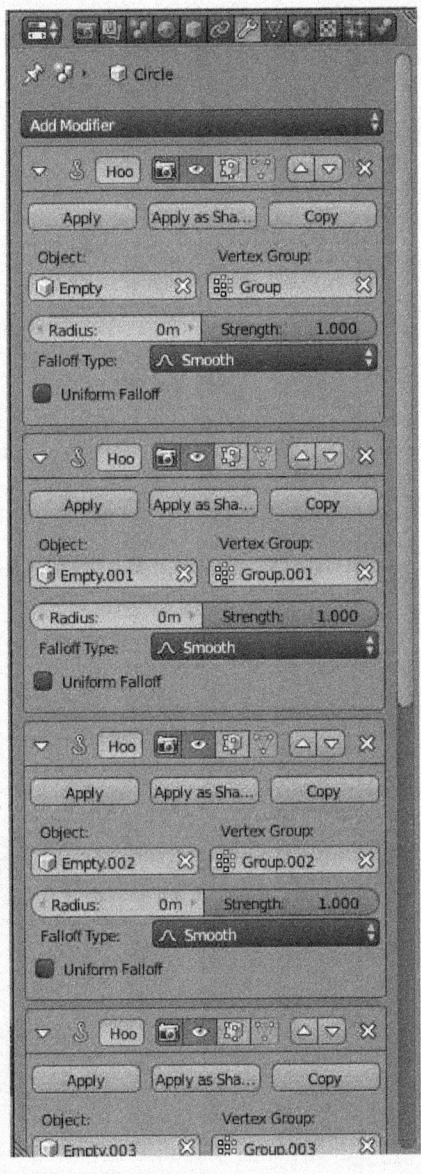

fig. 504 the *Hook* modifiers in cascade

Moving each hook you can see that the associated vertex group is consequently shifted, individually.

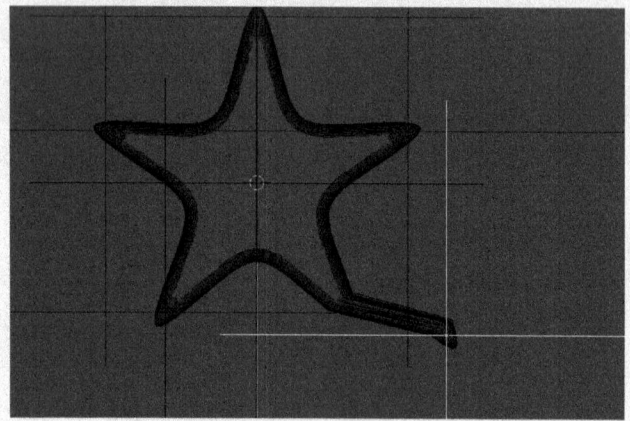

fig. 505 dragging of the *Vertex Group* by means of the associated *Empty Hook*

Select it and enter in *Edit Mode*, by selecting all the vertices associated to the hooks.

Associate all the selected vertices to a new further *Vertex Group*.

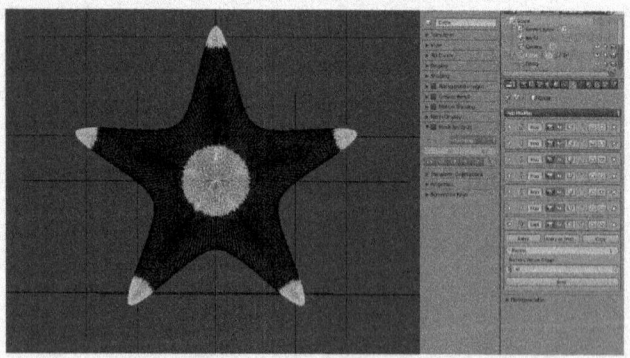

fig. 506 association of the *Vertex Group* to a *Laplacian Deform* modifier

Finally add, after having minimized all the *Hook* modifiers, the *Laplacian Deform* modifier, associating the vertices of the starfish tentacles and central body to the modifier.

Apply the **Bind** command.

Now, simply acting with the *Empty* movement and rotation, the associated *Vertex Groups* will undergo the same transformation, proportionally acting also on the surrounding vertices, achieving a regular and proportional deformation.

It is now the moment to place on the scene the starfish.

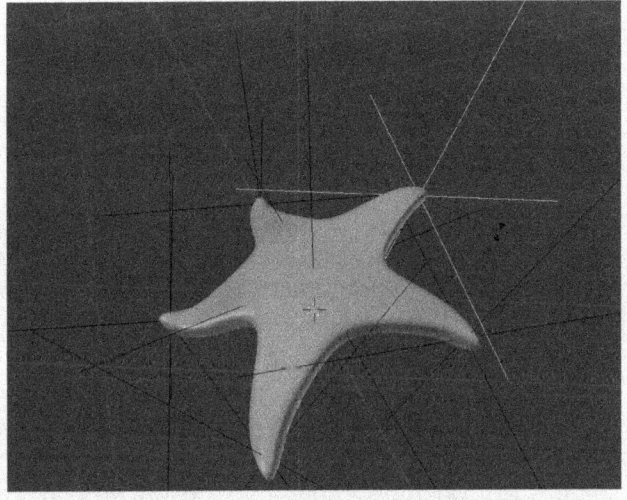

fig. 507 starfish placement

LATTICE

The **Lattice** modifier is a very powerful deformation tool.

427

Essentially it allows you to deform a high polygonal definition *mesh* to which is associated, by controlling only few vertices.

You need to construct a cage containing the approximate maximum envelope of the *mesh* and, acting on the few vertices comprising the cage, operating similarly to the hooks, the *mesh* will undergo a proportional deformation in correspondence of the vertices.

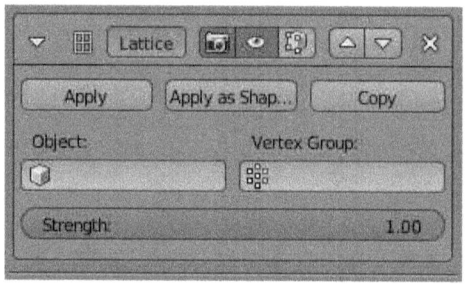

fig. 508 the *Lattice* panel

Once the *Lattice* parallelepiped has been placed, which for the sake of clarity may be renamed lattice, with SHIFT + A you can operate in the *tab Data Lattice* for defining the subdivision and control point number along the local axes *U*, *V* and *W*.

Then select the *mesh*, and apply to it the *Lattice* modifier, assigning in the **Object** box the relevant *Lattice*.
Of course you can restrict the modification only to certain vertices belonging to a specific **Vertex Group**.

Finally the **Strength** cursor (from 0 to 1) allows you to regulate the lattice intensity for the mesh vertex deformation.
Now you can select the *Lattice* object, enter in *Edit Mode* and shift, rotate or scale the vertices. In real time the *mesh* will undergo a proportional deformation.

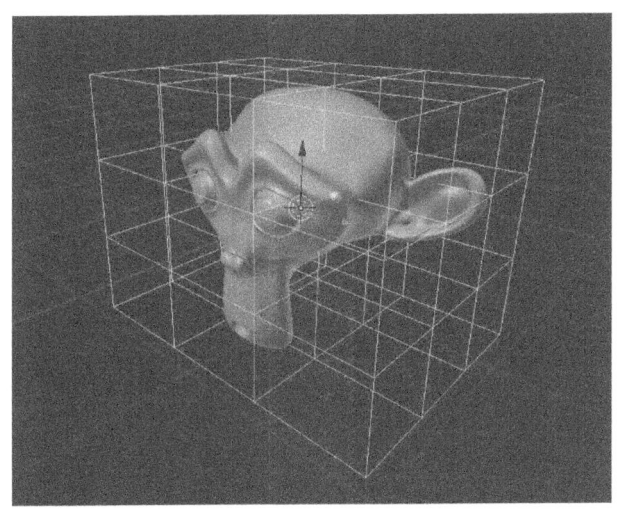

fig. 509 the *Lattice* with 4 subdivisions along *U, V, W*

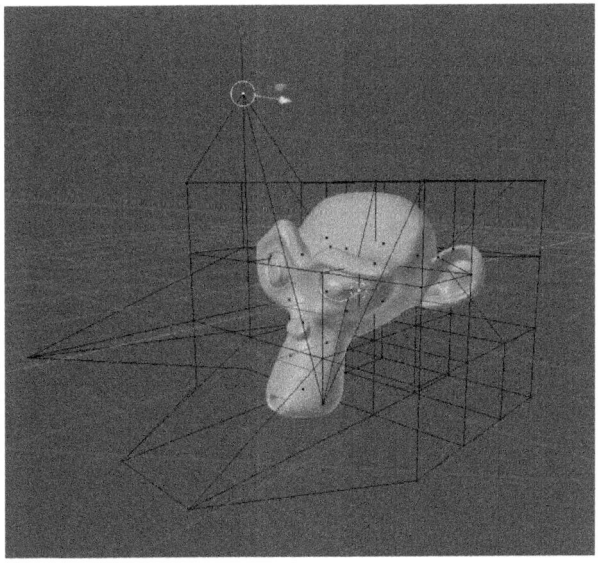

fig. 510 the *mesh* deformation according to the *Lattice* transformation

429

Mesh Deform operates similarly to *Lattice*, with the difference that the *mesh* will undergo a deformation with the control of some vertices of a corresponding mesh, of the same nature of the former, but with a much less detailed geometry.

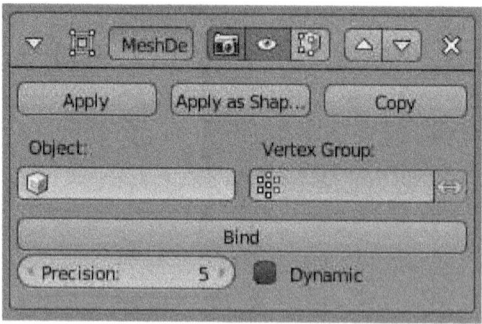

fig. 511 the *Mesh Deform* panel

For example, insert a cube and apply to it the *Subdivision Surface* modifier with 4 subdivisions. The cube will be transformed in a solid similar to a sphere. Rename it *"mesh"*.

Insert now a second cube, with the same starting dimensions and in the same position with respect to the previous one. Assign to it the *Subdivision Surface* modifier with only 1 subdivision. Apply the modifier on this second cube. Rename it *"Deform'*.

Select now the *"Deform"* solid and, in the *Display* panel inside the *tab Object* of the *Properties* editor, enforce the *Wireframe* view in the *Maximum Draw Type* menu.
This will visualize the solid with a wireframe for any global visualization in the 3D scene.

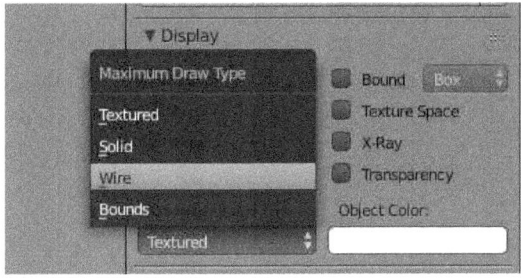

fig. 512 *Wireframe* visualization for the second cube

Select now the cube renamed "*mesh*" and assign the *Mesh Deform* modifier, setting the *Deform* cube as **Object**.

Enter now in the modifier panel and click the **Bind** button for computing the transformation. After few seconds you will be able to start to operate on the "*Deform*" cube vertices and the "*mesh*" cube will be deformed in real time.

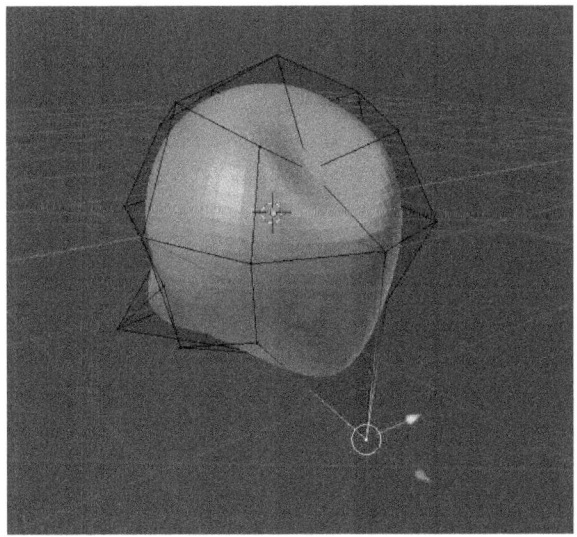

Mesh deformation with *Mesh Deform*

The **Precision** parameter controls the deformation definition, whereas the check **Dynamic** allows you to dynamically re-compute the *Bind* on the top of all the other modifiers in cascade.

SHRINKWRAP

This modifier, analogously to the other previously analyzed tools in the 3D *menu* view, allows you to project a *mesh* on another *mesh*.

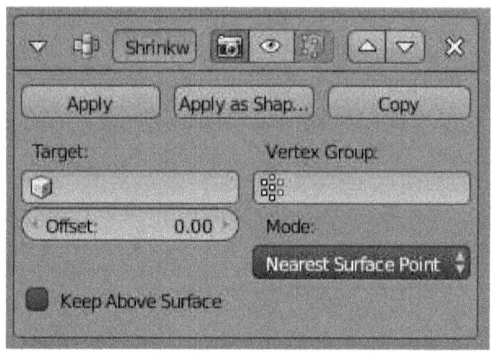

fig. 514 the *Shrinkwrap* panel

This modifier requires a high enough definition for the mesh vertices to be projected on the second *mesh*.

The modifier must be applied to the *mesh* to be projected, after both the meshes have been suitably subdivided with *Subdivision Surface*.

In the **Target** menu you need to insert the name of the *mesh* on which to project the selected one.
Vertex Group allows you to project only the vertices belonging to a specific group.

Offset allows you to separate the projected mesh from the surface by the selected value. For negative values, the *mesh* will be distanced outward; for positive, will partially penetrate the second *mesh*.

The **Mode** menu defines the method for the mesh projection, i.e.:

- *Nearest Surface Point*, such as each vertex be projected on the closest surface area on the second *mesh*;
- *Nearest Vertex*, such as each vertex be projected on the closest vertex of the second *mesh*;
- *Project*, such as to project the vertices along the direction of an axis (*X*, *Y*, *Z*) chosen in the options which will be visualized. The vertices which are not touching the second mesh after the projection, will not be projected. The flags *Positive* and *Negative* allow you to direct the projection along the selected axes. The *Cut Faces* menu allows you to prevent any projection on the front side *Front* (or on the back side, *Back*) of the destination faces. The face side is determined by its normal.

Auxiliary Target allows you to insert a further *mesh* for the projection.

 EXERCISE n. 18: BILLIARD BALL NUMBER 8

Let's make a practical example of the use of *Shrinkwrap*. We will model a billiard ball with the number projected on it.

Insert a cube and assign the *Subdivision Surface* modifier with 4 or 5 subdivisions.

The cube will be transformed into a solid tending to a sphere with all quadrangular faces.

Insert a text, enter in *Edit Mode* and, after having deleted with CANC *Text*, type the number 8.

Rotate of 90° with respect to the x axis the text and transform it into a mesh by typing ALT + C and choosing *Mesh to* Curve. Apply the *Subdivision Surface* modifier also to the text, with at least 3 subdivisions.

Go in frontal view (1 NUM) and center the number 8 on the sphere, then in *Top* view (7 NUM) drag the number out of the sphere.

Assign to the number the *Shrinkwrap* modifier and set the cube, now transformed into a sphere, as *Target*.

The number will be printed on the ball. The more defined the two mesh geometries, the more detailed the projection.

Try to play with the parameters and with the *Mode* menu to achieve satisfying results.

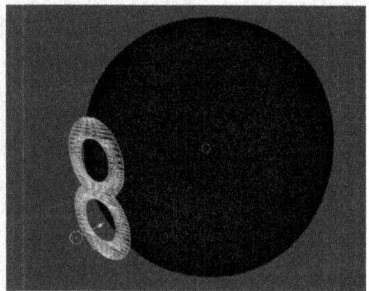 

fig. 515 projection of the number 8 on the ball

This modifier allows you to deform a *mesh* choosing one of the three deformation options along the *z* axes:

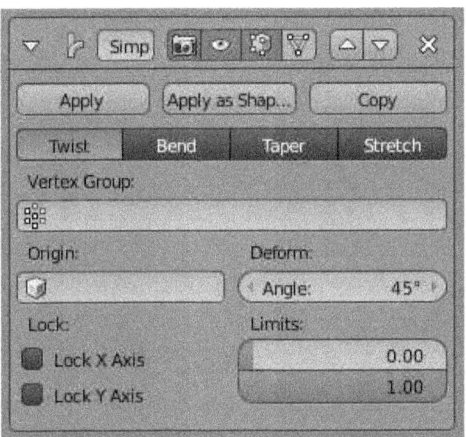

fig. 516 the *Simple Deform* panel

- **Twist**, twisting the *mesh*;

- **Bend**, bending the *mesh*;

- **Taper**, tapering the *mesh*;

- **Stretch**, stretching the *mesh*.

For each of the four modifiers some options are the same, as **Vertex Group**, for which only the vertices assigned to a specified group are transformed; **Origin**, defining as transformation center the origin of an external object; and **Limits**, whose two parameters define the lower and upper deformation limits of the *mesh*.

Other parameters will be activated depending on the selected modifier type. Let us see them in detail.

a) Twist

- the **Deform** counter express in degrees the twist mesh rotation;
- **Lock X Axis / Y Axis** if checked prevent the twist effect respectively along the *x* and *y* direction.

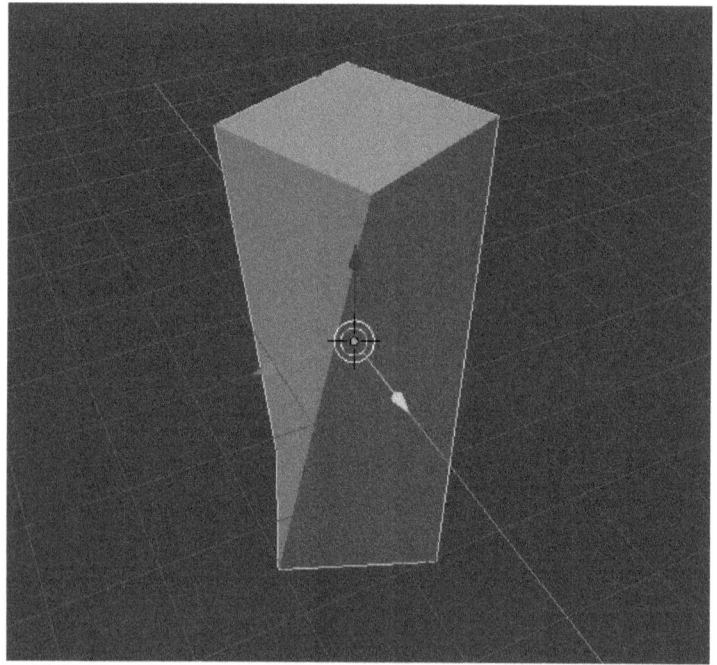

fig. 517 *Twist* applied to a parallelepiped

b) Bend

The *Deform* option is available, specifying the bending degrees.

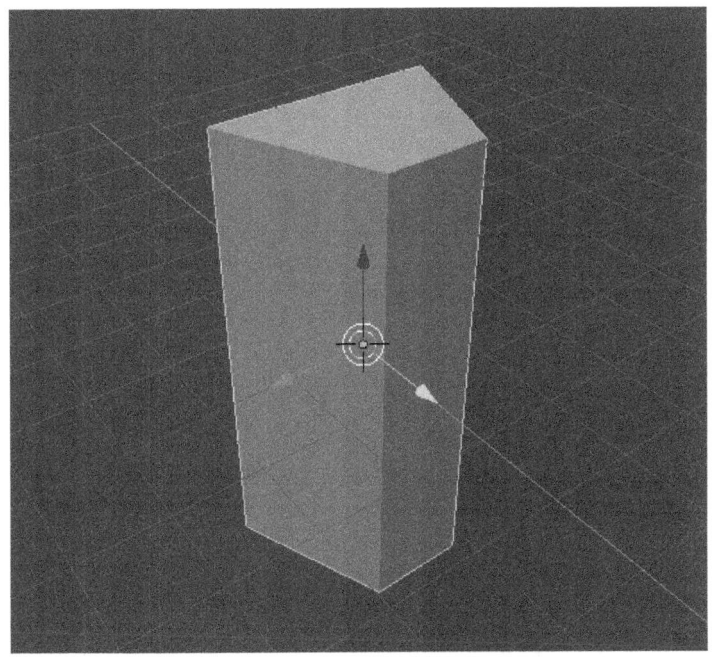

fig. 518 the *Bend* modifier bends the *mesh*

c) Taper

The *Deform* parameter is expressed by a *Factor* value determining the taper transformation amount and the direction. Moreover the *Lock X Axis / Y Axis* check options are available

437

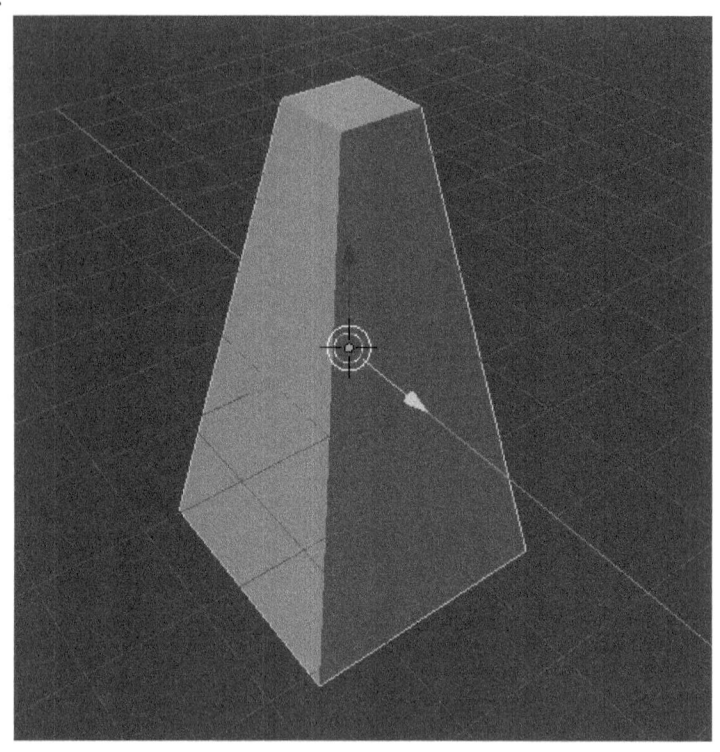

fig. 519 the *Taper* modifier action on the parallelepiped

d) Stretch

Has the same parameters of *Taper*, which uses for stretching the mesh.

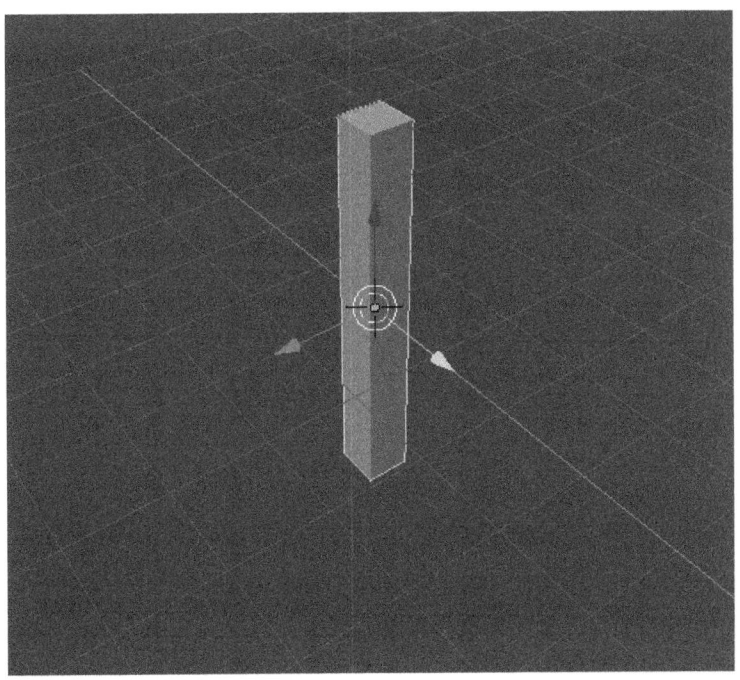

fig. 520 the action of the *Stretch* modifier on the *mesh*

SMOOTH

Smooth, not to be confused of the homonym shader, is used to really smoothen and round, with the help of a detailed geometry, the angularities of the *mesh* to which is assigned.

The algorithm affects the vertex replacement near the edges between the mesh faces, depending on the **Factor** parameter, determining the modifier action intensity.

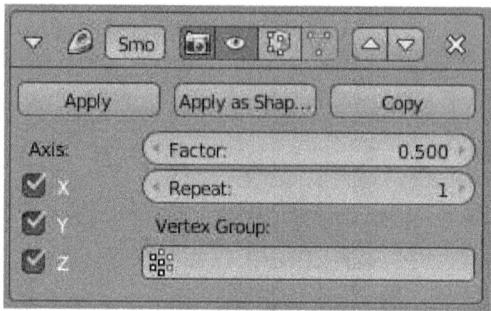

fig. 521 the *Smooth* panel

Repeat defines the algorithm repetitions, each one adding a further smoothing.

Inserting a **Vertex Group**, the modifier will act only on the assigned vertices.

The flags on *X*, *Y* and *Z* prevent the deformation along the specified axes.

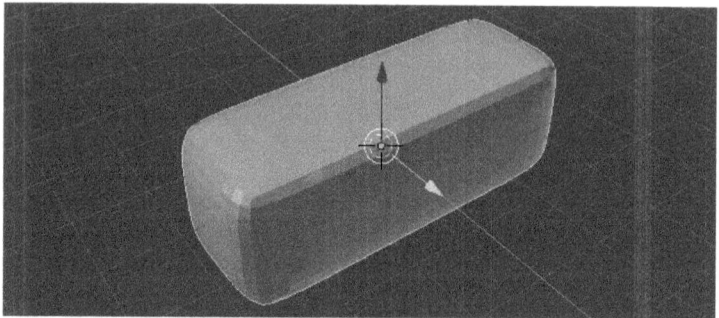

fig. 522 the action of the *Smooth* modifier with *Factor* = 2 and *Repeat* = 7 on a parallelepiped

Warp allows two external objects (usually *Empty* objects) to affect the deformation of the mesh to which the modifier is applied.

In particular the modifier operates on the *mesh* such as the two external objects (respectively indicated in the **From** and **To** boxes), act on the mesh vertices (suitably subdivided), as active elements resisting one to the other.

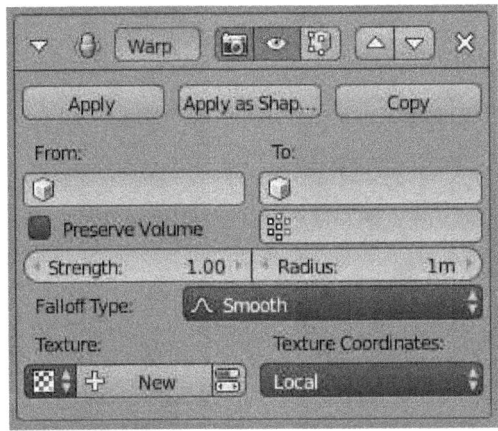

fig. 523 the *Warp* panel

For example insert a sphere and add geometry with a *Subdivision Surface*.

Insert then two *Empty* objects, one on the left and one on the right of the sphere, the first assigned to *From* and the second to *To*.

By moving the first *Empty* toward the sphere, the latter will undergo a concave deformation, whereas moving the second object till passing the sphere, the latter will be stretched.

441

In the **Strength** counter you can set the modifier strength of action, whereas in **Radius** the action range in the *mesh*.

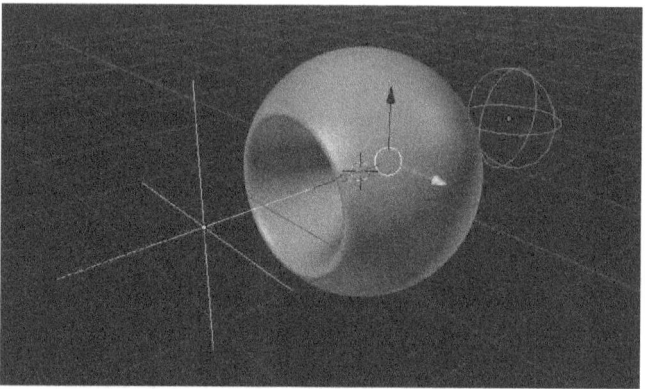

fig. 524 influence of the *Empty* indicated with a Cartesian frame

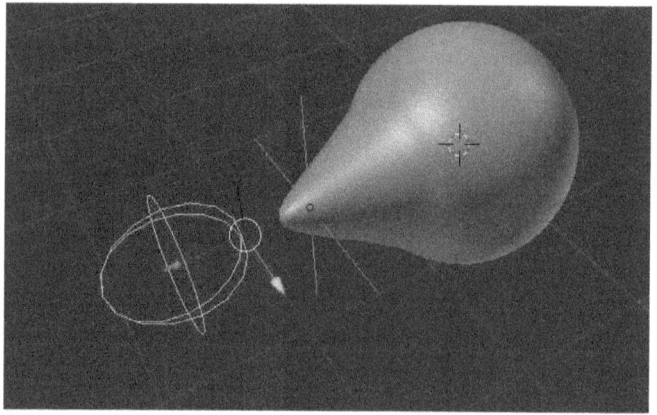

fig. 525 influence of the spherical *Empty*

You can also assign a **Vertex Group**.

Preserve Volume preserves the volume after the deformation.

Falloff Type opens a menu where you can choose the deformation method according to proportionality algorithms.

Texture Coordinates opens a menu where you can choose the reference axes on which performing the transformation, choosing among the local mesh axes (*Local*), the global system (*Global*), the local axes of an external object (*Object*) and the *UV* coordinates of the assigned texture (*UV*).

Finally you can assign a **Texture** (chosen from the *tab Texture* as previously seen) as deformation *Falloff*. The vertices during the deformation will the displaced depending from a *displacement* defined by the assigned texture gray scale.

WAVE

The last modifier *Deform* of the list is **Wave**, deforming a mesh, a curve, a surface or a text, applying a waved behavior to the vertices.

Of course a detailed geometry is required.

The modifier deforms vertices along *z* direction and propagates along the object with circular waves (if both the checks **X** and **Y** relevant to **Motion** are enabled), with rectilinear waves (if only one axis is enabled), parallel to the axis corresponding to the activated check *Y* and/or *X*.

For visualizing the animation you only need to type ALT + A.

The flag **Cyclic**, if activated, allows you to cyclically repeat the animation.

Normal (available only for *meshes*), if activated, shift the mesh vertices along the surface normals, instead of the object *z* axis, as by *default*).

fig. 526 the *Wave* panel

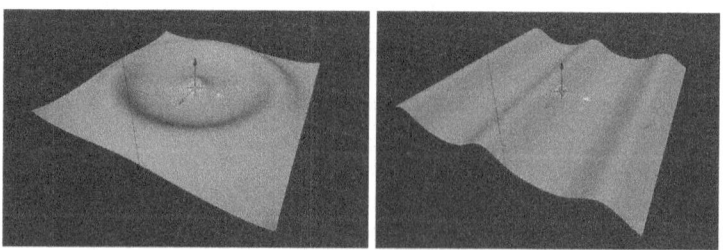

fig. 527 *Wave* with *X* and *Y* checked (on the left) generates concentric circular waves, whereas (on the right) with only one flag, parallel rectilinear waves.

444

The **Time** section contains the information on the animation and in particular:

- *Offset* determines the wave position of the initial frame;
- *Life* the animation duration, expressed in *frames*;
- *Damping* allows you to set a further frame number (*frame*) in which the wave will be softly damped from the maximum amplitude (at the indicated frame) to 0.

The **Position** section defines the *X* and *Y* position of the wave center, whereas **Falloff** controls the speed of the wave blurring while getting away from the above coordinates).

Start Position allows you to use and external object center as wave center.

Vertex Group assigns the modifier only to the vertices belonging to the selected group.

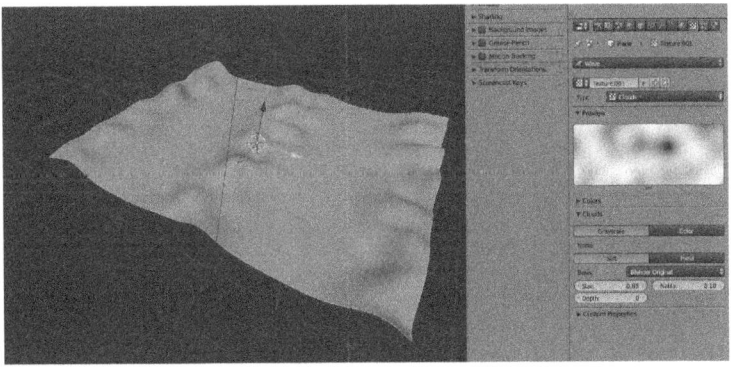

fig. 528 a procedural *Texture Cloud* set as *displacement* of the waves

Texture enforces a *displacement* (whose accuracy depends on the mesh geometry) to the waves. Like for the previous modifiers, you only need to add an external texture or a procedural one from the *tab Texture* and recall it in the homonym box of the modifier.

Like for *Warp*, **Texture Coordinates** opens a menu where you can choose the reference axes for the transformation. The following choices are available: the mesh local axis (*Local*), the global system (*Global*), the local axes of an eternal object (*Object*) and the *UV* coordinates (*UV*) of the assigned texture.

The **Speed**, **Height**, **Width** and **Narrow** cursors allow you to numerically insert parameters useful for the wave control and in particular, respectively, for the animation speed, the wave height, the distance between a wave and the next one (and so the frequency????) and the wave amplitude.

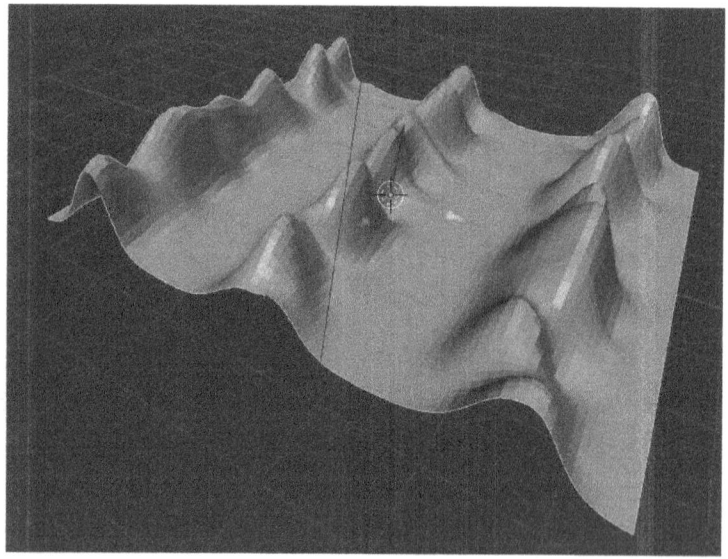

fig. 529 the modified dimensional parameters make more complex the wave shape

446

5.4. The sphere problem

At the end of this chapter we want to face an important problem for the 3D modeling: the sphere.
The sphere, from the modeling point of view, is an object to be accurately managed, most of all for a correct shading and mapping.

As we have seen and repeated many times, especially for the 3D modeling of meshes to be rendered with an *Unbiased* engine, the best thing would be that the spheres be subdivided in polygons as much regular as possible, and most of all quadrangular.

Since Blender (like other commercial software based on the same modeling criterion) operates by curve approximation, it happens to be forced to face triangulation problems, sometimes unavoidable. We know how much this is risky for the shading.
The *default* sphere (*UV Sphere*) (and also other solids derived from the sphere), in particular, is composed of a grid of parallels and meridians, all converging in a unique point to the north and south pole, generating triangular faces at these points.

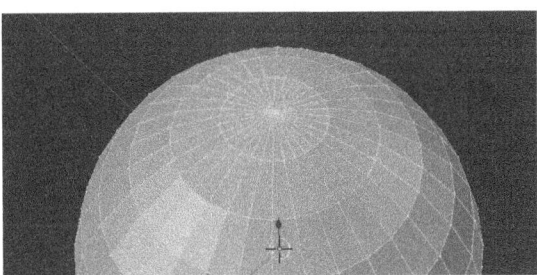

fig. 530 triangular faces of the *UV Sphere* at the poles

Depending on the detail level, it could be convenient and necessary to modify the geometry.

A method, provided the sphere meridians be a multiple of 4, is to cancel the vertices corresponding to the poles, selecting the circular *loop* of the first parallel and fill the surface with F.

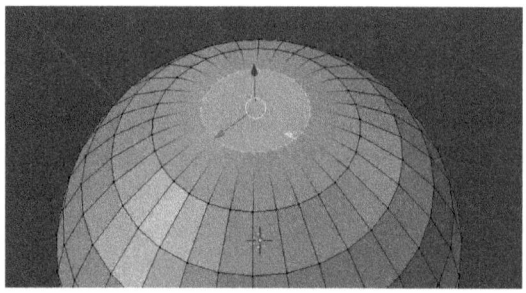

fig. 531 deletion of the vertices at the pole and *fill* on the first parallel

Once the face has been created, you can make a first *Inset* with I, then, passing in frontal view (1 NUM), gradually raise the *loop*, following the sphere natural curvature.

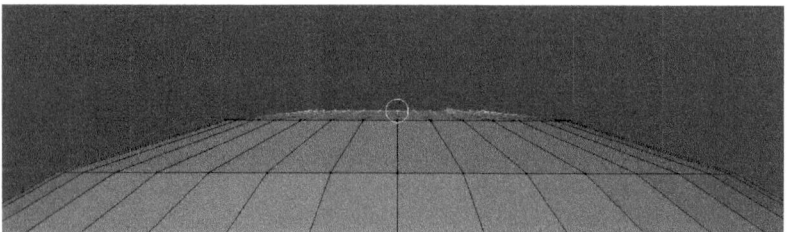

fig. 532 *Inset* and loop raise

Repeat a second time the same procedure.

In order to avoid that a polygonal face is left on the top, operating in *Top* view (7 NUM), make some cuts with *Knife* (K) alternating one vertex and two and passing from the center.

In this way the surface will be divided in many quadrangular faces.

You now only need to raise the pole according to the curvature radius.

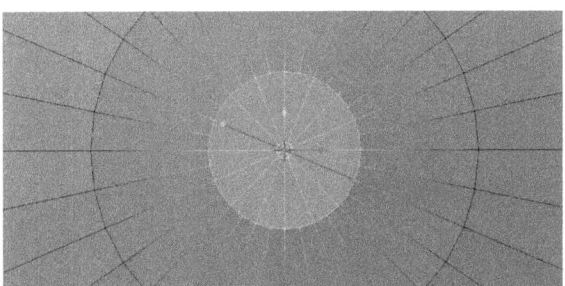

fig. 533 subdivision of the end face with *Knife*

A second method for obtaining a sphere subdivided in quadrangular faces is to insert an icosphere (divided in triangles) and apply to the latter a *Subdivision Surface* modifier. This modifier will suitably subdivide the *mesh* creating quadrangular faces.

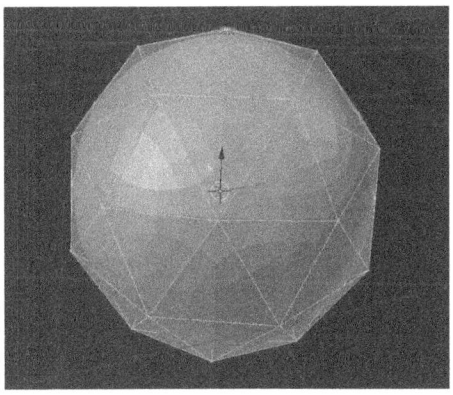

fig. 534 subdivision of an *Icosphere* with *Subdivision Surface*

We know that *Subdivision Surface* subdivides a *mesh* and rounds its edges.

Inserting a simple cube in the 3D view with the modifier applied to at least 4 subdivisions, the solid will be transformed tending to a sphere. We want to stress the word *"tending"*, because it will not be a perfect sphere, but a solid similar to a sphere with the base geometry of a cube. Theoretically with an infinite number of subdivisions the cube will the exactly transformed into a sphere.

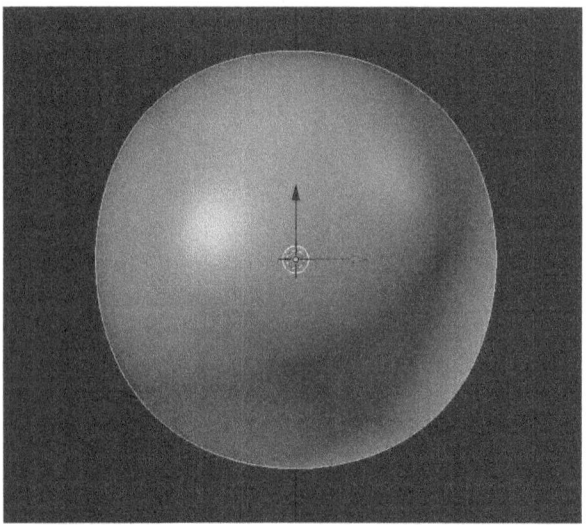

fig. 535 cube subdivision with *Subdivision Surface*

Perhaps the most precise method for creating a sphere, either for regularity and face homogeneity, is to insert a cube, with suitably subdivided geometry with W and *Subdivide* (at least 15 subdivisions for achieving a good result) and apply to it the *Cast* modifier where *Sphere* will be set in the *Cast Type* menu and 1 in the *Factor* counter.

fig. 536 the *Cast* modifier will deform the cube into a sphere, whose faces will be homogeneously placed, like those of a cube

6
CONCLUDING
REMARKS

6.1. Conclusions and acknoledgements

I want to thank all who have contributed to the development of this first volume of **Blender – the Ultimate Guide**, my family, my collaborators, my friends who have supported and advised me, like, among all, Francesco Andresciani (who developed the cup decoration used in exercise n. 19 on *Texture Paint*), the 3D *artist* Alan Zirpoli with whom I developed the kitchen models represented in this volume, Massimiliano Zeuli, Giovanni Caruso for the translation in English of this books, obviously all the *Blender Community* and the *Blender Foundation*, all the people following me and the web site www.blenderhighschool.it, and all my editors.

I want to dedicate to all of them the success of this book.

Thanks.

Andrea

6.2. Support bibliography

For the writing of this volume all the following digital and print sources have been consulted:

- Francesco Siddi - Grafica 3D con Blender - Apogeo 2015
- Oliver Villar Diz - Learning Blender - Addison Wesley 2015
- Andrea Coppola / Francesco Andresciani - Blender - Area 51 Publishing 2013-2015
- Francesco Andresciani - Blender: le basi per tutti - Area 51 Publishing 2014
- Gabriele Falco - Blender 2.7 Grafica e Animazione 3D - 2014
- Gordon Fisher - Blender 3D Basics - PACKT Publishing 2014
- John M. Blain - Blender Graphincs Computer Modeling & Animation - CRC Press 2012
- Ben Simons - Blender Master Class - 2012
- Andrea Coppola - Blender Videocorso (modulo base e intermedio) - Area 51 Publishing - 2014-2015
- Andrew Price - The Architecture Academy - 2014

Moreover the following web sites have been consulted:

www. blender.org (Cloud)
www.blenderguru.com
www. blendtuts.com
www.francescomilanese.com
www.blenderclick.it
www.blender.it
cgcookie.com/blender
www.blenderhighschool.it

6.3. About the Author

Andrea Coppola, born on 1971, is a polyhedric professional: architect, *designer*, 3D *artist* and builder (and many years ago also a musician, arranger and producer).

He lives both in Roma (where he works as an interior designer, designer and trainer) and in Kenya (where he has designed and constructed five house residences in Watamu: (for information see www.lamiacasainkenya.com). In Kenya he is also founding partner of the construction company Hendon Properties Ltd.

Holder and founder of the architectural firm in Roma L.A.A.R. (www.laboratoriodiarchitettura.info), he worked and presently works as interior designer and designer (having designed, in particular, the two kitchen models "Nairobi" and "Skin" for Reval Cucine s.r.l. and the chair "Cra Cra" for Art Leather).

He also worked as security responsible in building sites and as university assistant tor the architecture faculty of the University of Rome "La Sapienza", teaching some master classes.

Passionate about computer graphics and in particular about Blender, regularly teaches courses, through the web site www.blenderhighschool.it, one of the main referenceы in Italy for Blender and official partner of Blender Italia (www.blender.it). Through this web site, connected with www.blenderclick.it (managed together with Francesco Andresciani), the Author tries to give his personal contribution to Blender development, thanks to his versatility, offering tutorials, tricks, books and products for free or not, in addition to modeling and rendering services.

As consultant he has developed catalogs for kitchen firms (together with Alan Zirpoli) and for the Mars Society of Bergamo, an interactive project using the real maps of the red planet provided be the NASA (together with Francesco Andresciani).

Besides this guide, he has published 8 e-books on Blender, 1 book on PBR Theory, 1 on the 3D print, 87 video courses, 1 Thematic Academy on Blender; 3 e-books on Autocad; 2 e-books on Arduino 1 course about sound design and 1 *thriller* ("L'Altra Specie"), all edited by Area 51 Editore of Bologna (www.area51editore.com) and Lulu (www.lulu.com).

He's one of the 6 Italian BLENDER FOUNDATION CERTIFIED TRAINERS.

Contacts:
blenderhighschool@gmail.com
www.blenderhighschool.it

For any question, please, use the Author's free Helpline: .
http://www.blenderhighschool.it/helpline.html

www.ingramcontent.com/pod-product-compliance
Lightning Source LLC
Chambersburg PA
CBHW071409180526
45170CB00001B/26